Praise for *Living Above the Store*

"*Living Above the Store* breaks the mold on business writing. It is a book about the greening of business to be sure, but it is literature first, brilliant disquisitions and narratives that place commerce within the broader context of history, culture, and the cherished human values that bind us together. Martin Melaver has enlarged the vocabulary of commerce and restored it to a place of honor, a timely gift in an era of disillusionment."
—PAUL HAWKEN, author of *The Ecology of Commerce*

"Martin describes the evolution of his ideas and practices with refreshing candor and humility. He is a role model for me, my students, and anyone interested in building a values-based, sustainable business."
—JOHN VOGEL, Adjunct Professor,
Tuck School of Business at Dartmouth

"Martin Melaver's beautiful retelling of his family and business experience provides valuable professional management directions for realizing ethically based business practices that are crucial to our society's health. General readers will also be inspired by the author's advice, personal journey, and approaches to the challenges he's taken on."
—MICHAEL SINGER, artist/designer

"*Living Above the Store* is the right book for these difficult times, when business needs to regain trust. Melaver starts with specific stories of running a family business, sharing successes and failures, frustrations and joys, and then broadens out to illuminate general principles for running a sustainable business. These stories still stick in my mind, long after I have put the book away."
—MARC GUNTHER, contributing editor, *Fortune*

"The most sustainably growing family business leaders, I find, are philosophers of management. *Living Above the Store* is a compelling example. Further, it is a wonderful story built on wonderful stories. All

business leaders will be inspired by the power of connecting driving values with convincing stories."
—JOHN L. WARD, Clinical Professor, Kellogg School of Management and Principal, The Family Business Consulting Group

"There is a third century teaching that says, 'Do not separate yourself from the community.' Commentators since have interpreted this to mean that even if one can accomplish more alone, distancing oneself weakens the entire community. The unique contributions of every individual are critical to the dialogue and discussion which nourish the community. Martin Melaver offers his own commentary on the building and sustaining of community. Each chapter is multi-layered and engaging. Not only does Melaver aspire to connect his actions to a vision of 'Building a Business That Creates Value, Inspires Change, and Restores Land and Community,' but he inspires others to do so as well."
—RABBI NINA J. MIZRAHI, Director, Pritzker Center for Jewish Education, Jewish Community Centers of Chicago

"At long last, a visionary work that reminds us what businesses once were, and can once again be. Martin Melaver has shared with us the story of his remarkable real estate company, eloquently teaching us how to run a business that is not solely about making a buck, but about building a sustainable society. Mandatory reading for leaders from all sectors—business, NGOs and government—who believe that our work should make the world a healthier, kinder and more prosperous place."
—EILON SCHWARTZ, Director, The Heschel Center for Environmental Learning and Leadership, Tel Aviv

"Creating a sustainable economy requires a transformational shift in the thinking of business. *Living Above the Store* embraces this challenge and is a compass for businesses, large and small."
—DENNIS CREECH, Executive Director, Southface Energy Institute

LIVING ABOVE
the
STORE

BUILDING A BUSINESS THAT CREATES VALUE, INSPIRES CHANGE,
AND RESTORES LAND AND COMMUNITY

Martin Melaver

CHELSEA GREEN PUBLISHING
WHITE RIVER JUNCTION, VERMONT

Project Manager: Emily Foote
Developmental Editor: Joni Praded
Copy Editor: Robin Catalano
Proofreader: Margaret Pinette
Indexer: Lee Lawton
Designer: Peter Holm, Sterling Hill Productions

Printed in the United States
First printing, April, 2009
10 9 8 7 6 5 4 3 2 1   09 10 11 12 13

Chelsea Green Publishing Company
Post Office Box 428
White River Junction, VT 05001
(802) 295-6300
www.chelseagreen.com

The Chelsea Green Publishing Company is committed to preserving ancient forests and natural resources. We elected to print this title on 30% postconsumer recycled paper, processed chlorine-free. As a result, for this printing, we have saved:

17 Trees (40' tall and 6-8" diameter)
6,337 Gallons of Wastewater
12 million BTUs Total Energy
814 Pounds of Solid Waste
1,527 Pounds of Greenhouse Gases

Chelsea Green Publishing made this paper choice because we and our printer, Thomson-Shore, Inc., are members of the Green Press Initiative, a nonprofit program dedicated to supporting authors, publishers, and suppliers in their efforts to reduce their use of fiber obtained from endangered forests. For more information, visit: www.greenpressinitiative.org.

Environmental impact estimates were made using the Environmental Defense Paper Calculator. For more information visit: www.papercalculator.org.

Our Commitment to Green Publishing
Chelsea Green sees publishing as a tool for cultural change and ecological stewardship. We strive to align our book manufacturing practices with our editorial mission and to reduce the impact of our business enterprise on the environment. We print our books and catalogs on chlorine-free recycled paper, using soy-based inks whenever possible. This book may cost slightly more because we use recycled paper, and we hope you'll agree that it's worth it. Chelsea Green is a member of the Green Press Initiative (www. greenpressinitiative.org), a nonprofit coalition of publishers, manufacturers, and authors working to protect the world's endangered forests and conserve natural resources.
    Living Above the Store was printed on Natures Natural, a 30-percent post-consumer-waste recycled, old-growth-forest–free paper supplied by Thomson-Shore.

Library of Congress Cataloging-in-Publication Data
Melaver, Martin.
  Living above the store : building a business that creates value,
inspires change, and restores land and community / by Martin Melaver.
      p. cm.
  Includes bibliographical references and index.
  ISBN 978-1-60358-085-4
  1. Management--Environmental aspects. 2. Business
enterprises--Environmental aspects. 3. Social responsibility of
business. 4. Sustainable development. I. Title.
  HD30.255.M45 2009
  658.4'083--dc22

                    2009000035

This is for Dana and Alon,
who from time to time would play this
duet on their guitars:

אני ואתה נשנה את העולם,
אני ואתה אז יבואו כבר כולם,
את זה קודם לפני, אמרו
אני ואתה נשנה את העולם.-לא משנה

You and I, we will change the world,
You and I, then all the others will come,
It's been said before,
It doesn't matter—you and I, we will change the world.
—Arik Einstein, "You and I"

CONTENTS

FOREWORD

As a latecomer to the community of environmentalists (my conversion happened the summer I turned sixty), I have been struck by a recurring observation: While surely all the smart people are not environmentalists, every environmentalist I have met has been a smart person. One of those is Martin Melaver, the author of this book, and it is an honor to pen this foreword.

As one of my associates at Interface, Inc. (the company I founded in 1973), observed, "There is just no such thing as an *ex-environmentalist*." I think he's right. Once you get it, you simply can't un-get-it. That suggests, of course, a kind of ratchet-like movement. One smart person at a time wakes up, is converted to heightened sensitivity to the plight of the Earth, and never goes back to his or her old view of reality. The mind, once expanded, never returns to its previous state. Thus, the movement grows.

In August 1995, one year after my own eyes and mind were opened by reading Paul Hawken's treatise, *The Ecology of Commerce,* I was invited to present the opening plenary speech at the annual conference of the US Green Building Council (USGBC). The council was in its third year of existence; the green building movement was still nascent.

Before speaking, I counted the audience. That was easy; there were only 135 people there. Since the USGBC is a membership of organizations, there were fewer than 135 "members" in attendance (several groups had sent multiple people).

Ten years later at Greenbuild (as the annual conference had come to be named), Paul Hawken and I shared the opening plenary with Janine Benyus, author of the stunningly important book *Biomimicry.* Attendance that year in Atlanta was more than twelve thousand people. Two years later in Chicago, the official attendance was better than twenty-two thousand (some estimated that as many as forty thousand actually showed up). By that time, membership had skyrocketed to more than nine thousand organizations—architects, engineers, designers, developers, building owners and operators, manufacturers, consultants, government agencies, nongovernmental organizations—a huge cross section of the entire building and real estate industry. From 135 to more than 22,000 in twelve years: That, you might say if you are a business-person, is a growth curve to die for!

Green building is alive, well, flourishing, and rapidly moving into the mainstream. And not a minute too soon.

Maybe we participants in this movement can pause for a moment and celebrate the progress that has been made. But let us not pause for too long, and let us not celebrate too long, because we still have a long way to go; there's no place for complacency. And I am pretty sure we don't yet know the destination. That is, I don't think we would all agree just yet on what would define a truly sustainable built environment.

So how should we be thinking about the goals to which we aspire? In other words, what is "green enough"?

Let's say, hypothetically, that we adopted and agreed on this definition: "A *sustainable built environment* is one that creates no net new environ-mental impact into the indefinite future." Whoa, you say! That's setting the bar pretty high, don't you think? *No* net new footprint (impact) into the *indefinite* future? Just how long is that indefinite future? Seven genera-tions? No. A thousand generations? No. Ten thousand generations? . . . No, longer than that; as long as humankind inhabits the Earth. That *is* pretty indefinite, come to think of it. But that has to be the planning hori-zon for true sustainability, as *impossible as it seems*.

Which leads to another question: Even if we agreed that our objective was to achieve sustainability in such rigorous, unrelenting, challenging terms, how the *hell* would we ever hope to get there, or even set a course in that direction?

To begin to get at an answer, I can only fall back on our experience at Interface. Because that is precisely the goal we *have set* for ourselves in the tiny slice that we occupy in this great industry: zero environmental impact by 2020. We call it "Mission Zero."

If you're feeling satisfied with the depth of green in yourself, or your organization, or your last project, I invite you to think again.

Maybe right here, I should back up a bit for those who don't know me, and introduce myself. I am simply a husband, the father of two daughters, and grandfather of five terrific grandchildren; and I am an industrialist—some would say a radical industrialist, but I assure you that I am as competitive as anyone you know, as profit-minded as anyone you know. I founded my company, Interface, from absolute scratch in 1973; served as its CEO for twenty-eight years, and still chair its board. All I had at the beginning was an idea about producing carpet tiles in America for the emerging Office of the Future. Today Interface is a global company, with production in six countries (on four continents). Sales—in 110 countries—totaled more than $1 billion last year, and we are a recognized leader in industrial sustainability.

In 1994, Interface's twenty-second year, I set this third child of mine (after my two natural daughters) on the path to total sustainability. Paul Hawken's book *The Ecology of Commerce* convicted me as a plunderer of the Earth, and I set myself and the rest of Interface on this new and daunting path.

My involvement with sustainability is thus largely in the context of an industrial enterprise—one petro-intensive for both materials and energy—and I write out of that experience, hopefully to provide a better understanding of the kinds of profound changes that are required by the concept of total sustainability as I define it: zero footprint. I draw from lessons we have learned at Interface since 1994, as we have been climbing this high, high mountain named "Mount Sustainability." They are lessons that I think apply at a human scale (you and me); a company scale (your organization and mine); a societal scale (industry, city, state, nation); and a macro scale (the world).

Thinking at the macro level: My premise is that we, individually and collectively—humankind—are an integral part of two closely interrelated global systems. Let us call one the *technosphere*. The other key component of the technosphere, besides ourselves, is the industrial system. The technosphere—we and the industrial system—coexists intimately with the second global system, the *biosphere*. The biosphere consists of all the living and life-support systems of the Earth—the forests, rivers, oceans, wetlands, soil, fields, atmosphere, aquifers, hydrological cycle, climate regulation, ultraviolet radiation shield, pollination, seed dispersal, and more—*and* all life on Earth, *including us.*

So we have the technosphere. We have the biosphere. And we have the coexistence of the two, in a thin, spherical shell that is eight thousand miles in diameter (the diameter of Earth) and about ten miles thick. Notice that we humans are the common element in both; and relatively speaking the thin shell is the thickness of Saran Wrap on a basketball-size planet.

From that premise, a restatement of the definition of sustainability, then, might be: *the continued healthy, balanced coexistence into the indefinite future of the technosphere and the biosphere in this thin shell.* Another name for the biosphere is *nature.*

Yet it is manifestly clear that today this coexistence is so unbalanced and threatened that it is *not* healthy. On a global scale, every living system is in decline. Biodiversity plummets. The human footprint increases. The planet warms. The weather goes nuts! The technosphere continues to expand *at nature's expense.* The question arises: How can this go on and on into the indefinite future? And the answer is, clearly it cannot, unless we somehow miraculously find the biosphere (nature)—the Earth itself—to be infinite in its ability to supply the stuff (the resources) *demanded* by the technosphere, and to absorb the poison (the pollution) *produced* by the technosphere.

This imbalance—this *dis*equilibrium—is a serious problem that we are feeling already ourselves and, far worse, are creating for our grandchildren and their grandchildren. The recognition of the imbalance has given rise to the environmental movement and, within it, the green building movement.

How then do we reverse the frightening trends, eliminate this problem, and bring these two systems, technosphere and nature, into harmonious, healthy balance in a way that will last a thousand human generations, ten thousand human generations?

Can anyone rationally claim we have done this yet? I think not. So how green is green enough? How far do we have to go? How do we bring these two spheres *back into* harmonious balance?

This is the fundamental problem we have addressed at Interface over the years since 1994, at the level of the firm, and we have had some good help in our quest. For example, Dana Meadows.

Dana was one of the smartest people I have known—an American biophysicist, expert systems analyst, author, syndicated columnist, college professor, and farmer. She died tragically early. Dana, in her prime, published an elegant paper titled "Places to Intervene in a System, in Increasing Order of Effectiveness." Number nine on her list, the least effective place to intervene that even made the list, is to adjust the numbers, the resources going into the system—more of this (people, money), less of that (subsidies, taxes). Working down (or up) the list toward *more* effective, we find such things as: adjust the regulating negative feedback loops of the system; more effective, drive the positive feedback loops of the system; still more effective, change the goals of the system.

Number one on the list, the most effective place to intervene, according to this brilliant woman, is to challenge the mind-set behind the system—the paradigm, the perception of reality, the mental model of how things are that underlies the system in the first place. Dana said that this is the most effective place to intervene, but she also acknowledged that it is the hardest.

Now, we have systems all around us. Within the technosphere, we have our transportation systems, our communication systems, our production systems, our computer systems, our production planning systems, our management systems, our systems of government, our accounting systems, our educational systems, our systems for managing our households, our system of taxation, our regulatory systems, our banking system, and so on. Altogether these make up the *industrial system* that has arisen out of the industrial revolution.

What is the paradigm behind the modern industrial system? Is it an accurate view of reality? Or is it flawed? I suggest that it is seriously flawed, and that we need a new paradigm—a more accurate perception of reality.

The truth of a *new* paradigm doesn't just spring into existence. It will have been there all along. It will just have been obscured by the old, flawed view of reality. The Earth was always round, even when everybody *knew* it was flat. It always circled the sun, even when everyone *knew* it was the center of the universe. The divine rights of kings were considered the natural order, even as revolution was fomenting in the New World's colonies and in France.

If you look carefully at how the industrial system operates, you know it originated in another day and age. And it still views (or acts as if it views) reality as it did way back then, nearly three hundred years ago, when Thomas Newcomen invented the steam-driven pump in 1712.

Here's the eighteenth-century view of reality—in part—that still pervades our thinking:

- The Earth is an inexhaustible source of natural resources. We'll never run out. There will always be substitutes available. The market will find them. The first lesson in any economics textbook and, generally, taken for granted.

- The Earth is a limitless sink, able to assimilate our waste, no matter how poisonous, no matter how much . . . not mentioned at all in economics textbooks.

- Relevant time frames for the consequences of our decisions are, maximum, the life of a human being; more likely, the working life of a human being; sometimes, especially in business, just the next quarter. In politics, the next election.

- The Earth was made for humans to conquer and rule. *Homo sapiens sapiens* (the self-named "wise, wise man") doesn't really need those other species except for food, fiber, fuel, and maybe shade on a hot summer day.

- Technology is omnipotent, especially when coupled with human intelligence, specifically left-brained intelligence (you know: practical, objective, realistic, numbers-driven, results-oriented, unemotional). These will eventually prevail.

- And how about this one? Adam Smith's "invisible hand" of the market is an honest broker.

- Or this one? Business exists to make a profit.

- Or this? The way to abundance for all is through increasing labor productivity. It was natural enough to think this way in the eighteenth century, of course, when people were the scarce resource and nature was bountiful.

Our work at Interface to create a sustainable company, with zero environmental impact, leading to a sustainable industrial system that will be sustainable into the indefinite future, has convinced me that every element of that paradigm, which is still so very pervasive, is wrong— dead wrong. Survival of our species depends on a new industrial system developing, and quickly, based on a new paradigm—a new and more accurate view of reality, one that acknowledges:

- The Earth is finite (you can see it from space; that's all there is!), both as a source (what it can provide) and as a sink (what it can assimilate and endure). It has a carrying capacity for us humans, and we are already exceeding it.

- There will come an end to the substitutes that are possible. We cannot substitute water for food, air for water, food for warmth, energy for air, air for food. Some things are complementary, and not even the market can change that. The first lesson in economics textbooks needs to be rewritten.

- Relevant time frames for considering the consequences of our decisions are evolutionary in scale. We must, at least, think beyond ourselves and our time on Earth—so brief— and think of our species and all the others, not just ourselves, over evolutionary time, the true long run. Here, for starters, we could adopt the indigenous peoples' standard of seven generations, then build on that. What if every decision we made regarding resource usage took into account the effect on resources available seven generations into the future? What, indeed, if we thought a thousand generations ahead and really cared about our distant descendants? For one thing, we would shut down the nuclear industry until there was a solution to the nuclear waste problem—a 240,000-year problem!

- Humankind was made for Earth, not the other way around. Earth doesn't belong to us; we belong to it. And the diversity of nature is crucially important in keeping the whole web of life, including us, going sustainably over evolutionary time.

- Technology must fundamentally change if it is to be part of the solution instead of a major part of the problem. The technologies we have grown up with, and take for granted, share some common attributes. They are extractive (they take from the Earth); linear (take–make–waste); driven by energy from fossil fuels; wasteful; abusive; and focused on labor productivity.

- The new technologies must be renewable (not extractive), cyclical (not linear), solar-driven, waste-free, benign, and focused on resource productivity (the productivity of all resources, not just labor). In the twenty-first century, it is nature that is scarce and diminishing, and people that are abundant.

- The right side of the brain—the caring, nurturing, artistic, subjective, sensitive, and emotional side (in business, the "soft side")—is at least as important as the left side, and perhaps a good bit more so, since it represents the human spirit.

- And the market? The market is opportunistic, if not outright dishonest, in its willingness to externalize any cost that an unwary, uncaring public will allow it to. It must constantly be redressed to keep it honest. Does the price of a pack of cigarettes reflect its cost? Not close! A barrel of oil? Not within $150! The revered "invisible hand" is blind as a bat if it ignores the externalities. How can it be an honest broker, or allocator of resources, stumbling along in its blindness?

- Business exists to make a profit? I beg to differ. Business makes a profit to exist. It must surely exist for some higher purpose. Who among us really expects to stand before our maker someday and talk about shareholder value?

- In a world of four billion very poor people and too little nature, the route to abundance for all must surely be through increasing resource productivity—putting people to work using material resources more efficiently. For clearly, the greatest moral and ethical challenge humanity faces is to lift the poorest among us out of grinding poverty while healing our already badly damaged Earth.

In our own way at Interface. we have chosen to intervene in the system as we operated it for twenty-one years, from its inception in 1973 until 1994, when we woke up to its *un*-sustainability. The US Green Building Council has also chosen to intervene in the system, whether or not its members have thought of it in these terms.

From this new mind-set—this more accurate view of reality—the four thousand people of Interface have devised, and are executing, a plan to climb Mount Sustainability clear to the top, that summit representing our goal: the transformation of our petro-intensive company into a sustainable one by 2020; said another way, to bring our company into complete, healthy, harmonious balance with nature. Is this possible? As physicist Amory Lovins has said, "If something exists, it must be possible." When we are successful, we will no longer be taking anything from the Earth that the Earth cannot naturally and rapidly renew—not another fresh drop of oil for energy or materials—and we will be doing no harm to the biosphere.

This, I am suggesting, corresponds to a no-net-new-impact standard for the entire construction industry. Which brings us back to the question: How? For sure, we will not get there with LEED 2.1 (not even Platinum). More likely it will be closer to "LEED 99.0."

That's the challenge at the macro level, but what about the micro level, where the action is? Martin Melaver and his company, Melaver, Inc., headquartered in Savannah, Georgia, are integral parts of the USGBC, and leaders in this movement. Martin has chosen to intervene in the system. His story of that intervention—told at an intimately personal level—will take you inside the workings of a superior mind and a fascinating company. It will take you through the challenges met and conquered in building a new kind of real estate development company.

How should we think about what is green enough? You will not find a better, more detailed map than this book. Read and get to know two great gifts to the Earth—the man and his company.

RAY ANDERSON

WHO WE ARE

Corporations can and should have a redemptive purpose.
We must understand that reaching our potential is more
important than reaching our goals.
—Max De Pree, Leadership Is an Art[1]

"No": A Story of Affirmation

"No. We won't do that."

The words came from Colin Coyne, our COO. The ensuing quiet around the Balch & Bingham boardroom that Monday morning in Birmingham was awkward and disconcerting. After six months of intense work to propose a build-to-suit, $70 million office tower for the largest law firm in Alabama, our team was prepared to walk away from the deal, just like that, because of who we are.

The project was an important one for our company, Melaver, Inc. We had acquired the old Federal Reserve Bank, built in the 1920s, and hoped to renovate it and the adjacent annex building, as well as add an office and hotel complex abutting the existing structures. It would be our first mixed-use sustainable development of significant size outside our home state of Georgia. Birmingham, decades after abandoning its downtown core in the aftermath of its stance against integration, seemed ripe for the type of renaissance our project could augur.

We had commissioned a top green architectural firm, BNIM out of Kansas City, to deliver an iconic design that we hoped would catalyze redevelopment in the downtown area. The iconic part was challenging, since we wanted a design that would fit into the turn-of-the-century architecture while suggesting a new chapter in the city's history, befitting the first change in the skyline in almost twenty years. We were looking to include a host of community stakeholders in the project, so that the final product would inject new life into the downtown's staid nine-to-five-and-go-home rhythm. The potential client—Balch & Bingham—was vacillating between staying in their current offices or signing with us to build them a new signature office complex. Many movers and shakers, prominent people not only in Birmingham but from the entire state, were seated around the board table that morning, creating a golden opportunity for us to advocate the merits of sustainability.

Sustainability—such a hot topic these days. It's virtually impossible to pick up any newspaper in this country without reading some article on the subject, from green building and technologies to organic agriculture to global warming and other aspects of environmental degradation. There may be no consensus about what the term means, but there is definitely a general feeling that we know it by its absence. There's no lack of sobering statistics conveying the degree to which we have degraded our habitat—our air, our waterways and groundwater, our soils and landscape. Perhaps the most sobering statistic of all is the notion that we currently need 1.2 planet Earths to accommodate our consumption of resources and our discarding of waste. If all the world's population lived the standard of life in the United States, we would need five planet Earths to provide for us all. It doesn't take a scientist to tell us that things are out of whack.

But it is not just that we are degrading our environment, or that we have become the only species on the planet that is literally modifying its host environment on a global scale. We are degrading ourselves, perhaps without even being cognizant of the fact. It's not a message most of us care to hear, particularly given the advances our civilization has realized since the Industrial Revolution and what those advances have provided: increase in life span and leisure time and wealth, improvement in health, the relative freedom to shape one's own destiny, and so many other benefits. We seem to know so much more than we did even a century ago, and this knowledge carries with it a sense that it will set us free. But is this really the case? Or has our vast increase of knowledge enriched us in certain narrow contexts while impoverishing us in others?

The food we Americans eat travels an average of 1,500 miles to arrive on our tables. Separation between us and what we eat is indicative of a more fundamental displacement between ourselves and nature, the cycle of the seasons, and our connection to where we live. At what point do we grasp that the food we eat is filled with some of the 80,000-plus synthetic chemicals in our environment, the consequences of which are only vaguely understood? With 40 percent of the world's population living on less than two dollars per day, how can we not see that we are feeding ourselves mythologies of health and progress, both physical and metaphysical?

One of my favorite books is *Flatland,* written in 1884 by the British teacher and theologian Edwin Abbot. The book tells the story of a two-dimensional world in which one "character," a line, begins to imagine a three-dimensional world that is literally beyond his flat, physical reality. The challenge *Flatland* poses for us today is this: How do we step outside a world that has brought us so much knowledge and advancement and see another dimension, one that enables us to recognize that our ethical orientation toward the world is flat and misguided and not so much enabling progress as leading to our own demise? How might we see that the turbocharged pace of life for so many of us today is lacking in a calm, deliberative, purposive sense of direction? How do we go about the process of living sustainably, and what can a business do to facilitate this movement?

Oddly enough, underlying this very focused business meeting in Birmingham, Alabama, were deeper questions such as these. Building sustainably, living sustainably; this is what our company, Melaver, Inc., has been about to a large extent since its inception in 1940. The built environment in the United States accounts for 36 percent of total energy use and 65 percent of electricity consumption, more than 40 percent of greenhouse gas emissions, and 35 percent of all nonindustrial waste.[2]

Part of building sustainably means reducing waste, using less energy and water. It also means using and reusing local materials, as evidenced in our proposal to rework the old steel piping throughout the Federal Reserve Bank building, originally manufactured in the steel mills around Birmingham. And building sustainably means utilizing paints and flooring and furnishings made from healthier materials. As part of our company's overall commitment to sustainability, we develop all of our buildings to Leadership in Energy and Environmental Design (LEED) standards—standards established and evaluated by the nonprofit U.S. Green Building Council. In addition, all our company's staff members must at least study for and take the LEED exam, resulting in approximately 80 percent of our staff being LEED accredited.

But building sustainably, for us, means more than the physical structure. Our company has grown slowly and deliberately over the decades, sustaining itself in large part by keeping pace with the needs of our community. And so sustainability entails a social component as well as a physical one. It entails working within the urban core of a community so as not to contribute to the hundred-plus acres of open land that get converted to concrete and asphalt every day, so as not to exacerbate urban sprawl, greater congestion and commute times, and greater dissolution of communal life. Building sustainably calls for injecting social programs into our developments so that we contribute to the overall reinvigoration and health of a community. It means using our projects as levers to bring along a broad group of stakeholders—educators, government leaders, health and social workers, artists, nonprofit advocates, urban planners—to work collaboratively on enhancing community. Our company's statement of purpose neatly summarizes our sense of what this type of sustainable development entails: "Enveloping our community in a fabric of innovative, sustainable, inspiring practices." To us, restoring the Federal Reserve building was nothing less than the opportunity to be envelopers, to catalyze the restoration of downtown Birmingham.

Building sustainably, for us, however, extends even beyond the social context of how our work fosters community. Building sustainably is part of a larger business model, in which how one earns a living flows seamlessly into a set of ethical beliefs and practices promoting the overall health and well-being of our land and community. Managing a sustainable business entails connecting our viability as a successful business to the viability of our human and natural environment. Granted, this is a more idealistic vision of a business than one typically sees. *Maybe, just maybe, it's this mission-driven ethos that gives us the reputation for being so difficult to deal with* was one of the thoughts running through my head that morning in Birmingham. *Can we afford to be so idealistic in this case?*

Like most businesses, we don't like to find ourselves in situations where we are forced to negotiate from a position of weakness. But we had no backup tenant prospects looking at the Birmingham Fed project—hardly an ideal position from which to take a strong negotiating stance. We badly wanted—and needed—this deal with Balch & Bingham. For starters, there just wasn't a lot of big-tenant demand for significant commercial space in downtown Birmingham. Inking a deal with Balch would enable us to prelease at one fell swoop about two-thirds of the project. With this prelease in hand, it would be relatively easy to entice a lunch-dinner restaurant to locate on the premises. The remainder lease-up activity would likely move ahead with similar ease. A deal with Balch would also fast-track our financing negotiations and facilitate discussions we'd been having on lining up New Markets Tax Credits, a complex funding mechanism that assists with loans in areas designated by the federal government for critical urban renewal. Adding to our challenges, this was our development debut in the Birmingham market. Our entire team felt the pressure to make this debut successful.

The Birmingham Fed project was also important to our team on a personal level. This wasn't surprising. Our staff reminds me a lot of the sandlot baseball team in Disney's movie *The Bad News Bears*: a team of talented, kick-ass malcontents who are hell-bent on playing the game their own way, trying to earn respect from their peers but not willing to earn that respect by the same old methods. Our controller, Karen Stewart, who has worked with us for almost fifteen years, came to our company after raising her two kids. She had put a promising accounting career on hold to manage a family, and as she told me at her initial interview many years ago, she wanted to spread her wings and find out just how much she could accomplish. Randy Peacock, a good ol' country boy who grew up building cheap stick tract housing and is now in charge of our green construction, wanted to prove to the change-resistant construction industry that building green not only made sense but was the only way to build. Denis Blackburne, our CFO, left a successful career working for some of the largest and most prestigious companies in the world in order to make a difference. And me? As the CEO of a third-generation family business, I knew only too well that while only one-third of successful family businesses make it to the third generation, and just one-sixth make it to the fourth. I did not want to be the weak link that broke a chain reaching back seventy years.

As I looked around the conference room table in Birmingham that Monday morning, my thoughts drifted to the fact that it isn't always so easy to deliver on our aspirations to become a sustainable business. Sometimes it feels as though I am asking our team to run a relay race in Birkenstocks. It isn't just that we are trying to promote a different way of building, although that is challenging enough. Part of the challenge involves jettisoning traditional business conventions in lieu of different management practices designed to realize a business's highest potential. We weren't just trying to restore an old Federal Reserve building in Birmingham. We were also engaged, each of us, in an ongoing process of restoring who we are. Partly to console my worries, partly as whistling in the dark, I thought about former Herman Miller CEO Max De Pree's words—which open this chapter—on a company needing a redemptive purpose. *That's easy for him to say*, I thought. *Maybe, just maybe, we've gone too far this time?*

The issue on the table, posed by the newly annointed managing director of Balch & Bingham, was this: "Guys, we love your work and we love many aspects of your proposal. But we don't get this sustainable stuff. Would you be willing to develop this project for us, but not do it sustainably?"

The question may have been directed at Colin, but I felt all eyes in the room on me. I looked over at Colin and we shared a brief smile. It seemed like minutes before he responded, though it was only a few seconds.

In retrospect I think the folks at Balch & Bingham were shocked by our response, though I don't know if they were taken aback more by our refusal or by the fact that such a monumental stake was placed in the ground by someone other than me. As it turns out the decision to say no and the fact that this decision was made and articulated by a colleague are fundamentally related.[3] While our *no* that day in Birmingham took only a fleeting moment to utter, it took decades of collective groundwork to build the foundations underlying what was being said. The remainder of this book will be devoted to fleshing out the affirmative principles embedded in our *no* that day: the management principles and practices that shaped this foundation-building work, the journey we took as a company to realize who we are, and the moves we are making to become a sustainable business.

Defining This Book

Living Above the Store is about a lot of things. It is primarily about the almost two decades I have spent working with a remarkable group of people to foster a sense of community, rework the way business is practiced, and restore our sense of self in the process. It is about striving to become a restorative business.

The coming pages describe the business culture my colleagues and I have shaped together and the use we have made of this culture to serve as an instrument for social change and foster greater health and well-being of our land and community. These issues—engendering a strong sense of community through shared values and practices, promoting social change, and fostering a land-community ethic—comprise the three interlocking themes of this book.

The book also portrays the restorative principles and management practices that inform everything we do at Melaver, Inc., to become more sustainable. It is intended to encourage other businesses to step outside the familiar, conventional dimensions of how a business is typically run and gain a new perspective on how a business can be run. Much of what you will read here flies in the face of most conventional business tenets. But, as you'll see, there is a viable case to be made for challenging business-as-usual practices.

These days there is a profound need to tell good stories about what the role of business should be and what a business is capable of when it sets its heart and mind and soul to being part of a restorative movement. *Living Above the Store* strives to tell that story

There are a few terms in this book, used rather often, that beg a host of questions. At the risk of sounding academic, I'd like to briefly flesh out these terms a bit.

Restore/Restorative. It may seem anomalous to focus a book of management practices around the notion of restoration. More commonly, *restoration* is thought of in the context of renovating a house or a piece of furniture or a work of art. Thinking more broadly, the term *restoration* connotes something spiritual, as an action that is restorative in nature, returning one to some healthy and/or exalted state. Neither definition seems the stuff of business.

If that weren't troubling enough, there's the challenging question "Restoring to what, or when?" Is there some particularly idyllic time in the past to which we seek to return? If so, when was that and how do we get there? Or is it more a mental state of being, returning to some prelapsarian nirvana that has passed us by? If so, what does that look like? Who gets to determine why that ethos is compelling? Underlying these queries are questions of a more philosophical nature. *Restoring* suggests fixing a brokenness or state of disrepair. By what standards is such an assessment made? While it seems clear that humankind has strayed far from living at one with the natural world, my use of the term *restoration* has less to do with returning us to some Edenic union with nature and more to do with returning us to a more authentic sense of ourselves. This is an ethical reorientation, calling for a careful reconsideration of the disruptive, destructive practices we are engaging in. It calls for thoughtful reflection on what has moved us so far from our responsibilities toward one another and the land we inhabit. It calls for reconnecting with those elements of our individual nature that renew our sense of self and our sense of purpose.

Business has been responsible for many remarkable achievements. But in the process, business has evolved into an end in its own right. The job description for management has become simply the perpetuation of the institution. Rather than serving to help realize our highest potential, as Max De Pree would say, business only serves to realize its highest earning potential. *Living Above the Store* is about redirecting the compass of business in the direction De Pree points us.

We. Throughout this book, I use the collective *we* often to invoke a shared sense of purpose and direction. Who is this? My colleagues at Melaver, Inc., who work alongside me? The larger group of stakeholders with whom we engage in business? Americans? Humanity? The larger the scope of inclusiveness, the more universal the stakes involved, the more hubris in the undertaking. I have tried to be careful in my use of *we*. In the early chapters of this book *we* focuses on my colleagues at Melaver, Inc. Later on the scope widens to include the stakeholders with whom we work, and then the community at large. Toward the end of the book, *we* extends to the major sectors that comprise a complete society or culture—business, government, academia, and nonprofit organizations. As our company engages in efforts to restore who we (at Melaver, Inc.) are, we extend our actions outward to the larger community to restore who we (humankind) are. Restorative efforts on a small scale (the individual, colleagues at work) are intimately connected to restorative efforts on a larger scale (community, region, nation, planet).

Perhaps the most challenging definition is that of *sustainability*. There have been numerous trenchant critiques of the term, most of which are pretty much on the mark.[4] First, there is the tricky matter of balancing the triple bottom line on which sustainability is based: economic profitability, environmental stewardship, and social enrichment. As mathematicians John von Neumann and Oskar Morgenstern argued many years ago, only one variable in a system can be maximized at any given time.[5] As such, sustainability, with its three variables, is susceptible to giving preferential treatment to one variable—economic profitability—over the other two.

Second, *sustainable* means a host of different concepts to different users. There is no underlying philosophical rigor to the term, making it easily co-optive. What is being sustained? And for whose benefit? Are we trying to sustain the lifestyle to which we have become accustomed? Or trying to return Earth to its carrying capacity, to the point where we are consuming fewer resources than our planet generates and creating an amount of waste that is within the limits of our planet to absorb? And if so, carrying capacity for whose consumptive practices—the first world's, those one billion inhabitants on our planet who earn less than a dollar a day, or someone in between?

Finally, there's a basic anthropocentric bias to the term *sustainable*, the notion that we as humans should manage nature for our own uses. If we could, for instance, manage forests in a sustained-yield way, just because such management addresses human demands does not necessarily mean that nature is being conserved or well served.

In short, sustainable can serve as a smokescreen for business as usual. It lacks broad agreement on its meaning. It potentially frames nature as a commodity and a resource for human consumption.

There is no question that *sustainability* is a problematic concept and can mean virtually anything to anybody. The term, by its loose nature, has invited a vast array of participants to the table who want to know more about what sustainability means to them and to the larger world. Rather than feeling despair that such an important concept means so many different things to so many people, I think this is cause for hope. All of us among the various sectors of society are, for once in our history, at least in the right church, if in different pews. Granted, the church is immense, with numerous nooks and crannies for people to pray in their own way. But at the very least we are beginning to create meaningful dialogue around economics and ecology.

For us as a company the meaning of the term *sustainable* is perhaps best explained by its Latin root, "having to do with sustenance; that which feeds us, nurtures us." There are critical metaphysical, spiritual, and physical connotations to the term. Managing a sustainable business entails fulfilling a range of needs, providing the sustenance for life and living. An overview of these needs includes:

1. Creating and nurturing a work environment that enables each individual to realize his or her highest potential

2. Fostering a business culture that provides for the growth
   and maturation for all who work there
3. Helping to make work deeply meaningful, so that work is
   integrated into all that we do
4. Broadening the influence of the company's mission to the
   community at large, so that staff members feel there is an
   overarching purpose to what they do
5. Articulating, embracing, and implementing a philosophy
   that enhances ethical sensibilities, particularly the sense that
   how we degrade or restore the way each of us lives is intertwined in the relative health and well-being of our land and
   community

Evoking a Land-Community Ethic

Living Above the Store is a business book about sustainable management practices that challenge conventional tenets of how a company
should be run. More fundamentally, it is about linking the practices
of a business more closely to the workings of the natural world. It is
about being part of what the naturalist Aldo Leopold once described as
a "land-community ethic."

It is difficult, perhaps foolhardy, to ignore the considerable literature
cataloguing how our natural world is collapsing. About two-thirds of
the world's commercial fisheries have dried up, with projections that
these will collapse completely by 2050.[6] We have lost half the globe's
forests since 1950. Average animal species population has declined
30 percent since 1970, with estimates of some 55,000 species becoming extinct every year. Fifty percent of the planet's rangeland is over-
grazed and deteriorating into desert. Ninety percent of the world's fresh
water is tied up in glaciers that are melting at an unprecedented rate,
and the remaining 10 percent is being severely compromised through
overpumping of aquifers and degradation of surface waters. It is estimated that by 2025, 40 percent of the world's population will suffer
from chronic water shortage. And so on. The real kicker, of course, is

addressing our runaway emissions of greenhouse gases, which if left
unabated are likely to result in planet-changing consequences.[7] The list
of ills humankind has perpetrated on the environment isn't just linear
in its decline, but part of a complex feedback loop. To write a book
about business practices in light of this collapse seems like fiddling
while Rome burns, precisely at a point in time when viable, actionable
solutions are demanded.

What is the role of business in the context of these changes? "Not
much" is one mordant response. Humanism, with its overweening ego
and anthropocentric orientation toward life, got us into this mess. And
this same arrogant humanism—with its foolish belief that all problems
are solvable and that all problems are solvable by people—will keep on
feeding another foolish belief, that we can figure out a way to survive.[8]

It's sobering stuff.

We could, I suppose, shrug and invoke the Ecclesiastical homily of
"eat, drink, and be merry," and simply stay the course. For tomorrow
we will die. But such an approach, I think, moves us too quickly from
a position of denial of impending collapse to one of despair. The world
may indeed be going to hell in a handbasket, perhaps without us along
for the ride. And it may be the height of humanistic arrogance to assume
we can solve our way out of this jam. But it's at least worth trying.

Numerous writers on business and the environment at some point
seem compelled to say whether they are optimists or pessimists regarding humankind's capacity to change our current trajectory of planetary
degradation. To me, this question is a nonstarter, or perhaps it's a question of recontextualizing our language. A Japanese word for optimism
is *rakkanteki,* conveying not a notion of utopian faith but the sense of
having enough challenges to give life meaning.[9] It matters less how we
characterize ourselves; much more that we face the facts squarely and
ask ourselves what we plan to do about this state we have created. It will
take considerable collective will to step beyond our current consump-
tion-driven ethic to see things in a new light. I hope this book will help
pull us in that direction.

The challenge of fostering a paradigm change in the way humankind
engages with the larger world extends well beyond the practices of one

business or even business generally. It will take a global village for this land-community ethic to gain momentum and eventually take hold. For those working in the major sectors of society, my hope is that some of the basic aspects explored in this book of fostering community within a business context will apply to similar community-building in other sectors of society. Granted, the challenges each sector faces are different. I hope some of these differences can be subsumed by a broader shared concern for restoring the overall health of our ecosystem.

I also hope these other sectors recognize that a revolutionary sea change is now happening in the way business is conducted. While business has traditionally viewed itself as an island, we are now seeing an unprecedented emphasis in the business community on collaboration and partnering. This is a critical time to take advantage of the more open platform in the business world, to take the collaborative tendencies of the other societal sectors and connect this to the workings of the business community. We face an unparalleled need to set aside the distrust inherent in each of our sectors. I hope that this work helps facilitate a more trusting environment or at least facilitates discussion as to what a more trusting social order might look like.

The Need for Good Stories

While *Living Above the Store* is essentially a business book focused on sustainable management practices that foster a land-community ethic, it is also the story of one company's evolution over three generations from a corner grocery store into a real estate business. It is a business book written mostly through storytelling.

A number of writers on the environment and business share a sense that there is an indispensable need for good stories,

> . . . stories about how people and land come together, about present generations joining hands with past and future ones, about people regaining intimacy and friendship with other species, about nature's inherent mystique and the limits of human knowledge,

about the joys of communal life, and about the resettlement of the American land.[10]

This call for stories is a tall order. Many of the stories told about our company in the pages ahead are writ small. It always feels to me a bit odd to share these narratives with wider audiences. They seem to be so trivial and insignificant when placed in the context of the efforts of global companies and of huge moves the business community must make to redress our various excesses. But even small stories are opportunities to reflect on the nature of business and community and people. These vignettes capture critical moments in the evolution of our company. They enable me, my colleagues, and you, the reader, to step back and view this evolution from a more detached perspective.

Our stories help shape the sense my colleagues and I have of being part of a distinct company culture and history. They also mentor, enabling us to shape future decisions. And these accounts help shape collective memory: In the retelling of moments that shaped our journey into sustainability, we pass these stories on to the next generation of company leaders as well as to others in business who might find them helpful.

I hope that through such stories business leaders, among others, will reflect more deeply about the stories we need to attach ourselves to. Which tales resonate with us over time, long after events have transpired? What makes for a good story? I like to think that a good story speaks across generations, linking a past culture to present and future ones. What makes for a really good story? I like to think that a really good story has the capacity to highlight values that are basic to the human condition. What makes for a classic story? A classic is is a very good story that endures, by engaging an entire canon of writings, causing us to rethink and reinterpret the wisdom we have held dear.

The story of our own company is largely the story of learning to think more deeply about these issues. How we evolved over the years, what lessons we learned, which values nurtured our growth; these are some of the topics that this chronicle addresses.

My grandmother Annie Melaver ran a corner grocery store, opened in 1940, originally called the M&M Food Store. Miss Annie, as she was always called, would on occasion close the store to deliver soup to a sick neighbor. Many of her customers, still in the throes of those late-Depression years, bought food on credit and paid when (and if) they could. My father, Norton Melaver, delivered groceries to folks' homes, the bags balanced carefully on the handlebars of his bike. After college, he joined his mother in the business, moving the old store to a new location nearby and heralding the move with a grand name change that would remain for the next four decades: M&M Supermarket. The original store eventually measured up to the name and grew into a regional chain that operated fourteen grocery stores in and around Savannah, Georgia, before it was sold to Kroger in 1985.

Those years in the grocery business dominate my childhood memories and inform my sense of running a business to this day. I remember the nightly phone calls from customers, interrupting the family dinner hour. My sisters, Tovah and Ellen, and I would dutifully take the messages, and our father would return the calls that same night, but only after we had finished eating and put the dishes away. Family and business at our home were intertwined, but somehow, managing a sustainable business suggests that family comes first.

Managing a sustainable business also means taking courageous stances on social issues of the day, even at the risk of losing business. Our family business took a proactive stance in hiring minorities in managerial positions well before it was done in the Deep South. Our open support for desegregation resulted in our being picketed by a group of angry white segregationists. When we sold the grocery business in the mid-1980s, about 15 percent of the sale of the business was set aside for the community at large and half of that was distributed among all the employees at the company who had worked with us for at least a year. Managing a sustainable business means taking care of the unrelated "family" members who work with us.

Though we sold the grocery business in 1985, we still owned the real estate where the stores and warehouses were located. Although we had never thought of ourselves as real estate developers and property managers, we discovered that this had been a corollary to running a supermarket operation for decades. The sale of our business not only made us aware in a way that we had not been before of this corollary business activity; the sale also forced us to confront the nature of this real estate business that was both familiar and new to us. Everything changed. We began to consider the consequences of development, what it meant to develop for other uses (not just retail) and for other clients (not just for our own business).

That period, about the time I started working for Melaver, Inc., was a soul-searching one for us as a family, since we did not like most real estate practices. We did not care for the tendency to make one development look similar to every other development in the country, the aesthetic banality of this sameness, the general indifference to greenfields and open space and trees. The feeling we shared as a family was that the real estate profession generally built without any true connection to a community and its needs. Our journey as a company, a journey charted throughout this book, is one of trying to shape a set of business practices in the real estate profession that connects us back to a communal ethos that began with Grandma Annie's corner store.

Although the specific stock in trade of our business has changed over time, certain underlying values have remained intact. Those values—having to do with the ways in which business and community merge into one another; the sense that *how* one conducts oneself is as important as *what* one does and *how well* one does it; the commitment to ongoing, lifelong learning; the belief in giving back to the community on a regular basis and not just at the end of a long, successful career; the belief that work entails personal and spiritual growth—connect our work today at Melaver, Inc., to the M&M Food Store founded almost seventy years ago. While our company has evolved over the decades, we have remained close to our roots, maintaining a sense of living above the original corner store, intimately immersed in our community.

This sense of living above the store goes to the heart of running a sustainable business. To us, this isn't just a matter of being "green" but of building a set of integrative practices in which the human-made environment is in harmony with itself as well as with nature. That's a mouthful. It will take most of this book to elaborate more precisely on what I mean. This notion of integrative practices linking the built to the natural has to do with nurturing within the company a sense of personal and collective responsibility for the community as a whole. It entails a ripple effect, in which personal growth of all our staff members shapes the growth of our stakeholders (shareholders, tenants, vendors, partners), which in turn shapes the growth of the larger community. *Living Above the Store* is fashioned as a series of stories that start small and radiate outward into bigger contexts, starting from who we are as individuals living in concert with others, into who we are as a business, then to embracing community and land.

It is probably no accident, though it was hardly intentional on my part, that the notion of restoration evokes the retail roots underlying the story told here. The family store serves as the basis for our restorative practices at Melaver, Inc., connecting aspirations for the future to past practices and beliefs. What will the fourth-generation business—if we reach that point—look like? I don't know exactly. William Greider, toward the end of *The Soul of Capitalism*, envisions a new type of business more in sync with the needs and aspirations of its citizenry:

> I can imagine corporations that are, on the whole, smaller and more nimble, more responsive and cooperative, interconnected with other firms and social interests. . . . The principles of economics would look utterly different, since the meanings of profit, loss, and productive output would be revalued to conform better with society's understandings of what is gain and what is loss.[11]

I would like our company to live up to Greider's vision, in which profit, while certainly a measure of a company's health, takes a secondary position to its capacity to provide meaning and purpose, for those who work for it as well as for the larger community. I hope the type of business we are nurturing today evolves into a more mature, more empathic, more aesthetically pleasing, more meaningful, and more valuable endeavor tomorrow. And I hope part of the legacy of our current business will be fostering practices in other businesses that amplify and extend our own. Beyond that, I hope that the legacy of our company will be that we served as an agent for social change, to demonstrate that business, working in concert with other major social sectors—academia, nonprofit organizations, and civil service and government—can evolve beyond its more narrow, *Flatland*-like perspective to serve as a catalyst for a restorative ethos.

Five Principles of Restoration

The stories told and the management practices discussed in this book are grounded in five underlying principles, each the subject of an ensuing chapter:

1. **Recovery.** This is based on the Platonic concept that learning and growth are about tapping into what we know instinctively to be true.[12] Recovery entails taking stock of the context— place and people, land and community—that shapes who we are. Recovery also entails unlearning numerous rules of thumb and mythologies that have been taught to us over time. This unlearning process calls for a constant, critical questioning of what we often take for granted. Recovery creates a business environment that not only encourages questioning and dissent, but also facilitates a deep trust in what one knows to be true, irrespective of what one has been taught.

2. **Restraint.** As a management principle, restraint involves "staying within who we are." This means that while we push all of our staff to reach their highest potential, we accept the differences and limitations in each of us. Perhaps paradoxically, those differences also need to work their way into alignment with one another. Managing a sustainable business restrains authoritarian top-down mandates and cultivates a bottom-up, participatory style of stewardship that brings out all the voices of a company. Restraint also means that while we push ourselves to be agents of social change, we are always cognizant that we cannot push our company

beyond its natural capacity. We can grow and evolve, but only so far and so fast at any given point in time. Restraint means recognizing there are limits to growth. Where we grow, how we grow, when we grow, with whom we grow, and indeed whether we grow at all—these questions inform every decision we make. Restraint is about economic and spiritual quality, not quantity.[13]

3. **Synthesis.** This requires taking the disparate values of individuals within a company and integrating them into a more holistic vision. Synthesis also builds upon a company's capacity for sociability and solidarity and integrates these two elements with the values of the company so that all aspects of a system cohere. For the individual staff member, this means that work, living, and play are in balance with one another. As a business model, synthesis entails connecting the essential nature of what a company *is* to what a company truly can *become*. As a company, synthesis entails not only integrating the disparate voices from within, but also integrating the knowledge and experiences of a broader group of partners.

4. **Covenantal action.** Rather than viewing the practice of business as a right, we view it as a covenant, requiring the permission of the community, of nature, and of ourselves. As a management practice, this entails fostering a "brain trust" of diverse, committed professionals across multiple disciplines, all working together through a sense of conjoined intelligence. Covenantal action also involves integrating economic, social, and environmental measures of performance in order to create a covenant between land and community.

5. **Congruence.** This links the efforts of business to activities occurring in the other three major sectors of society—government, academia, and the nonprofit world—so that all four sectors begin to coalesce around a land-community ethic. For us as a company to act as change agents for

restoring land and community we need to link our efforts with those of the other social sectors.

Fashioning a Business of Restoration

The five management principles woven throughout the pages of *Living Above the Store* serve as a counterpoint to many canonical business texts. I don't mean to suggest such business texts are untenable—just incomplete. For instance, though many of the tenets found in James Collins's popular *Good to Great* and James Collins and Jerry Porras's *Built to Last* are compelling, the story of our own evolution as a company begs such questions as "Great . . . at what?" and "Built to last . . . for what purpose?" Are superior returns to the market over an extended period of time the sole benchmark of a company's greatness? Should they be? And is longevity necessarily desirable? If a company had managed to stay in business for a hundred years by running a sweatshop, would that be something to celebrate?

Business holds so much promise. It calls for a blend of skills and knowledge across multiple disciplines and thus demands as much creativity as any profession I know. It involves synthesizing ideas and practices, large strategies and microtactics in ways I find meaningful and invigorating. It has the capacity to demonstrate how financial, social, and environmental capital can be integrated into each other. And yet it is dismaying to see such leadership potential go to waste. The business writer Stephen Covey once noted that a leaderless business is analogous to successfully scaling the highest tree in a jungle without ever considering whether that is the right tree to climb in the first place.[14] I could not agree more.

We Americans have become quite good at scaling trees, with frightening speed and efficiency. Americans now work more hours than almost any other nationality. Is such a heavy emphasis on work sustainable? The old business cliché about needing to work smarter, not harder, begs the question: With all of our technological innovations, are we now working smarter and harder but less wisely? Business has embraced the sense that it needs to be competitive on a global scale. How does that mind-set square with cost-reduction strategies that result in a major portion of our national workforce lacking health insurance? Or in cost-reduction strategies that move jobs to countries where workers earn less and environmental and labor regulations are less protective? Are we scaling the right tree?

A business is rewarded (or punished) on the basis of its most recent quarterly returns, and business leaders are compensated hugely on those returns. Where is the room, or inclination, to plan for the long-term needs of that business and the larger communities where it resides? The business literature is replete with writings on moral leadership, and yet our culture seems to worship icons of bottom-line profit, much as we celebrate the home-run exploits of a steroid-laced hitter. What we have come to regard as standard business practices and metrics, such as sole focus on the financial bottom line or growth in assets, will probably be with us for a long time to come. *Living Above the Store* provides at least an alternative accounting.

The principle of *recovery* calls for us to slow down and take stock of our surroundings rather than accept on blind faith many "blow-and-go" practices that treat people and places as little more than homogeneous and interchangeable parts. The concept of *restraint* responds to the unquestioned notion that businesses must grow with the goal of achieving global competitiveness. Restraint raises the issue of placing limits on growth. The principle *synthesis* calls for a business to integrate—rather than destroy and replace—the essential aspects of what a company has been in the past with the potential for what it can accomplish and integrate the values of staff members into a coherent whole. The principle of *covenantal action* looks to substitute the traditional and narrow notion that a business is beholden only to its shareholders with the notion that business should be accountable to a broader constituency of stakeholders. *Congruence* is intended as a more viable business model than the current business rage over globalization and vertical, global supply chain practices. Congruence has more to do with horizontal organizational design, where a sustainable business spreads its sphere of influence across a culture, integrating itself into the fabric of a particular place and integrating its practices with the other segments of a society.

The business of restoration challenges other standard business conventions. For the much-vaunted concept of scalability (using a core business model and replicating that model on a much grander scale, such as a franchise operation), this book posits a faith in place-focused economies and economic quality.[15] While our own company, for example, has the capacity to deploy a small, core group of colleagues to develop a vast proliferation of homogenous buildings throughout the United States, we have chosen instead to develop fewer projects that are well integrated with the needs of communities closer to home. In contrast to the conventional business emphasis on competition and differentiation strategies, this book promotes a more open platform, sharing what we know and do with others, so that our ostensible competition also takes up the charge of restoration. As such, in lieu of competition our company focuses on collaboration and emphasizes consilience of knowledge and action. In contrast to notions about change management, whereby a business imposes one new trendy management practice after another on its haggard staff, we emphasize adaptation, where the entire company evolves slowly together. Instead of developing a human resources program built around a total compensation package, our approach to hiring and retention is built around providing a calling for each staff member. Instead of business leadership, this work promotes a notion of stewardship.

To sum it all up, if a traditional or conventional business is built around a mechanistic system of policies and procedures with an authoritarian governance structure, the restorative company sees itself as a living system[16] governed by a sense of nurture.[17] Where the conventional business defines its purpose in narrow, economic terms that maximize financial returns, the restorative business utilizes its economic health for the purpose of shaping a greater sense of meaning for all who come into contact with the enterprise. A conventional business focuses on short-term returns on equity. A restorative business looks to the long-term optimization of value for itself, nature, and community. A conventional business feels it must answer to its shareholders. A restorative business feels beholden to a much broader collective of stakeholders. Whereas a conventional business tends to be structured in silos of functional activities, parcels out authority and power in a hierarchical fashion, and tends to house knowledge and innovation in a priestly class of experts, the restorative business works through cross-pollination, shared leadership, and collaboration. The conventional business is defined in large part by contractual relationships. A restorative business is shaped by a powerful sense of covenants. A conventional business works to differentiate itself through various strategies of outcompeting the competition. A restorative business looks to shape congruence among disparate sectors of society, because it will take such congruence to restore human endeavor to the habitat we have degraded.

Constructing a Road Map

Each chapter of this book begins with a story having to do with one management principle. These tend to be stories where we stub our toes as we stumble around seeking some small measure of enlightenment. The stories and management principles in each chapter build upon one another. By telling how we built a foundation for community within our company and broadened that effort to include stakeholders, neighbors, and then the larger social community, I hope to depict the gradual widening of a sense of shared commitment to a land-community ethic. The overarching picture tries to capture the centrifugal, outward rippling effect of a pebble dropped in a body of water, enveloping us all in a restorative set of beliefs and practices.

We begin by an act of recovery (chapter one), taking stock of the place we live and of the people who live around us and, of course, of ourselves. As we take stock of self, we begin to restrain those external influences that have perhaps diverted us from what we know and feel instinctively to be true. The principle of restraint (chapter two) then informs a set of management practices that foster a culture of bottom-up, collective questioning, searching, and dialectical engagement. We don't all agree with one another. Nevertheless, this dialectical culture resolves itself rather magically in a synthesis of values (chapter three). That synthesis brings together not only our shared sense of who we are as a company, but also a sense of the company we can potentially become. In lieu of competing with other business firms, we face a more serious challenge:

competing against our own inherited sense of "success" in order to shape a sustainable business that is in harmony with the natural world. As we work together toward that larger challenge, we foster covenants (chapter four) with a broader group of stakeholders—first key partners such as architects and engineers and contractors, then the neighborhood around us, to eventually shape congruence among all sectors of society (chapter five). Shaping congruence, where an entire social order coalesces around a set of ethical practices and beliefs, moves us toward a greater integration of land and community. It links us to a set of practices and beliefs grounded in place and people, of being in and of community, of living above the store (chapter six). I conclude the book with operating instructions for managing this set of sustainable principles over the long haul.

Throughout this book, I will be returning to a map that charts the evolving process of a business moving toward becoming more sustainable. This Restorative Process Map, viewed as an outline or template, is pictured below.

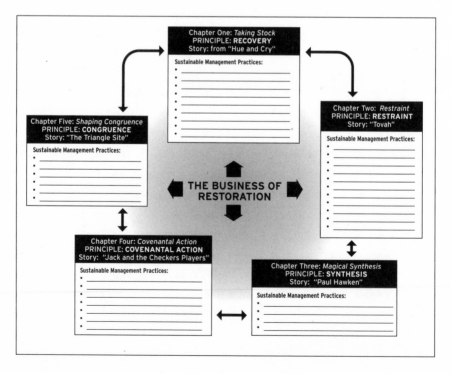

Pictorial representations such as this Restorative Process Map can sometimes be a challenge to read. This one is circular, with bilateral arrows between boxes, rather than linear because even though managing a sustainable business involves sequential steps, it is not a linear process. In the chapters that follow, each principle of a restorative business may indeed build upon the preceding ones in a linear fashion—and the map will be completed as the principles are explained. But in a sustainable and restorative business, as the circle of engagement with community expands to include ever greater numbers of stakeholders, each principle is revisited; hence the circular movement of the map. Viewed in this way, the Restorative Process Map recapitulates the rippling outward effect of a sustainable business enlarging its sphere of influence as it evolves.

Coda

We began this chapter with a story about a potential development project in downtown Birmingham. That story centers primarily around saying no to a client, a big client, who posed the question about building the project contrary to our values and beliefs. I would love to say that there is a happy ending to this story, that the potential client respected our mission-driven stance and decided to partner with us on the Birmingham Fed project—in short, a nice, neatly packaged lesson about the good things that occur when one stands up for what one believes.

But that's not exactly the case. We lost the deal. The prospective client chose to remain in the conventional office building it had occupied for several decades. We haven't abandoned the Birmingham Fed project, and have instead moved beyond our initial plan built around a single large tenant to develop a mixed-use project. Sure, we would have preferred to have landed that deal with Balch & Bingham. But sometimes the fit just isn't there. It's a lesson that courses through much of this book in terms of the people we hire, the places we decide to work, and the broad group of stakeholders with whom we engage. Other lessons learned? Maybe that saying no is sometimes painful, that it sometimes does not lead to the fairy-tale ending we would like. Another lesson is that taking a stand for doing things differently oftentimes results in others entrenching themselves more obstinately in what is known and familiar. Change can be intimidating.

I believe that our stance that day in Birmingham reinvigorated us as a company rather than made us feel dispirited. Not one of my colleagues has ever once looked back on that event and thought wistfully about the road not taken. On the contrary I think we came away from that experience sharing an even greater sense of moving in the right direction. Sometimes the most significant thing we can do in our business dealings is to learn to say no: no to areas where we feel we should not build, no to types of buildings we feel should not be constructed, no to prospective partners and stakeholders who we feel are not aligned with our sustainable philosophy.

But the path toward a restorative direction cannot be paved with a series of negatives. Utopian experiments in the United States, to cite just one example, often managed to survive for many years by creating a strong negative identity, in essence saying, "We are defined in large part by not being like those communities that surround us." There is something artificial about this type of boundary setting. It lacks transportability to other communities. It lacks integration with a larger order. And in the end, an identity based largely on negative criteria is difficult to sustain. Kibbutzes in Israel, originally established as a reaction against bourgeois European sensibilities of the early twentieth century, have either faded away over time or have incorporated many of the practices of the larger culture. For a culture to sustain itself over the long haul, something affirmative (and life-affirming) is called for.

My father ran a grocery business for forty-five years. Among the many lessons he taught me during his tenure, one will remain with me all of my life: No matter how difficult any day was for him, he always returned home upbeat, feeling that things would turn out for the best. He never said as much. We just knew, my sisters and I, that despite intense pressures from international franchise operations, despite rising interest rates during difficult economic times, despite the ongoing poaching of our key employees, we would be OK. If I could have only one quality to pass along to my own kids, it would be this overarching sense that things will turn out all right.

I can say that without any qualms or misgivings when it comes to our project in Birmingham or to our business generally. Despite the setback of not inking the Birmingham deal, despite the financial credit crisis of 2008 that has the world in turmoil, things will indeed turn out all right. Unfortunately I cannot say the same to my kids when it comes to the state of the planet. To do so would cross the line from bravura to prevarication. I can, however, tell them that we are doing our best to right some serious wrongs.

Living Above the Store does not so much imagine happy endings as suggest promising beginnings, primarily those written small, at the local and regional level, by folks wielding everyday tools such as common sense and empathy. The implementation of small changes day by day at the community level gives me the greatest hope. When a fourth-grader, returning home from a field trip to one of our sustainable projects, asks her mom to replace the incandescent lightbulbs in the house with compact fluorescents or LED lights; when someone stops one of my colleagues on the street to say "Thank you for what you are doing for our community"—these everyday moments in the ongoing life of our business link a past history to present practices to the legacy we will leave future generations. I'm hopeful about the capacity of these stories to restore us to who we are. If, according to Emily Dickinson, "hope is the thing with feathers that perches in the soul," then we need ways in which to embody that hope and give it wing.

CHAPTER ONE

TAKING STOCK

In the century ahead we must chart a different course that leads to restoration, healing, and wholeness. . . . To do that, we do not need research as much as rediscovery of old and forgotten things.

—David Orr, *The Nature of Design*[1]

Don't we all come to feel equally possessive about the places that set the contexts of our lives? And isn't that a good starting place? What about our problems? Do we own those collectively, too? The loss of our eelgrass worlds, our salt marshes. Isn't that home, too? What if we just go with that? Expand that sense of place of ownership outward. Own what's beautiful and what's ugly both, until the island that our community is drops away, and we stand on the still blue-green globe?

—Tim Traver, *Sippewissett: Or, Life on a Salt Marsh*[2]

Picture a small corner grocery store, sometime in the 1950s, in the downtown of a sleepy, Southern town. There's a produce aisle as you walk in, with white porcelain scales hanging from the ceiling for customers to weigh their tomatoes and apples and such. A wood-lattice bin of watermelons at the start of the aisle beckons. At the end of the aisle is the produce prep room, where a black thirteen-year-old is working. His name is Thomas Brown, and he works with Miss Hester, the manager of the produce department. She calls him Tommy. Up at the front of the store are four registers and a small office. Thomas's younger brother, Edward, or Eddie, works up front where he bags groceries and carries them to the customers' cars for tips.

Thomas is a character in the short story "A Matter of Vocabulary" by Pulitzer Prize–winning author James Alan McPherson. McPherson's story provides numerous insights into how a business is woven into the fabric of place and people.

THE STORY

Thomas Brown got his first job when he was thirteen. Both he and his brother worked at the Feinberg Super Market, owned by Milton Feinberg and his sister Sarah Feinberg. . . . Thomas had worked himself up from carry-out boy and was now in the Produce Department, while Edward, who was still new, remained a carry-out boy. . . .

[Tommy's] job was bagging potatoes. It was very simple. Every day after school and all day Saturday, he would come in the air-conditioned produce room, put on a blue smock, take a fifty-pound sack of potatoes off a huge stack of sacks, slit open the sack and let the potatoes fall into a shopping cart next to a scale, and proceed to put them into five- and ten-pound plastic bags. It was very simple; he could do it in his sleep. Then he would spend the rest of the day bagging potatoes and looking out of the big window, which separated the produce room from the rest of the store, at the customers. . . .

He thought of the window as a one-way mirror which allowed him to examine the people who frequented the store without being noticed himself. And it seemed as though he was never really noticed by any of them; no one ever stared back at him as he stood, only his head and shoulders visible behind the glass, looking out at the way certain hands fingered items and the way certain feet moved and the way some faces were set and determined while others laughed with mouths that moved in seemingly pleasant conversation. But none of them ever looked up from what they were about or even casually glanced in his direction. It was as if they could not see beyond the glass. . . .

Milton, and his sister Sarah Feinberg, liked him. He could tell it by the way Sarah Feinberg always called him up to her office to clean. There were always rolls of coins on her desk, and scattered small change on the floor when he swept. But he never touched any of it. Instead, he would gather what was on the floor and stack the coins very neatly on her desk. . . . And when she came back into the office . . . Sarah Feinberg would smile at Thomas from behind her little glasses and say: "You're a good boy, Tommy."

"I like you," Milton Feinberg told Thomas. "You're a good worker."

Thomas could think of nothing to say.

"When you quit school, there'll be a place in the store for you."

"I ain't gonna quit school," Thomas had said.

Milton Feinberg smiled and chewed on his green cigar. "Well, when you finish high school you can come on to work full time. Miss Hester says you're a good worker."

"Yeah," said Thomas. But . . . he was thinking of how far away he was from finishing high school and how little that long time seemed to matter to Milton Feinberg.

[Shortly thereafter, a crisis occurs. Eddie, Tommy's younger brother, accidentally places an order of groceries in the wrong car, and the customer leaves without discovering the mistake. Sarah Feinberg is furious at Eddie, so Eddie goes back into the produce department to avoid her anger. But she follows him to vent her displeasure.]

"Why are you back here?" Miss Sarah Feinberg asked Edward.

"I come back for some water."

"You know you lost twenty-seven dollars' worth of groceries up there?"

"It wasn't my fault," said Eddie.

"If you kept your mind on what you're supposed to do this wouldn't have happened. But no! You're always talking, always smiling around, always running your mouth with everybody."

"The people who got the wrong bags might bring them back," Eddie said. His nose was still sweating in the cool room. "Evidently somebody took my cart by mistake."

"Evidently! Evidently!" said Miss Sarah Feinberg. "Miss Hester, you should please listen to that. Evidently. You let them go to school and they think they know everything. Evidently, you say?"

"Yeah," said Eddie. Thomas saw that he was about to cry.

. . .

"You get back up front," said Miss Sarah Feinberg. And she shoved her way through the door again and out of the cool produce room. . . .

"I'm goin' home," [said Eddie.]

"You ain't quittin'?" said Miss Hester.

"Yeah."

"What for?"

"I dunno. I just gotta go home."

"But don't your folk need the money?"

"No," Eddie said.

He took off his blue smock and laid it on the big pile of fifty-pound potato sacks. "I'm goin' home," he said again. He did not look at his brother. He walked through the door and Thomas watched him walk slowly down the produce aisle and then out the front door, without looking at anything at all. . . .

"You going to quit too, Tommy?" [asked Miss Hester.]

"No," he said.

"I guess your folk do need the money now, hunh?"

"No," he said. "We don't need the money."

. . .Thomas . . . did not want to think about his brother or his mother or the money. . . . He decided that it would be necessary to record the faces and bodies of new people as they wandered, selectively, with their shopping carts beyond the big window glass. He liked it very much now that none of them ever looked up and saw him watching. That way he did not ever have to feel embarrassed or guilty. That way he would never have to feel compelled to nod his head or move his mouth or eyes, or make any indication of a greeting to them. That way he would never have to feel bad when they did not speak back.[3]

Recovering the Context of Stories

This passage, from the first story in James Alan McPherson's short-story compilation *Hue and Cry*, might not seem connected to the idea of sustainability. But sustainability begins with the principle of recovery, of taking stock of one's context. And that is precisely what this passage from *Hue and Cry* is about. In this story, Tommy is literally taking stock of the place he lives and works, taking stock of the people who make up his world. And while Tommy is taking stock of place and people, he's asking some basic questions: Can I truly live here? Do I belong? Where can I find true community? The story provides us with an opportunity to step into Tommy's shoes and ask ourselves these same questions.

McPherson, the story's author, resembles Tommy. McPherson grew up in Savannah, went on to study law at Harvard, and earned an MFA from the University of Iowa, where he now teaches creative writing. McPherson doesn't often come back to his hometown. He's taken stock of where he grew up, evaluated what he learned, and moved elsewhere. You might say that McPherson took stock of Savannah and found it wanting.

When McPherson was about Tommy's age, he worked in a local grocery store, the M&M Food Store, which became M&M Supermarkets, which became Melaver, Inc., the company that's the subject of this book. Milton and Sarah Feinberg are apparently modeled after my father and grandmother.

As a kid, I remember family members referring once to *Hue and Cry* during our regular Friday night dinners together at my grandmother's house. And I remember them saying, almost too casually, that they appeared in the book and that the portrayals were not flattering. That was it: mentioned briefly, never to be mentioned again. *It's not worth explaining further; that's all you need to know,* their reticence seemed to say. It was a long time before I picked up the book and read it. I simply took what other family members said at face value, without investigating for myself.

Interesting the way certain so-called truths are handed down to us and blithely accepted without our ever making the effort to delve deeper. I remember my ninth-grade classmates finding amusing many of the stories created by the ancient Greeks and Romans to explain the natural order, as well as the question our teacher posed to us in response to our hubris: Are there any myths we hold sacred today, myths that on closer examination simply don't hold water? We chuckled derisively with all of our ninth-grade certainty. *Myths,* we thought. *We are way too modern to believe in myths.*

The act of recovery entails coming face-to-face with the mythologies that have been handed down to us and uncritically accepted. Recovery is in large part a demythologizing act.[4]

There are indeed some unflattering portrayals of people I care about deeply in McPherson's short story. Milton and Sarah Feinberg are not the paragons of racial tolerance that I had not only proudly associated with my family but with Jewish merchants in town generally. The M&M Food Store portrayed in McPherson's story looks different from the nostalgic images I still have of that place. For me, the store was our family livelihood and an integral part of the community. It was where I worked on weekends and holidays and on summer vacations, taking inventory, waiting on customers. I bagged potatoes, just like Tommy, looked out of that prep-room glass window just as he did. But I remember the same produce aisle from a different perspective, my work there part of a young white boy's rite of passage rather than a potential no-exit job of a young black man such as Tommy.

I learned valuable lessons from finally picking up and reading

McPherson's story: lessons about the need to explore for myself and not accept at face value the stories others handed down; lessons about the value of stepping outside my own skin and seeing things from a different perspective; lessons about disenfranchisement and what it must feel like to be set adrift from everyone else; lessons about my hometown. Among other things, though, I also discovered that this moment in the grocery store occupies only a small space in McPherson's depiction of Tommy's youth and that there is a wealth of positive insights about community mixed in with McPherson's critique. His was a much more complex tableau of communal life than I had been led to expect.

Sustainability begins with a process of recovery, of demythologizing what one has taken for granted as true, of inquiry into one's context, of taking stock of place and people. This process of taking stock is something that must be done deliberately, and it will inevitably uncover a mixture of assets and liabilities, of positives and negatives. But it's a critical step. If we are to find some antidote to making one community look and feel like every other locale, we need to dig down and uncover its uniqueness. Most people are probably familiar with philosopher George Santayana's remark that "those who cannot remember the past are condemned to repeat it."[5] Similarly, those who don't study and value the uniqueness of one's context are likely to repeat the sameness found elsewhere. That doesn't mean we shouldn't try to change and improve our community. But it does mean that we need to understand a community for what it is—and what it is not—in order to realize what it has the capacity to become.

Let's take a closer look at this process of recovery, which requires examination of both place and people. The two are largely inseparable. In fact, over the course of this book, we will constantly be turning our attention to these two halves of culture, trying to attend to one while keeping the other in focus. It's a challenging balancing act. For the sake of discussion in this chapter, we will consider place and people sequentially, mindful, however, that the two, like foreground and background parts of a print by the graphic artist M. C. Escher, shape and are shaped by one another. I will also be using my hometown of Savannah, Georgia, as the focus of our exploration of place and people. It is, after all, the context I know best. The issues involved in examining this particular locale, though, are germane to places elsewhere.

A Coastal Place

Taking stock of place entails so much that it's daunting. History, geology, agriculture, biology, botany, hydrology: These subjects only scratch the surface of a thorough grounding in one's environment. I certainly had no clue of the place I lived in growing up. Until high school, my life was largely confined to a small triangular patch of ground, bounded by our home, Pulaski Elementary School two blocks away, and the Jewish community center where I spent afternoons playing Ping-Pong and basketball before returning home for dinner. My friends and I got around on foot and on bikes, and we played baseball in the street outside our house because there was so little traffic. Add working in the grocery store, visiting my maternal grandparents in Americus, Georgia, every month or so, and Friday-night dinners with my grandmother Annie and aunt Millie, and that was my whole world. Part of my sense of place evolved naturally and intuitively as a part of living in this close-knit world. But a part of coming to understand my sense of place has also occurred later in life, and it is these later discoveries that I want to dwell on here.

For a few weeks every summer our family rented a place on Tybee Island, one of fourteen barrier islands that protect the hundred-mile Georgia coast and located only twenty minutes east of the city. For many years, I had no idea what a barrier island was, much less that Tybee was part of an ancient chain of Pleistocene (120,000 years old) and Holocene (6,000 years old) land formations. What I knew as a kid was that every so often dredging machines would arrive, take up accumulated sediment from the south end of the island, and deposit it along the full stretch of beach to keep it from eroding. The wet, dredged mud made the beach look ugly and smell horrible. But in short order, the beach was considerably wider, making it easier for us to play half-rubber, a game unique to our part of the world, involving a broom handle for a bat and a cut-in-half rubber ball that, when thrown, dips and curves with a viciousness that would make any major-league knuckleball pitcher envious.

Still, after a few years, the beach would again erode, and so once again local leaders and politicians would lobby the federal government for funds to conduct additional dredging. It was only as an adult that I began to understand the Sisyphean pattern. Barrier islands move, with dunes that shift and drop forward and back. It doesn't make sense, financially or otherwise, to fight the slow but persistent shifting of sand and water along our coast. The natural erosion on Tybee, moreover, is exacerbated by the ongoing dredging of the Savannah River to accommodate the shipping trade. As the harbor is deepened, sand that would naturally be deposited on the north end of Tybee accretes elsewhere. The result is a combination of natural and human influences on the island that is slowly whittling away the beach. In light of such impacts it does not make sense to build houses and put infrastructure on the edges of the beach. When we do, we are playing a losing game with time.

In 2006 a prominent local businessman gave a talk about growth coming to the Georgia coast. He noted that when you fly at night from Maine to Florida, all you see is an endless string of lights—until you hit the Georgia coast, which is all dark. That hundred-mile stretch of darkness, the last frontier of darkness on the entire East Coast, this businessman was saying, was about to experience explosive growth. The aim of the speech was to get listeners pumped up about finally bringing light and growth to this last little remnant of darkness. And indeed, there was palpable excitement throughout the room that day.

Uncanny how right Santayana was about being condemned to repeat a history we resist recovering. In the fifties, local residents in Savannah were in the process of tearing down much of the eighteenth- and nineteenth-century homes in the historic district—until the Historic Savannah Foundation came into existence to save most of our local architectural treasures. Today, with tourism in Savannah's historic downtown area the major economic driver for the region, no one would dream of demolishing our historical context. But back then? Who knew the extent to which restoration would be intertwined with economics? A rare few.

The same issue is at stake on our Georgia coast today. As the local businessman droned on about bringing light and prosperity to our poor backwater of coastal darkness, my thoughts ran to the fact that this place is home to one-third of all the salt marsh on the entire Eastern seaboard and that this semipristine, precious land provides our local population with so much for free if we are willing to leave it alone. Our estuaries and back-barrier islands serve as a speed bump to the northeasters that pound the Georgia coast from early summer to late fall. They filter impurities flowing from the five major rivers originating to the west and north. They abound with nutrients that provide the feeding and spawning grounds for our local shrimp and oyster populations. Taking stock of place entails recovering such stories, if we'll listen.

If folks are attracted to this ever more valuable piece of estuary located in southeast Georgia, are we killing the golden goose by developing it and lighting it up like every other bit of the East Coast? Shouldn't we instead be setting this invaluable land aside in perpetuity? As the island botanist Paul Godfrey said tersely prior to Hurricane Katrina, "Nature always bats last at the shoreline."[6]

An Agrarian Place

Taking stock of place does not solely involve recovering our sense of the natural world; it is about understanding how the natural and human-made have engaged with one another over time. This intertwining of worlds becomes clearer when we consider the complex lessons provided by the settling of Savannah in the mid-eighteenth century.

My roots are in a town, Savannah, that echoes Einstein's well-quoted line about paradigm change: "No problem can be solved by the same manner of thinking that created it." Savannah, founded by James Oglethorpe and underwritten by a group of English philanthropists formally referred to as the Trustees, was envisioned from the outset as a response to the cycle of poverty in England, where debtors languished in jail until their debts were paid. The London philanthropists shaped the Georgia Plan to "restore those whom they perceived as deviant to their proper activity in a healthy English society." Key components of the plan included:

- Landholdings for the "worthy poor" were limited to fifty acres per person.
- The fifty-acre holdings included a house lot in Savannah proper, a garden lot of 4.875 acres on the edge of town, and a 45-acre farm farther out.
- Settlers had to cultivate the land within ten years and raise one hundred mulberry trees on the property in order to keep it.
- "Adventurers," who came to Savannah at their own expense, were allotted five hundred acres, with similar requirements of cultivation.
- Land speculation was forbidden, with the intent of inhibiting the assemblage of large land holdings. Envisioned instead was a community of yeoman farmers living on small landholdings.
- Slavery was forbidden.

The Georgia Plan was based on the seventeenth-century notion of agrarianism, an economic-political philosophy that linked ownership of land to industrious work, citizenship, and political authority. Distribution of power was viewed as proportional to the distribution of land. Small, equal allotments of landholdings such as those found in Savannah were intended to shape a society of politically engaged citizenry. Wealth and profits that came from pursuits such as land speculation—profits that seemed to be derived easily and without patience and diligence—were perceived to be injurious to both the individual and society. Tellingly, the motto for the trusteeship establishing the colony of Georgia was *Non sibi sed aliis*, Latin for "Not for themselves, but for others."

There is a good bit in this sketch of my hometown I find compelling. The city itself was founded on a paradigm shift away from untenable English practices. The health of the land and of the citizenry were linked, with an emphasis on restraining the tendency of some to grow at the expense of others through massive land assemblage. Governance was shaped as a covenantal bond between the philanthropic Trustees and a larger social order they sought to improve.

There is also the compelling design of the place itself. Oglethorpe envisioned Savannah as a tight series of squares, a concept that even today is a benchmark of cutting-edge, mixed-use urban community planning. Given our company's focus on compact urban community development with green space, all we need to do is look outside our office window, located on one of Oglethorpe's original squares, to have a clear example of what we are all about.

However, the lessons provided by my hometown are a bit more complex. The original plan for Savannah, as it turns out, was based on a landscape imagined back in England, with only a hazy sense of the true Georgian environment. Crops and products that flourished in similar latitudes in Spain, North Africa, Persia, Japan, and central China—such as mulberry trees and silk, grapes and wine, oranges, lemons, sugar, and spices—were all unjustifiably expected to do well in Savannah. The pamphlets touting the new colony—a mixture of canny advertising and hubris—outlined a business plan of productivity and prosperity that seemed fail-proof. Unfortunately the colony never managed to survive without subsidies from the English crown. Perhaps the most significant failure of all, however, was the incapacity of the leadership, even Oglethorpe, to adapt to Georgia's existing conditions. They stubbornly expected the land to bear unlikely fruits well past the point when they should have known it could not.

That the Trustees exaggerated their depiction of the region is not surprising (marketers will be marketers). That they continued to act as if the environment were as they had portrayed it in the promotional literature, even after the experiences of the colonists contradicted this image, is unsettling. Early leaders of the colony stubbornly maintained notions about the prodigality and healthfulness of the Georgia landscape that they knew were at odds with the evidence around them.[7] Taking stock of place is as much about demythologizing as it about connecting the present to the past. Both efforts—questioning and connecting—are at play here.

On the wall of my office is a copy of an engraving, capturing Savannah in the mid-eighteenth century when it was just a village. You can see the young, raw look of the downtown squares Oglethorpe designed, the whole small town a clearing in the trees sitting on the bluff of the Savannah River, surrounded by forests on both the east and west sides and fading out, looking southward, into a wash of green canopy.

It was a long time before I connected the development of this raw new village of Savannah to the general obliteration of the Southeastern landscape, once blanketed by a hundred million acres of longleaf pine, 98 percent of which have now been lost. Considered one of the most diverse ecosystems on Earth, a longleaf forest is home to numerous rare plants and animals that survive only in this environment. It takes considerable time for a longleaf pine to grow, some eight-five years to reach a diameter of twelve inches. I've seen old pictures of longleaf pine forests, massive things with enough space between trees to drive a carriage through. There are only a few remnant stands of longleaf pine surviving today. Savannah's economic growth and prosperity in the nineteenth and twentieth centuries was built upon the decimation of this pine forest. The city was the railway terminus for logging in the hinterlands, and the shipping origin for destinations around the globe that used the lumber for shipbuilding and home construction, the sap for pitch and tar, resin and turpentine. When he addressed the 1902 Turpentine Operators' Association annual convention in Jacksonville, Florida, Governor W. S. Jennings spoke movingly of the loss of the longleaf forest:

> In looking over the State as I saw it first, I recall mile upon mile of lofty pine stretching away on all sides, standing like lofty brown columns, supporting arches of living green, through which the breezes, as they passed, made sweet music; but now as I traverse the same country, I see great areas of scrubby pines, jack oaks, and a little wiregrass. The cathedral arches have gone, nature's organ is silent, and the colonnades, with their ever changing vistas are no more. The hand of desecration rests heavily on the bosom of the earth, blackened stumps alone pathetically tell of the monarchs that once made the land beautiful and valuable, and I am told that the ancient order of turpentine men wrought all this desolation. . . . In the track of the naval stores and lumber men there are only blackened stumps to pitifully tell the story of the past, of a beautiful land left a ruin [by] ruthless, wasteful extravagance.[8]

The act of recovery, of taking stock of place, involves accounting for the losses we have endured and renewing our efforts to find a more restorative path going forward. That path needs to be found soon. Thirty percent of the rich ecosystems of my home, part of the much-maligned and poorly understood southeastern United States, are critically endangered—more than any other region in the country.[9]

A Lordly Place

I'd like to convince myself that wasteful extravagance in our region is all ancient history, having occurred well before my time. Unfortunately, that's not the case. With our longleaf pine forests now largely destroyed, our destructive practices have broadened in scope to include the serious deterioration of our lands, soils, water resources, and air quality.

In the summer of 1970, a group of students and a lawyer, under the auspices of the Center for Study of Responsive Law, arrived in Savannah to study the effects of the town's industrial plants on air and water quality along the Savannah River. The ensuing report, *The Water Lords* (1971), one of numerous publications by Ralph Nader's "Raiders," caused a national uproar. Front and center of the study's attack was the largest kraft paper mill in the world, owned by Union Camp, and the cozy business relationships the paper mill (and other plants) had with city leaders. Reading the account today, almost forty years later, is unnerving. The study chronicles immense dumping of oxygen-depleting pollutants each day into the river, huge consumption of groundwater from the Upper Floridan aquifer, dumping of raw sewage by the city, release of toxic levels of sulfuric acid, closed-door negotiations that indemnified industry from lawsuits, and political stratagems that insulated industries from contributing anything but nominal taxes to the city and county. The list goes on and on. Beneath the surface of Nader's measured, lawyerly introduction, you can sense outrage:

> The facts in this report compel an ethical conclusion. These
> Savannah-based companies are outlaws. The violation and

defiance of even the most modest laws does not fully reveal the enormity of the lawlessness. A self-answering question needs to be asked: by what right, legal or moral, do these companies destroy the property and health of innocent neighbors, and jeopardize the resources that our generation holds in trust for future generations?[10]

I didn't read *The Water Lords* when it first came out. Since I was thirteen at the time, its import would have been lost on me. It isn't now. A recent study by the U.S. Environmental Protection Agency on Toxic Release Inventory lists Savannah as among the highest in the region for carcinogen levels. Tellingly, the top offender—Augusta, Georgia, in nearby Richmond County—exhibits most of the elements of air and water pollution that *The Water Lords* cataloged long ago. There's a current push to deepen the Savannah River harbor to foster additional economic growth for the Georgia port, despite the numerous environmental ills this deepening would cause, including saltwater intrusion into adjacent wetlands and reduced dissolved oxygen necessary for marine life such as the endangered short-nose sturgeon. The noxious smell of the paper and chemical plants is still present, mostly impinging upon working-class and poor neighborhoods, such as nearby Fellwood Homes, one of the oldest public housing projects in the nation (discussed in chapter four).

Even so powerful an indictment provided by *The Water Lords* failed to note that the forestry operations of the 1960s caused roughly 60 percent of Georgia's lower coastal plain to be ditched and drained and denuded of bottomland hardwood wetlands that harbored a diverse habitat of birds, mammals, fish, reptiles, and amphibians. In place of this once-rich ecosystem, we now have inexpensive suburbia.

Recovering our sense of place entails delving into stories from the past, stories of economic history, such as *The Water Lords*, that inform our own business practices today, challenging us to consider whether the despoliation of the past is something we've left behind.

A Blue-Water Place

Traveling around Savannah, I'm aware in ways I once was not of the odd place names, derivations and amalgams and corruptions of early Creek and Spanish words. Tybee Island gets its name from the Uchee Indian word for *salt*. Wassaw Island, just south of Tybee and one of the few nesting places left on the Atlantic coast for loggerhead turtles, comes from the Creek word for *sassafras*. Ossabaw Island, the state's first Heritage Preserve, comes from the Guale word for *yaupon holly bushes place*. Many of the state's riverways and watersheds have similarly held on to early names. The Altamaha River, 137 miles long and containing eleven endangered mussel species found nowhere else in the world, has a long, torturous etymology of its own, including the phrase *treacherous waters*. The Oconee and Ocmulgee Rivers, both feeding the Altamaha, come respectively from the Creek for *water eyes of the hills* and the Hitchiti for *it is boiling*.[11] The Savannah River was once called Isundiga, a Creek word meaning "blue water." Perhaps the place name was a misnomer, as is now claimed, but perhaps it really once ran blue before industry moved in.[12]

Such place names serve as a cautionary tale, reminding us of a history and a connective tissue that is growing fainter with each passing generation, much like the 5,000 languages currently spoken worldwide, which are anticipated to dwindle to about 150 by the end of this century.[13] As we encroach and build upon these Creek-named barrier islands and waterways, even as we hold on to those place names, what wisdom from past practices and seasonal rhythms will we have forgotten? Recovering our sense of place, taking stock of it, necessitates seeking out what lies embedded in the names we take for granted.

Among the gaps in my knowledge of place, my lack of knowledge of pre-European civilization looms large. I have only a rudimentary understanding of how native agrarian practices, with an emphasis on mixed plantings, were supplanted over time with colonial monocultural plantations: first indigo, then rice, followed in turn by Sea Island cotton in our region.[14] Poor soils, farming practices that exhausted and eroded the soil, cash-crop economies, and slavery all melded together to degrade the landscape and culture of the region. Poor, sandy soils, lacking the mineral-rich loess deposited on the Midwestern prairies at the end of the last Ice Age, meant that the productivity of the land declined rapidly. The practice of the headright system—whereby fifty acres of land were provided to new immigrants—ironically fostered large land assemblages, in sharp contrast to the ideals of the Georgia Plan. These large holdings, planted with labor-intensive crops such as rice and cotton, were ripe for an economy based on slavery—yet another departure from the original intentions of the Trustees.

Our current notion of property rights is, like so many other concepts, a European import that differed from the Indian notion of property as a set of usufruct rights.[15] While the European notion of land ownership meant that one had full and total rights to all aspects of a property during the period of ownership, the Indian concept of land ownership meant a limited entitlement to work the land for a particular use. The fundamental divide between these two ideas of ownership leads us to many of the quandaries we face today over our natural capital. Should the water underlying one's property "belong" to the owner, as it is permitted in certain parts of the country? Should a landowner be responsible for runoff from property into adjacent rivers and the consequent damage that occurs downstream?[16]

Recovering a sense of the way prior cultures lived within the place we now call home prompts questions as to how smart our First-World technologies are.[17]

Taking stock of place entails a querying of our own assumptions about the way things have always been and whether, to avoid collapse on a macro scale, we need to reconsider some of our cherished notions about our core rights to place.[18]

Taking Stock of Place in a Business Context

Taking stock of place is about intellectual curiosity and celebration. I am struck by the multiplicity of disciplines called upon to make sense of place. Taking stock of place can also be an emotional undertaking. It can shake the foundations of what we thought we knew and open us up to stories that perhaps never made it into canonical accounts of history. It can lead us down byways into the past that we had complacently insulated ourselves from. Taking stock of place invites us to question the very paradigms that have guided our sense of self.

But what does taking stock of place have to do with running a business? Such knowledge is nice, but is it relevant for a business, its strategies, tactics, and operations? Should it? Does knowledge of place help a business prosper or is it just a "feel-good" nod to the local culture?

While these are questions I often hear posed in the business community, they seem to me a bit odd. Business is always taking stock of place. Consider language and basic customs of place. A business would be foolhardy to operate in an environment without understanding these cultural components. A painfully obvious example is Chevrolet's decision to use its Nova brand name in the Spanish-speaking world (*no va* translates as "no go"—not the best name for a car). How about conventions governing dress, social interactions, or basic business practices? Anyone doing business in China typically is briefed on the proper way to present a business card, on expectations regarding toasts at formal banquets, and on the pace at which business negotiations are conducted. How about knowledge of the regulatory environment? It would be financially irresponsible not to be thoroughly versed in the rules and regulations of the place where one conducts business.

Of course, various businesses differ greatly in the degree to which they engage with place. A local business is tied to its locale in a complex set of ties and relationships. Sometimes, as in our case, ownership dates back generations. Prior generations have left their own marks on their community, have made commitments to the community that encourage future generations to behave similarly. Local businesses also tend to know one another. They have a shared commitment to the locale in ways that larger corporations do not[19] and share a sense that they must support one another in business and in other endeavors both in their own self-interest and in the interest of the general community—because the two are joined at the hip.

A business is likely to be less engaged with place if its model is one of replication. Big-box retailers, franchise operations, and producers of commodity products typically fit this category. They locate in one place as happily as the next, setting off bidding wars among municipalities to have their facilities located here versus there. And they have the willingness and capacity to pull up stakes, vacate, and relocate just as quickly as they arrived. Still, even these types of businesses must attend to certain basic elements of place, whether they are municipal regulations or the vagaries of local weather patterns.

Finally, there are companies that fall somewhere in the middle of the spectrum of localized businesses and global producers of commodities. Some service-sector businesses, Shangri-La Hotels, for example, base their value proposition on culture-specific offerings. Shangri-La replicates a portion of what it provides from hotel to hotel but then adapts this general service offering to the place where a hotel operates.[20] Another example is the Langdale Company, a timber company based in southeastern Georgia that is one of the largest private landowners in the country and has begun to emphasize long-term land stewardship. It's a thin wedge of companies that operate in this arena, and it's difficult to evaluate with certainty how substantively such businesses dive into the culture of a place. But at least there is an identification between what a business does and where it is located.

In short, virtually anyone involved in business today takes stock of place in basic ways. A businessperson might not be fully aware of the degree to which this adaptation to culture takes place, but it is an elemental fact of business life. It also needs to go further, moving from a sense of obligation motivated by business survival ("When in Rome do as the Romans") to a deliberate choice motivated by a company's authentic belief that its own fate and that of the larger community are woven together.

Why would a business choose not to take stock of place in deep and meaningful ways? What would prompt a business to move in this direction? More importantly, why should it? Let's consider each question briefly.

The most obvious rationale for not taking meaningful stock of place is that doing so does not seem to have much to do with business. *We're not historians or biologists or geologists; we're in the business of maximizing profit for our shareholders.* This argument, one often linked to the writings of the Nobel Prize–winning economist Milton Friedman, boils down to an issue of cost and the belief that business should not be held accountable for impacts on its milieu.

There are other reasons why a business might not consider taking stock of place. Part of the problem is the enormity of the issues involved. Nature is complex, and we have only a limited understanding of the environment around us.

Another part of the problem rests with the apparent surfeit of natural capital around us. Our places don't seem to be in imminent danger of collapse[21] and give little hint on the surface of even incremental decline.[22] Gregory Bateson, the noted British anthropologist, is credited with illustrating this challenge through the simple example of placing a frog in tepid water and slowly turning up the heat until the frog boils to death without responding to the incremental change in temperature. Like the frog, we are slow to recognize gradual, dire changes in our environment.

The challenge of integrating a sense of place into daily commerce also has to do with a historical tendency to separate nature from humankind. We began the first Industrial Revolution, dating from the mid-eighteenth century, by converting nature into an abstraction. Earth began to be regarded as a system of land parcels with bundles of rights attached to them and containing Earth's living things to be used at our disposal as resources. The Trustees' plan for Georgia, laid out in England without actual experience on the land, is typical in this regard. The establishment in 1872 of Yellowstone as the first national park in the United States serves as a much-referenced example of cordoning off of nature from daily life.

Finally, the challenge of taking meaningful stock of place touches on ethical and epistemological considerations. Humankind is anthropocentric in its outlook. We make decisions based on what we perceive to be our own self-interest.[23] It's challenging for us to comprehend things from anything but our own perspective, despite arguments that we need to do so.[24]

Given these challenges, what would prompt a business to move in this direction? Five distinct motivating factors come to mind. A business could be required by government to comply with regulations and guidelines as the "cost of entry" into a particular market. Businesses operating in California, for example, are required to adhere to the state's relatively stringent energy code. The frame of mind with such businesses is *We're doing this taking stock of place, but only because we have to.*[25] A second type of business, which has a strong ethical orientation, is motivated by the belief that taking stock of place is the right thing to do. A business such as ShoreBank in Chicago, which provides micro-loans in poverty-stricken areas of the city, serves as a good example. The mind-set of such businesses is *We're taking stock of place because we should.* A third rationale for doing a deep dive into place is largely pragmatic. This approach holds that a business can do well precisely *because* it is doing good. DuPont's move in the direction of sustainable initiatives in the early 1990s is indicative of this type of motivation. A fourth approach is a utilitarian orientation, generally thought of as "the greatest good for the greatest number." A utilitarian approach tends to do well and do good but doesn't necessarily see a causal connection between the two. Finally, there is an integrative approach, in which place and business are seen as largely inseparable and where doing well financially and doing good for place are intimately connected.[26] An overview of these five orientations can be seen in Figure 1-1.

But even if businesses might be motivated to take stock of place, why should they? The question is only partially rhetorical. Why should McDonald's, for instance, care whether growth causes the degradation

Figure 1-1: Taking Stock		
Orientation	Rationale	Frame of mind in taking stock of place
Regulatory	Outside authority requires it	Doing
Ethical	It's the right thing to do	Doing good
Pragmatic	Makes good business/financial sense	Doing well because we're doing good
Utilitarian	Broad group of stakeholders expects it	Doing well and doing good
Integrative[27]	Spiritual sense that business and place are integrally connected	Doing well and doing good are inseparable

of the marshes in my hometown? The company uses sophisticated socio-demographic modeling that tries to anticipate and benefit from just such burgeoning growth. Speed to market, plug-and-play, efficient replication of what has worked elsewhere, marketing a product or brand that trumpets a certain worldly sophistication: This is the stock in trade of place-bereft businesses. And why not? Don't the stockholders of such companies expect these efficiencies as the basis upon which to maximize profits?

Should businesses conduct themselves any other way? Should business look beyond shareholder profits to maximize the value for a larger group of stakeholders in the community at large? A sparse list of business leaders and academics believe so. Still, while the number of businesses signing on to CERES principles—principles developed in 1987 to evaluate a company's environmental, social, and economic performance—is indeed growing,[28] the extent to which these signatories are doing a deep dive into place is still very limited.

Does it matter, in the end, whether a business takes deep stock of place? Is it in the best interest of the business to do so? Does a business need to take deep stock of place in order to be sustainable? I believe the answer to all these queries is yes.

It does matter greatly whether business takes stock of place, because business makes the greatest impact on place—for better or worse. If businesses continue to locate, use up a place, toss it on a junk heap, and abandon it for the next place down the road, we will have realized the nightmarish vision of Dr. Seuss's *The Lorax*. In that classic story, all the wondrous Truffula trees that once provided shade and habitat and economic vitality for an entire region are all cut down and the industry shuts down to move elsewhere, leaving a wasteland in its wake:

No more trees. No more Thneeds. No more work to be done.
So, in no time, my uncles and aunts, every one,
All waved me good-bye. They jumped into my cars
And drove away under the smoke-smuggered stars.
Now all that left 'neath the bad-smelling sky
Was my big empty factory . . .

The Lorax . . .
And I.

The story of the Lorax is not confined to fiction. The agricultural history of the South has modeled this process of plant-deplete-and–move on production.

If place needs the strict attention of business, business also needs place. Businesses need stability to function well. Both free-market proponents and conservationists agree that without attention to the environment there can be no sustainable place, that without a sustainable place there is lacking a sustainable culture, that without sustainable culture there can be no sustainable community, and that without sustainable community there is no sustainable business on a global scale.[29] Business owes it to itself to understand the fundamentals of the places where it operates. Business owes it to itself to understand the ecological stability of the places where it invests and its own impingement upon that stability. Otherwise it is degrading its own work environment and endangering its future.

Does it take time to study and think reflectively about place? Does it take perhaps an entire organization to synthesize discrete bits and pieces of knowledge of a place so that the pieces cohere? Yes to both these questions. But a business's lifeline is its ongoing capacity to learn and to adapt from what it learns. Taking stock of place, particularly the lessons place can teach us, constitutes the basic building blocks of a business's capacity to thrive for the long term.

Taking stock of place challenges the assumption that the march of time is also a march of progress. It challenges us to rethink our presumption that the world we know is the way things have always been or how the world should be. It also challenges us to consider whether we are learning from our context—or rather are repeating the mistakes we have historically foisted on our landscapes.

The philosopher Gaston Bachelard writes insightfully about the benefits provided by inhabited space. Our houses and our rooms provide the space for memories, provide nooks and crannies within which to curl up comfortably, extend us physical and emotional shelter, support our sense of stability, and enable us to dream. By recovering our sense of houses and rooms, Bachelard writes, in one of the most eloquent sentences I know, "We learn to 'abide' within ourselves."[30]

The same is true of our exploration of place. The process of restoring who we are, in short, begins with restoring our sense of where we are.

Taking Stock of People

Though businesses may ignore the concept of place, they pay closer attention to people. This makes sense. While few businesses view their business model as contingent upon maintaining close proximity to their places of operation, fewer still would ignore the people who buy their goods and services or the people who work to provide those goods and services.

There is no lack of well-regarded business books that focus on people. "Getting the right people on the bus" is the well-known tag line from James Collins and Jerry Porras' *Good to Great*. A 1997 McKinsey study of seventy-seven major corporations indicates that hiring and retaining top talent is the critical driver for a company's success. Crafting a strategy that enables a company to occupy a competitive space all its own is viewed as contingent upon creating a culture of trust and commitment that motivates people. Creating a sensibility of "felt leadership," where everyone in the organization feels the need for the company's vision, is considered important. So too is the need to have a "community of learners." In short, these days concepts related to business leadership focus on creating an empowered and meaning-driven workforce.[31]

These business books aren't wrong: Of course people matter, particularly if they are motivated and caring. And of course people work best when they have incentives to do so. The basic problem with this orientation toward people is that the focus is self-referential: A company looks to have people take stock in it, not the reverse. The direction is centripetal (swirling toward the center, in this case toward the company), not centrifugal (radiating outward toward others).

Strategies for managing a business typically amount to offering up a culture that attracts people inward toward the mother ship. Oftentimes business literature on culture evokes the sense that this culture can simply be served up on a platter to its staff, or that senior managers can create this culture *ex nihilo* in short order. But is business culture such a quickly shaped commodity that it can be molded in this way? Should it be? Is there an alternative approach to business-culture creation that evolves naturally over time and not something concocted by senior management, baked rapidly, and dished out to the rest of the staff?

These challenges can be seen most clearly in business literature that, ironically enough, seems to take stock of people and their need for meaning. Numerous business authors these days promote the idea of a culture of "soft control," envisioned as semiautonomous collaboration that fulfills the individual's desire for creativity while meeting the company's need for productivity.[32]

Most of us are probably familiar with this concept of soft control in one form or another, even (or especially) when it is well-intentioned. For instance, early on in my running of Melaver, Inc., I focused a lot of effort on creating a company culture that I personally would love to work for. And there's nothing fundamentally wrong with that—until one day you see a *Dilbert* cartoon tacked onto the refrigerator in the break room, lampooning the fact that the culture the boss thinks is wonderful and engaging is nevertheless a culture that has been imposed from above without much input from colleagues.

It's a tricky dynamic, creating the environment in which a workforce can be engaged without presupposing what that environment looks like. The tensions involved in this dynamic are unintentionally captured by Jeffrey Hollender, CEO of Seventh Generation and author of *What Matters Most*, when he notes:

> We've come to consider the company as a place in which to offer people an opportunity not just for material and economic growth, but spiritual and moral and personal growth as well. We've tried to create a corporate culture in which people are not drained by their work but energized by it, not alienated but fulfilled as members of an intentional community. We've tried to

be, in the largest sense, a satisfying company to work for and do business with, and a major part of that effort is having a well-developed vision of what it means to be a responsible business and a good corporate citizen.[33]

I like what Hollender is saying here. Nevertheless, his language contains a subtle but distinct implication of control from above. Much of the business literature on having an empowered and meaning-driven workforce seems little more than a disguised riff on top-down, managerially imposed social engineering. It may be well-intentioned engineering (and it may be much less benign), but at its heart, virtually all business writings on culture come down to a centripetal model that *presumes* a set of values for a workforce and uses that set of values to draw people in. Such a centripetal model begs this basic question: Has anyone instead thought seriously about taking stock of what a workforce itself cares deeply about? In lieu of a centripetal model of human capital, how about instead a centrifugal model, in which a culture is formed organically by those working at a company and then evolves over time as it engages with the larger community?

The act of recovery, then, focuses on fostering an environment that enables people in a social context (e.g., a business) to think profoundly about what matters most to them. Such an environment enables a group to recover its sense of meaning and purpose by not presuming what that sense of meaning is. While a conventional business model imposes culture, a restorative business model seeks to recover it.

At least one business leader, Max De Pree, the former CEO of Herman Miller, has given this issue considerable thought:

> The best people working for organizations are like volunteers, they choose to work somewhere for reasons less tangible than salary or position. Volunteers do not need contracts, they need covenants. . . . Covenantal relationships induce freedom, not paralysis. A covenantal relationship rests on shared commitment to ideas, to issues, to values, to goals, and to management process. Words such as love, warmth, personal chemistry, are

certainly pertinent. Covenantal relationships . . . fill deep needs
and they enable work to have meaning and to be fulfilling.[34]

Interestingly, while De Pree spends some time describing what the
experience of a covenantal relationship is like, he doesn't say much
about how it occurs. For him, a covenantal relationship is one in which
a company commits to enabling the employee to reach his or her fullest
potential. It entails what he refers to as certain essential employee rights:
the right to be needed, to be involved, to understand, to affect one's own
destiny, and the right to know.[35] For De Pree, work is viewed not so
much as a profession as it is a calling.[36] This sense of calling provides an
important insight into what taking stock of people is all about: fostering
an environment in which the underlying values of people in the workplace shape the business culture, not vice versa as is usually conceived.

This may be an odd notion to some. Do I really mean to suggest that
the employees create the culture of a company themselves, and not the
reverse? What if they wish to go in a direction diametrically opposed to
the company's historical practices or to the company's current strategic trajectory? How is consensus arrived at? How does one prevent the
company from reinventing its culture all the time, based on the inflows
and outflows of personnel? Do a company's business leaders no longer
control the show? Isn't this just a bit too anarchic to be workable? How,
in short, does this work?

Centrifugal Culture and Values

The ways a business facilitates taking stock of people are numerous and
diverse. In our organization, we rely on a variety of management tools
or processes: One is a bottom-up process involving values shaping and
reshaping. Another involves a collective hiring protocol. A third entails
creating space for meaning. These processes go to the heart of what a
business culture, functioning centrifugally, looks like.

When I began working at Melaver, Inc., in 1992, we had two employees: a bookkeeper and me. As we began to take on additional people
in the mid-nineties, each new hire was empowered to make significant
decisions on the fly. We needed a framework to guide our decisions, a set

of core values that would be at the center of all our actions. And so the first of many bottom-up processes was set in motion.

We began with a series of meetings at which we asked everyone at the company to name the values he or she held most dear. The list was long. We discussed each one, eliminating redundancies, subsuming "smaller" concepts like pride in one's work within larger ones, such as a commitment to excellence. Over a nine-month period, we reduced the list to four core values (ethical behavior, learning, service, profitability), each elaborated on by brief belief statements.[37]

Word-smithing those belief statements took longer than selecting our core values. Sometimes when a group engages in a process such as this, it is just an exercise. There is an unstated sense in the air that everyone is just going through the motions. Businesses have become so savvy about "managing process" (a euphemism for managing outcomes) that often the real value inherent in the process itself is eviscerated; *Check off the box of involving others and move on,* seems to be the underlying message. But done intently, patiently, genuinely, with an eye toward the moment itself and not the ultimate endpoint, focusing on recovering what people within an organization feel passionately about, such a bottom-up process facilitates meaning in its own right. The final "product" of our discussions did not come from me or from our senior management team. It was an effort of the entire company, an extended process that enabled everyone to speak directly about what mattered most.

We have since employed this same process with every important policy or philosophical document we've drafted. When we embark on one of these collective, bottom-up journeys as a company, the prospect of devoting extensive time and effort struggling over *words, for God's sake,* is daunting to all of us. Statements we generate together, however, aren't just words. Oftentimes most of my colleagues can't recall much of the verbiage we had worked so hard to create. Of greater significance is the collective act itself, as well as the unified sense of purpose that this process engenders. Sometimes, my colleagues groan when we begin such a process. "Just tell us what you are thinking," they say to me. "It would be a lot quicker." What they don't realize is that almost always before we start one of these sessions, I don't have a clue. Good things bubble up from within the company's collective conscience. That, to me, is what taking stock of people is all about.

Centrifugal Culture and Hiring

A second management tool we draw upon as part of our overall process of taking stock of people is our consensual hiring protocol. With certain, limited exceptions (summer interns mostly) we don't hire a new colleague without broad participation in the vetting process. Tedious? Probably. Worth the effort? Absolutely.

The logic behind such cross-disciplinary collaboration is fairly obvious. Since each job intersects with all others, we shape the new job description and vet the candidate pool from multidivisional perspectives from the outset. Once the hiring task force sifts through the stack of resumes, the short list of candidates is interviewed by many at the company, with the centerpiece of the process being an en masse conversation with the candidate around our conference table. Each candidate joins most of us in a spirited, freewheeling conversation that mimics the way we engage one another on a daily basis. There are very few stock questions. We may put on the table a thorny issue facing us at the time. For example: With whom does a sustainable company compete, and do we lose competitive advantage sharing our knowledge and experience with others? How do we work more collaboratively with a large group of stakeholders to ensure that the growth coming to coastal Georgia does not negatively impact our land and environment? All of us debate the issue around the table, involving the candidate in the discussion process.

The point is not to intimidate the potential hire. In fact, pains are taken to set the person at ease, to make him or her feel part of the group. Yes, we are taking stock of a particular person, trying to determine how well he or she will both complement and challenge the ways in which we work. And yes, we use the process as a means of enabling the candidate to take stock of us. But most important, we are using the process of collective hiring as a mechanism of renewal and recovery for those of us who are already working together. The insertion of a new colleague into the mix both reaffirms and modifies that mix in critical ways.

The literary scholar Frank Kermode, in a monograph titled *The*

Classic, defines an enduring work of literature by imagining a set of canonical texts on a long bookshelf. There may be thousands of well-known tomes on this shelf. According to Kermode, a new classic is a book that, when placed somewhere amidst these already established, older works of art, causes all the other books on the shelf to shift slightly from where they were resting. A new classic, in Kermode's metaphor, allows us to see all the older works in a different position, enabling us to view them in a different way from before.

That metaphor captures the essence of our hiring practices. We are looking for the new addition to cause us all to shift our viewpoints, to enable us to see what we do in a different and compellingly new way. A new hire allows us not only to take stock of ourselves, but also to query what we are doing, to assess the assumptions underlying our decisions. A new hire, in short, enables us to be better than we were. So while we often talk about looking to hire someone who is the right "fit," this language of alignment is a misnomer. We are actually looking for a certain creative friction or misalignment that corrects the natural tendency of a business to fall into groupthink. We use the process of consensual hiring to constantly reshape and refine our company's culture, rather than indoctrinate a potential new employee into a static environment.

The process of consensual hiring does beg the question, Is this a centrifugal aspect of culture creation or actually centripetal? Aren't certain types of people—mission-driven individuals with a sustainable ethos, for instance—drawn to a company such as ours in the first place? Is it possible that a company (1) starts out having a more centrifugal orientation, (2) over a period of time evolves into a mature identity, and (3) eventually becomes more centripetal in its structure?

Like so many other management practices we will be discussing over the course of this book, the issue of consensual hiring (and whether it is centrifugal or centripetal) comes down to the art of managing tension in creative ways. Yes, we do attract mission-driven individuals who have a passion for sustainable practices. But they come in all different colors and stripes, such that the mix created within our culture is very heterogeneous. That doesn't mean we don't have to monitor ourselves constantly. We do. Overemphasis on fit and alignment will indeed lead us into groupthink bias. Overemphasis on nonfit and misalignment will create chaos. Frank Kermode's metaphor is apt: We are looking for new classics that will fit on the shelf to begin with, but will also shift our collective thinking when they are placed alongside those already in place. To answer the question posed in the previous paragraph, collective hiring involves a centripetal-like attraction for the company culture to begin with but results in the constant addition of new colleagues who pull the company culture outward into new and uncharted territory.

Centrifugal Culture and Creating Space for Meaning

Underlying the collective shaping of values and shared hiring practices is the effort to provide open space to enable meaning to form. Peter Brook, eminent theater and film director and author of *The Empty Space*, captures this notion well:

> In order for something of quality to take place, an empty space has to be created. An empty space makes it possible for a new phenomenon to come to life, for anything that touches on content, meaning, expression, language, and music can exist only if the experience is fresh and new. However no fresh and new experience is possible if there isn't a pure, virgin space ready to receive it.[38]

A number of years ago, our staff was struggling to define *sustainability* and what it means in terms of company beliefs and practices. Over a series of bottom-up brainstorming sessions, we had developed an extensive list of economic, environmental, and social metrics. But you could tell the metrics weren't getting to the heart of the matter. Staff members were weighing in with thoughts and ideas, but the outcome seemed stiff and flat, making the brainstorming exercises seem rote.

We took a different tack, deferring these formal sessions in lieu of one-on-one sessions with all staff members during which we shared stories of what sustainability meant to us personally. Rhett, our head broker, recounted the story of his grandfather, a farmer in neighboring South

Carolina, who set up a school to educate the illiterate farmhands who worked for him. Angela, one of our property managers, talked about a garden she and her husband had created and that had become a focal point for the entire neighborhood to gather, learn about organic practices, and socialize. Karen, our controller, described a jewelry box she had handcrafted from local materials to hand on to her daughter, Katie. And so on. Over time we developed a small book of stories touching on themes such as education, community, conservation, waste reduction, legacy creation, stewardship, and intragenerational continuity. Eventually we returned to our initial exercise of defining sustainability. But this time, we crafted a statement that welled up from these personal stories. The stories had been there all along. But an analytical process, even a bottom-up analytical process, had failed to bring those stories to the surface. Lacking was the presence of an empty, open, and welcoming space to enable meaning to be expressed.

I'm a deep believer in the power of letting go and inviting the stories of others. But this process requires profound vulnerability and trust among members of an organization, critical components of team building.[39] When colleagues open themselves up through personal vignettes, there is considerable trust that these stories will not be made use of in any untoward ways, that the process of inviting this self-expression emanates from an authentic desire to understand one another better and not from some callous intent to mine and market personal sensibilities. Authentic intent from the outset—to allow meaningful expression to come forth—and authentic care and stewardship of these stories once they are on the table are absolutes. The result is deeply restorative, providing the company that takes such practices to heart with a substantive core that is irreplaceable.

Centrifugal Culture and Recurrent Practices

There are numerous other management tools and processes that exemplify the centrifugal nature of a restorative business.[40] We create cross-disciplinary teams for virtually all activities, for instance. This practice not only facilitates collaboration and collective buy-in for our projects and decisions, but, more important, fosters shared leadership.

In most companies roles and functions are parceled out by hierarchy. Senior management is responsible for designing the overall strategy of the company, midlevel managers are charged with overseeing the execution of the strategy, third-tier staff members are tasked with managing the day-to-day challenges of the work, and a fourth level of workers handles the most routine functions associated with maintaining the operations and administration of the business.

But in our cross-functional teams, the roles of strategizing, executing, managing, and maintaining are all mixed in together, with the result that the team takes charge of all levels of the work involved.[41] In this way overarching meaning and purpose are never far removed from the nitty-gritty details.

Other tools and processes we draw upon include a deliberate approach to naming, shared learning, collective ritual shaping, and coaching. These tools and processes help shape a culture emanating from the people who embody what we do. And, of course, centrifugal culture-shaping practices need not—in fact, should not—stop at the outer boundaries of a workplace but extend outward toward taking stock of people and their needs within the community at large (more on this in chapter four).[42]

There are times, especially when we collectively address a philosophical issue such as where we should or should not develop, when it feels as if we are revisiting the same issue over and over again, without resolution. My colleagues have a code name for this constant sense of return: Groundhog Day. It's a reference to the 1993 movie about a local weatherman played by Bill Murray, who is sent to Punxsutawney, Pennsylvania, to cover the annual Groundhog Day ceremony. The twist is that Murray keeps waking up day after day in Punxsutawney, reliving the day's events until the cycle is eventually broken by a sea change in his attitude toward the people and place around him. Initially staff references to our constant revisiting of certain issues as Groundhog Day were derisive, borne out of frustration and a sense that we were not able to make decisions and move on.

I've come to like this nickname though. It works. In the course of the movie Bill Murray's character uses his constantly returning day to best advantage: He becomes an accomplished pianist (ostensibly in one day), a close friend to many of the townspeople (ostensibly in one day), and a person who eventually sheds his veneer of cynicism and recovers his capacity to love (ostensibly in one day). In a similar vein, our constant returning to certain issues and challenges is not so much a repetition of the same debate but an opportunity to revisit issues and gain a little more insight and compassion and experience each time. The process of taking stock of people is about providing a social group the opportunity, over and over again, to recover a sense of something that will help make us more whole.

The Challenges of Time, Growth, and Size

Taking stock of people entails bottom-up processes. It calls for a centrifugal orientation toward the fostering and nurturing of a business culture. But how broadly can this be applied to other businesses? Let's consider some challenges associated with such an approach to business culture, more particularly the issues of time, growth, and size.

The first and most obvious concern is time. *We just don't have the luxury of time to engage in a bottom-up process on a consistent basis; it would kill our business* is a refrain heard often. The concern is valid. Most of us live time-starved lives, just keeping our heads above water, dealing with constant put-out-the-fire tasks. Who has time for reflection, especially when you're not talking about just a handful of senior executives but everyone at the company? How can a company afford a deep dive into the underlying need of all staff members for purpose and meaning in their lives? How can a company stop what it is doing long enough so that all staff members can interview a potential new hire? Why would a company want to engage in such collaborative processes, even if it could?

The questions of how and why are interrelated. Our collective experience as we worked through various bottom-up processes has been that the skepticism surrounding implementation (the how) is often a mask for underlying resistance (the why). As British poet and novelist Letitia Landon notes, "Whatever people in general do not understand, they are always prepared to dislike; the incomprehensible is always the obnoxious."[43] Let's first consider the issue from the standpoint of implementation (how), then address the deeper issue of resistance (why).

Virtually all businesses, irrespective of size or profession, involve at least four major types of work: designing, executing, managing, and maintaining. Moreover, virtually all businesses prioritize how much human and financial capital is invested in each of these four types of work. Devoting all of one's time to strategy could result in a well-wrought plan, but one lacking anything substantive to show for it. Alternatively, devoting all of one's time to executing will result in a business that lacks an overarching direction and a properly maintained set of assets. This challenge of balancing a company's time and energies can be depicted in

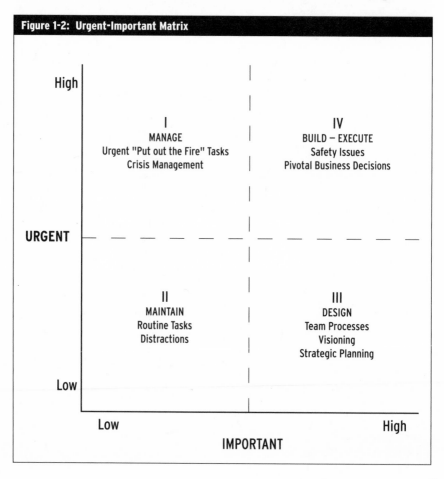

Figure 1-2: Urgent-Important Matrix

the Urgent-Important Matrix, which our company has constructed by synthesizing a similar matrix developed by Stephen Covey with elements of the Myers-Briggs Type Indicator typology (Figure 1-2).

Most companies devote time and energy to long-term design activities (quadrant III) but consign those activities to senior leadership and not to a broad spectrum of staff. The so-called rank-and-file are typically relegated to more mundane, less important tasks (quadrants I and II, managing and maintaining). In this conventional organizational structure, dating back to the Industrial Revolution, more or less invented on American shores with the "uniformity system" of mass production[44] and refined by management theorist Frederick Winslow Taylor at Bethlehem Steel and general managers such as Alfred Sloan at GM, roles in an organization mimic assembly-line production practices. Taking stock of people challenges this silo-like management structure, by engaging the full organization in the deeper design activities of the business, as well as the other quadrants.

But a troubling question remains: Why would a well-oiled, highly structured business organization retool its management style for the sake of processes that seem strange and potentially anarchic? Why would senior management voluntarily surrender control of the very activities for which they have climbed corporate ladders, activities that traditionally have defined the source of their power, prestige, and pay grade?[45]

First, a bottom-up approach, where all members of an organization bring their principles and values to the table, provides a business with the capacity to move faster, not slower. There is no substitute for having a workforce that feels passionate about what it does. Passion injects a mission-driven ethos into work and instills a sense, shared by all, that the work being done is both important and urgent. The ongoing process of taking stock of people is like building lasting foundations for a house: Once those passionate and heartfelt foundations are in place, the capacity of an organization to accomplish its more routine functions with intention and determination increases significantly.

A second rationale can be found in the context of hiring practices. A 1999 Millennium Poll on Corporate Responsibility, involving twenty-five thousand people surveyed in a thousand companies across twenty-three countries, found that a corporation's overall image is most affected by the degree to which it is perceived as fulfilling its social responsibility. This survey, conflated with several other studies, leads Bob Willard, author of *The Sustainability Advantage,* to conclude that a company's ability to hire and retain top talent will be based on how well it provides its employees with the sense that their employment serves some greater good or purpose.[46] Willard goes on to put a considerable price tag on recruiting and retaining talent, amounting to two to three times an annual salary.[47] So the question is not *Can a company afford to expend considerable time and effort with its hiring processes?* It's *What company can afford not to?*

But the practice of devoting significant time and effort in hiring or, further, the practice of consensual hiring practices is devoid of much significance if there isn't a value offering underlying the process. The significance of group hiring processes, from the point of view of the new hire, is not the prospect of being interviewed by a whole bunch of people. The significance is that the company is providing the potential hire with the opportunity from the get-go to shape the company's culture. In other words, the new hire is being asked to contribute a sense of personal meaning and purpose to the overall design of the company.

So why would a business choose to open its culture to ongoing, participatory redesigning? Because the market for talented people is pulling business in this direction by beginning to demand a culture of shared leadership as the price of admission. We're a very small company, located in a city that, while it has its attractions, is nevertheless hardly in the first tier of desirable places to work. Part of our strategy for attracting top talent to our company is insisting that they help shape our collective destiny. We feel that the business that learns how to take stock of people in authentic ways and learns how to provide an empty space for staff members to fill with purpose and meaning will have a distinct, competitive edge in the recruitment and retention of talented newcomers. While average corporate turnover in the United States is less than four years, our own capacity to hold on to strong talent for three to four times this average is, I think, testament to the value of participatory leadership.

Finally, businesses handicap themselves by making overarching planning the special provenance of a handful of specialists. Peter Schwartz, who for a long time has been associated with visionary scenario planning for major, global companies, notes that numerous organizations— from IBM to Apple to Honda—have all missed tremendous growth opportunities by not holding strategic conversations across a broad cross-section of staff. "There is often a profoundly depressing moment," notes Schwartz, "when the responsible managers realize that they *did* know what was going on or at least . . . had access to the necessary information." They never managed to connect the dots of strategic thinking across an organization.[48] Shared, bottom-up leadership is a systemic approach to connecting the dots across an entire company.

How does a business grow if it's constantly checking in with its broader staff before key moves are made? In a business climate renowned for the speed of change, can such a model keep up with the pace of business?

Taking stock of people is *not*, as is sometimes thought, a practice that constrains growth. In fact, there is no shortage of businesses, including large, successful ones (Starbucks, The Body Shop, Patagonia), that have done well in part by devoting time and effort to nurturing their employee base.[49] Instead a more subtle issue is at stake: Is a company's often unquestioned push to grow aligned with the needs of its workforce? While the process of taking stock of people need not necessarily constrain a business's growth, how many companies utilize the process (taking stock of people) as a means of exploring how to grow or whether to grow at all? My guess is not many. Should businesses engage in such exploration? I believe so.

The issue of growth is critical, not just in the context of this book or in the context of our company, but in the larger context of viability both for humans and nature. Population growth, technological efficiency, and consumption patterns are identified as the three critical components influencing our overall impact on nature. Business growth plays an integral role in consumption. As environmental educator David Orr points out:

> There are unspoken taboos against talking seriously about the very forces that undermine biological diversity. I am referring to

our inability to question economic growth, the distribution of wealth, capital mobility, population growth, and the scale and purposes of technology. These subjects have not yet entered the public dialogue because they are not considered realistic. But until they do, we are not likely to conserve much.[50]

Orr's comment may appear to be less widely true these days, with a recent flurry of business literature at least putting the issue of limits to growth on the table for public discourse.[51] Nevertheless, there is still a fundamental gap in our culture between talk about limiting growth and actual practices, much like someone who knows he has an addiction but resists doing much about it.

In the earlier years of running our business, I turned a deaf ear to limiting our company's growth. It took considerable time and reflection to come to terms with the notion that one person's (my) label of underachievement could be another person's moniker for reasonable restraint.[52] Even today it's a subject of much discussion among my colleagues (and the subject of the next chapter, devoted to the principle of restraint). Our own struggles during the credit crisis of 2008, with too much equity tied up in nascent development projects, are a partial result of my willingness/desire to push our company's pace beyond its natural capacity. If not an actual taboo, seriously proposing (not to mention actually practicing) limits to growth seems downright un-American and anticapitalist in most circles, even among some environmentalists.[53] But if this book accomplishes just one thing, I would hope that it at least fosters a wider debate over what constitutes appropriate growth for a business.

Paul Hawken, in *Growing a Business*, argues that every business has its natural rate of growth and that the challenge of leadership is to manage change within this bounded state.[54] To which I would add: It is the challenge of stewards of a business to engage its entire workforce in a dialogue of managing (and limiting) quantitative growth as well as managing (and optimizing) qualitative growth. The process of taking stock of people helps tease out these two distinct notions of growth and enables a business to create a more sustainable model in which the growth of a company and the growth of its workforce are more aligned.

The final major challenge to taking stock of people concerns the issue of size. It's one thing to carve out time for democratic discussion when your company is as small as ours (fewer than three dozen); quite another when you have thousands of employees spread over numerous locations. The logistics seem insurmountable. Just how practical is it to implement such bottom-up practices? Does there come a time in a company's growth when it becomes too large to involve everyone in discussing the philosophical issues facing the business, when it is too unwieldy to have everyone sign off on a new hire? Absolutely. And beyond logistics is a more fundamental concern: Can a large company—large in size and scope and complexity of operations—be worker-intimate? Can a large company provide meaning and purpose for its workforce?

Responses to these questions fall into two distinct camps. For classic environmentalists, the point of reference is usually economist Fritz Schumacher's seminal work *Small Is Beautiful* (1973), which focuses on small-scale, nonviolent technology that enables work to be fulfilling and creative.[55] Other writers and business-thought leaders, following from Schumacher, have argued that smaller entities are better informed, more adaptable, and more responsive to a fast business climate, enabling them to step in and provide leadership where big business and governments have abnegated their responsibilities.[56]

The second camp, that of big business, is represented by former Canon CEO Ryuzaburo Kaku, who contends that while individuals (and governments) have roles to play in implementing meaningful social change, they lack the "degree of wealth and power that corporations have."[57] It's a pragmatic argument, a sense that if needed change is going to occur and occur fast, it will need the top-down influence and significance of some of the world's largest producers. The Natural Step, a nonprofit organization originating in Sweden and providing consultancy services worldwide to assist major companies in reducing their environmental footprint, shares this pragmatic approach. Its focus is fostering maximum systemic change by partnering with those companies whose environmental policies and practices are felt globally. Companies such as

Interface, Scandic Hotels, Collins Pine Company, Nike, Ikea, IntraWest, Starbucks, and CH2M Hill all feature prominently in case studies published by The Natural Step.[58]

The critical issue in this debate is less one of size than intention. How serious are the stewards of a business about fostering a culture of meaning and purpose with the people around them? If the intention is present, the organizational tactics to take stock of place can be devised and implemented regardless of a company's size. The issue is not so much *can* a large corporation work with its staff to create meaning from within as it is *whether* a larger corporation *wants* to do so. When you have commitment and passion from a business leader, the answer is clearly yes, it can be done. Will that commitment continue over the long haul? Will it sustain itself as leadership succession passes from one person to the next? The question hinges on whether meaning and purpose is nurtured from within the organization from the bottom up (through shared stewardship), or whether meaning and purpose has been presented as part of a fully formed and static culture (through leadership mandate).

Even cutting-edge businesses tend to follow the second path, working from a more mechanical, formulaic standpoint. Change management is viewed and executed as a top-down process. Leaders have a sense of purpose, create a sense of urgency around that purpose, and build a top-level coalition that develops and communicates a vision, which then filters downward to methods of empowering staff across the entire company.[59] This may be an effective way to implement change that the leadership du jour wishes to see. But it's not necessarily the way to sustain meaning and purpose and passion over the long haul.

Beyond the issue of intention, though, looms size: the challenge of taking stock of people in large companies. "Spare, lean organizations," notes organizational expert Peter Senge, "are best able to promote the creativity needed to achieve any vision, about sustainability or anything else."[60] A general rule in business organizational literature is that companies of up to about 160 people make decisions large and small based on compelling logic (rational decision making), that companies beyond that size and up to about 750 people make decisions based on policies (bureaucratic decision making), and that companies beyond this size make decisions based on power and influence (political decision making).[61] An innovative work-around is to limit divisions in a large company to fewer than 160 staff members, an approach that has several advantages. The approach enables a larger company to work more creatively and entrepreneurially. This approach also enables a larger company to be more cognizant of and responsive to revolutionary changes in business practices.[62] Finally, and perhaps most important, such an approach enables smaller, decentralized teams to work collaboratively through all four roles captured by the Urgent-Important Matrix. Few large businesses, however, have adopted this innovative approach.[63]

Synthesizing People and Place

Over the years, our own efforts as a company to take stock of people and place have become so intertwined that they are part of the air we breathe. When we consider a potential development deal, for instance, my colleagues are likely to ask: *Does this community need more upscale condominium housing? Doesn't this project exacerbate sprawl? Are we helping catalyze needed economic growth for this area?* What my colleagues are doing, oftentimes without realizing it, is saying, *This particular project doesn't resonate with me, it doesn't make me feel that I'm doing something for the overall health of my community, and it doesn't inspire me with a sense of meaning and purpose.* Their sense of ownership in our decision-making process flows seamlessly into the sense of meaning and purpose they have from being part of our company, which flows seamlessly into a very personal slant on how our business decisions affect our community.

Taking stock of place enriches a business's efforts to take stock of people—and vice versa. The two enterprises are woven into each other, involving a process of deep engagement with context. This notion is akin to the familiar nostrum about marriage: You don't just marry your partner; you marry your partner's entire extended family. A deep engagement with people leads to those aspects of place and culture to which people are rooted. A deep engagement with place leads to a more profound understanding of the people who have put down roots there. Drawing upon these two evaluative touchstones is how a business becomes more restorative. The environmental and the ecological flow seamlessly into the social and the human.[64]

Some businesses, usually local in nature but not necessarily so, manage to successfully emphasize place *and* people. These companies—the focus of business case studies elsewhere—include Judy Wicks and the White Dog Café in Philadelphia, PA, Doc and Connie Hatfield of Oregon Country Beef, ShoreBank in Chicago, IL, Interface (Atlanta, GA), Patagonia (Ventura, CA), Ben & Jerry's (Waterbury, VT), Tom's of Maine (Kennebunk, ME), Stonyfield Farm (Londonderry, NH), Seventh Generation (Burlington, VT), Collins Pine (Portland, OR), and Righteous Babe Records (Buffalo, NY), among many others.

Other businesses, typically larger in scope, seem to place greater emphasis on the people component of what they do rather than place. In this category would be chains (Starbucks, The Body Shop) whose commitment to corporate social responsibility (CSR) leans heavily on issues like health insurance and employee ownership.[65] But because they are chain stores such companies do not root themselves deeply into particular locale.

Still other businesses seem to make their mark most powerfully on place, including the development company IntraWest and the engineering firm CH2M Hill. Timberland, with its program of providing an environmental scorecard for its shoes, and Herman Miller, with its focus on creating cradle-to-cradle products, might also be considered in this category, as they seek ways to limit carbon emissions—a type of place-centric emphasis in a global context. Finally, other businesses, typically huge in scope with a model focused on replicability, largely ignore both scales.[66] Such businesses, while financially successful, do little to enhance the environmental and social aspects of where they engage in commerce.

The People-Place Matrix (Figure 1-3), while an oversimplification, provides an overview of the degree to which various entities engage in stock taking.

This People-Place Matrix is conceptual, placing types of businesses

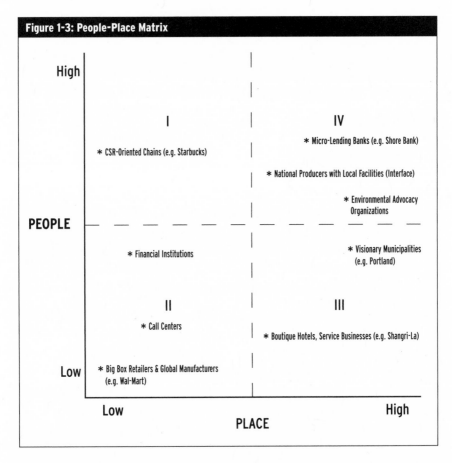

Figure 1-3: People-Place Matrix

High

I

* CSR-Oriented Chains (e.g. Starbucks)

IV

* Micro-Lending Banks (e.g. Shore Bank)

* National Producers with Local Facilities (Interface)

* Environmental Advocacy Organizations

PEOPLE

* Financial Institutions

* Visionary Municipalities (e.g. Portland)

II

* Call Centers

III

* Boutique Hotels, Service Businesses (e.g. Shangri-La)

* Big Box Retailers & Global Manufacturers (e.g. Wal-Mart)

Low

Low   PLACE   High

into quadrants based on stereotypes. Despite the stereotyping, there's a certain accuracy to the rough categorizations. Big-box retailers tend to have a one-size-fits-all business model and treat both place and person as commodities (quadrant II). Boutique hotels (e.g., Shangri-La) are reputed to have uniform management practices from place to place but adapt the look and feel of their hotels to their specific cultural contexts, making them relatively place-centric (quadrant III). CSR-oriented chains, by contrast, such as Starbucks, pay relatively little attention to the uniqueness of place but place significant emphasis on the needs of their employees (quadrant I). And, finally, businesses such as ShoreBank seem to be attentive to both people and place (quadrant IV).

One could easily challenge these categorizations based on one's own knowledge and experience of a particular company. The point is not to categorically pigeonhole businesses into specified places on the matrix but to suggest an analytical framework for evaluating a business's sensitivity to context. This matrix also begs additional questions. How might a company become a better steward of its land and community over the long term? What is the role of leadership in this equation? In a bottom-up, shared-leadership culture, who, if anyone, is leading this charge? Such questions are the focus of the next chapter.

Coda

We began this chapter with two stories, both focused on the principle of recovery. The first story, a passage from McPherson's "A Matter of Vocabulary," considers work in a small-town grocery store from the perspective of one who is removed from the dominant social context. The questions implicit in young Tommy Brown's detached observations are ones we all must ask: *What is the background behind this town I live in? What are its strengths and weaknesses? Who are the people that live around me? What is the nature of community that they (and I) have created? What do I want from the land and community of which I am a part? Do I belong here? Can I belong here?* The second story, my own recovery of the McPherson narrative, moves us toward an exploration of these questions.

Recovery begins, then, by opening ourselves up to the manifold stories around us. It entails stepping out of our own skins to view our context through others' eyes. It calls for us to demythologize many presumed truths. Beyond these general traits recovery necessitates a process of taking stock of the natural world of which we are part. It involves both questioning and connecting to past practices. It enables us to see the sometimes fine line between vision and hubris, where, for example, the well-wrought ideas of the Georgia Plan conceived in London confront the actualities of climate and geography in the nascent colony. Recovery invites us to reflect upon the nature of progress and our often unquestioned assumption that what we practice today is an improvement upon what we once did. It is about a robust education that integrates various fields of knowledge into wisdom. Recovery requires an ethical grounding in place and people.

That ethical grounding informs how a sustainable business culture is built: from the bottom up, through a set of practices whereby a business serves its people and place, not the reverse. Centrifugal culture creation conveys this sense of a business being pulled toward the essential needs of the community around it. Taking stock of place and people comprises the first steps in a centrifugal movement that will be with us the remainder of this book.

The initial stage in the process of shaping a sustainable business can be seen in the accompanying Restorative Process Map (figure 1-4). Much of this map still remains blank and will be filled in over the ensuing chapters.

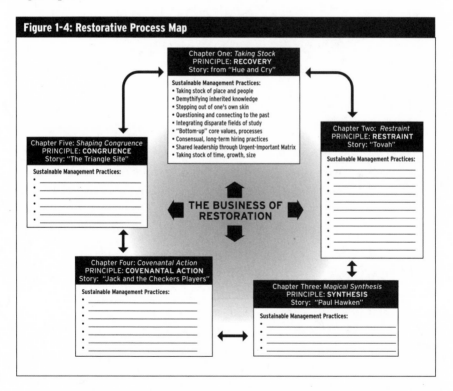

Figure 1-4: Restorative Process Map

Chapter One: *Taking Stock*
PRINCIPLE: **RECOVERY**
Story: from "Hue and Cry"

Sustainable Management Practices:
• Taking stock of place and people
• Demythifying inherited knowledge
• Stepping out of one's own skin
• Questioning and connecting to the past
• Integrating disparate fields of study
• "Bottom-up" core values, processes
• Consensual, long-term hiring practices
• Shared leadership through Urgent-Important Matrix
• Taking stock of time, growth, size

Chapter Five: *Shaping Congruence*
PRINCIPLE: **CONGRUENCE**
Story: "The Triangle Site"

Sustainable Management Practices:

Chapter Two: *Restraint*
PRINCIPLE: **RESTRAINT**
Story: "Tovah"

Sustainable Management Practices:

THE BUSINESS OF RESTORATION

Chapter Four: *Covenantal Action*
PRINCIPLE: **COVENANTAL ACTION**
Story: "Jack and the Checkers Players"

Sustainable Management Practices:

Chapter Three: *Magical Synthesis*
PRINCIPLE: **SYNTHESIS**
Story: "Paul Hawken"

Sustainable Management Practices:

CHAPTER TWO

RESTRAINT

In any biological system the first principle is restraint,
that is, the natural or moral checks that maintain a
balance between use and continuity. . . . We can make
ourselves whole only by accepting our partiality, by
living within our limits, by being human, not by trying
to be gods. By restraint [we] make [ourselves] whole.
—Wendell Berry, *The Unsettling of America*[1]

We began our exploration of *Living Above the Store* by looking at the
principle of recovery and the process of taking stock of people and place.
But the act of taking stock of one's context should also include taking
stock of oneself—a process of self-reflection that involves the principle
of restraint: learning to evolve within our own capacities.

Most of us in the business world would prefer to do anything but
take stock of self. We are typically people of action, not reflection.
Mainstream business cultures get leery when their leadership becomes
contemplative. Still, self-reflection is a fundamental step that numerous influential scholars on business leadership—James Collins, Warren
Bennis, and Joseph Badaracco, to name three—insist must occur for
high-performance companies to remain self-sustaining.[2]

What prompts a steward of a company to become more self-reflective?
Is it something genetic, "hard-wired" into the character of some people
more than others? Or is it prompted by some external factor: a disrup-

tive event, personal pain, an outsider who serves as a Socratic gadfly?[3] Why are some people more receptive and adaptive to self-questioning, and others less so?

There are also practical issues to consider. How do business stewards manage the day-to-day tasks of running a business and yet also carve out time for reflection? How do you nurture a business culture that facilitates both reflection and action? How can a business give voice to those leadership voices in the middle ranks of the company, voices that are often best positioned to question a current course of action? And how does a company manage a creative tension that poses questions without creating analysis paralysis, a creative tension that also ensures alignment of a workforce without lapsing into rote groupthink?

From these pragmatic questions, other, broader questions come to the fore: Aren't self-reflection and stock-taking just a little bit antiquated? Business, after all, seems to be about moving quickly, innovating, competing with other businesses by creating a differentiation strategy[4] before others appear on the scene. In our global economy, the emphasis is all about creative destruction—"the perpetual cycle of destroying the old and less efficient product or service and replacing it with new, more efficient ones."[5] Where is there space or time or inclination for reflection? The principle of restraint is offered here as a tentative response to these questions.

In this chapter, we begin with a story about a moment that, for me, prompted greater self-reflection. It's a story that highlights the critical role of others, in this case one of my sisters, to lead from the middle. The debate I had with my sister and the internal dialogue this debate fostered help illuminate a larger phenomenon that occurs within sustainable businesses: a dialectic of alignment and misalignment among staff and the principle of restraint undergirding this dialectic.

THE STORY

In 1985, our family sold M&M Supermarkets, our grocery business of forty-five years. It was time. It's a tough business, based on slim margins of between 1 and 2 percent. My father,

Norton Melaver, had been running the company since college, had grown the business from one small downtown store to a chain of fourteen supermarkets around Savannah, and he was tired. At a time when independents were closing left and right in the presence of major chains, our business had two-thirds of the local market. When our family (six of us: my parents, Norton and Betty Melaver, my two sisters and I, and Millie Melaver, my father's sister) sold M&M Supermarkets, we discovered that we didn't just sell a business. We parted company with something that was closely associated with all of us.

We discovered something else as well: We had been in the real estate business all along, developing stores and warehouses that we then operated. We also discovered that we didn't all like the real estate business very much. In fact, our family was split between those who felt we should become a socially responsible real estate company (whatever that was) and those who felt that as long as we gave back to the community, how we made our profits wasn't an issue; means versus ends.

Our family would come together in the late 1980s for quarterly meetings and argue about doing real estate differently. There were tenants some family members felt we should not rent to, places we shouldn't develop, ways of building that we shouldn't imitate. In the meantime, I was trying to shape consensus from the two sides of this familial debate. *Shape* is a misnomer. What I was trying to do was placate Tovah, the elder of my two younger sisters. You might have a member of your own family like my sister Tovah: someone who comes to a family gathering—Thanksgiving or Christmas/Hanukkah or New Year's—and serves as the conscience of the family, reminding the rest of us of our responsibilities regarding social and environmental justice.

And quite frankly, back then, fifteen or twenty years ago, I didn't want to hear it. I was just starting out overseeing the company in the early nineties, and here was my little sister popping into town every three months saying she disliked what the real estate world was doing to our communities, to our land. She disliked the sprawl that put people in cars for major parts of the day. She couldn't stand the fact that every development she saw—whether it was an office or industrial park, a retail shopping center or mall, or a residential community—all looked the same. She hated the idea of cutting down trees; not just clear-cutting a site, but cutting down any trees at all.

Here I was trying to learn a new business. I wanted this business to be successful, and I was determined that this business—the legacy of my grandmother and father—was not going to tank on my watch. About the last thing I wanted was for my sister to look over my shoulder and ask me to do real estate differently. I felt a knot in my stomach every time she rolled into town for our quarterly meetings.

But I went through the motions as we debated. We decided that there were certain types of tenants that we would not lease space to (pet shops; tenants involved in some aspect of the defense industry) and certain areas where we would not develop (counties, for example, that formally or informally espoused antigay practices). But it wasn't enough. Tovah began voting against my proposals to develop in other areas because they would entail cutting down trees or because they seemed to contribute to sprawl. She was an impediment to doing business as usual, to the point where I was meeting with our family CPA to discuss buying Tovah's shares in the family business.

As a company, we were beginning to move slowly in a more environmentally sensitive direction, researching energy-efficient HVAC systems and plumbing fixtures that would use less water. But the research was slow going, with the daily demands of growing the business taking precedence over the larger issues Tovah was driving us to consider. I can't say that I was doing much to hasten the direction toward more sustainable practices.

I'm not proud of those early days when I first became CEO of the company, and it does not give me much pleasure to write about them now. But the experience of those days helps

illustrate a number of key management practices that are critical for a sustainable business, namely the ethics of beginning
at home through a process of self-reflection, cultivation of
leadership from others throughout an organization, and use
of this leadership of diverse voices to shape alignment within
a business culture. Ultimately, these practices boil down to the
principle of restraint: learning to restrain one's own unbridled
ambitions, learning to restrain oneself from imposing a monolithic vision of a business upon an entire staff, learning how to
enable a company to grow within its own natural limits. Let's
consider each of these concepts in greater detail.

The Five Whys Dialogue

Toyota revolutionized the auto industry with its just-in-time approach to
assembly. At the heart of Toyota's change management program was a
system called the Five Whys, where management used a series of Socratic
questions as a way of probing into the root causes of a problem.[6] Toyota's
systems approach has applicability to any business examining the root
causes of problems it faces. For instance, one of our property managers
might need to investigate a roof leak on a relatively new property:

Q1: Why is the roof leaking?
A: Because some nails were left on the roof and punctured the
   membrane.

Q2: Why were the nails there in the first place?
A: They were left by a private air-conditioning contractor called in
   by a tenant to repair a roof-mounted unit.

Q3: Why are there problems with this new unit?
A: We undersized it. It's insufficient to cool the tenant's space.

Q4: Why did we specify this particular size unit?
A: We based the size of the unit on rule-of-thumb calculations about
   how much tonnage is needed to cool this space.

Q5: Why isn't that rule of thumb accurate here?
A: We never took into account the fact that the tenant's space is
south facing and contains significant glass, causing heat gain.

This Five Whys process, not unfamiliar in the business world, has broader applicability and can be used on a more personal level,[7] as an internal dialogue, as if looking self-reflectively into a mirror.[8] It's particularly helpful when used to reflect on my debates with Tovah many years ago:

Q1: Why is it that I resisted my sister Tovah?
A: Because I felt she was trying to undermine my authority as head
of the company.
Q2: Why was this a concern?
A: I was new in my role running the company. I wanted to make my
mark and succeed in running this real estate business.
Q3: Why did I feel that Tovah's suggestions would get in the way of
my desires?
A: Because I felt success meant doing what everyone else who was
successful in the real estate business was already doing. I wanted
us to be like everyone else.
Q4: Why did I want that?
A: Because I felt that was the way a business executive would be
acknowledged and respected. I didn't want people to think I was
some strange tree hugger.
Q5: Why did I feel that conforming to traditional ways would result
in acceptance?
A: Because that's the way everyone else got ahead. And because I
was afraid to trust myself to understand what was truly important
to me.

This self-reflection did not happen at once. It's difficult, in retrospect, to pinpoint the beginning of this process. Initially I was resistant to Tovah's persistent questioning, and then, beneath that resistance, was a vague sense of fear: fear of appearing indecisive to my staff, fear of being tested in the early going of my tenure with the company and the concomitant fear of failure that came with it, and fear of being taken into unknown territory.

At a certain point in such circumstances, I think the natural tendency is to fight back (resistance), flee (ignore the problem and hope it goes away), or confront the demons head-on and reflect about the issues being raised. What I discovered in the process of pursuing this last option, or rather rediscovered, was something I did not want to own up to: my own ambition and drive to succeed. The conventional real estate practices I wanted to pursue had everything to do with growing the company (at warp speed) as a testament to me and much less to do with what family shareholders wanted for the business or what would be best for the business itself. I rediscovered something else in this reflective process. I agreed with Tovah's critique. I didn't much care for the development practices of our profession. Her voice tapped into a deep-seated desire I had not felt entitled to even recognize, much less vocalize—a desire to be part of a group that would transform real estate practices and help make a difference in the community.

Despite the extended time it took me to take this more reflective path, the Five Whys dialogue-in-the-mirror process is relatively easy. Let's face it, you get to ask the questions and provide the answers. It's a controlled exercise (and private as well, unless you care to air this stuff in a book). Much more challenging, however, is using this process in a group setting, such as our business, where the straight-talk Q&A becomes more public and complex, involving numerous other voices. At that point the Five Whys dialogue becomes particularly valuable.

On my own authority I had hired (this was back in the days before we developed collaborative hiring practices) a new chief operating officer. He was a great guy, encyclopedic in his knowledge of construction practices, something of a perfectionist. And he was driving the rest of our management team nuts—to the point where they approached me one day with an ultimatum: Either he had to go, or they were leaving. At once and en masse. After considerable discussion, we decided to send each person on the management team individually to a weeklong retreat called a High Impact Leadership Seminar (HILS). The seminar is intended for business executives who are "stuck," capable when it comes to hard skills needed to manage a business but lost at sea when it comes to the softer, people skills. I was one of the first on our management team to go.

Robert F. Kennedy Jr. writes about the powerful effect that wilderness has on leaders, contending that only in the wilderness are we able to come to terms with ourselves in fundamental ways. Warren Bennis, a well-known authority on business leadership, similarly argues that by stepping away from the familiar and taught environment one can reach self-understanding.[9] That short time away from my business at HILS, in the company of strangers, was a form of wilderness experience, activating a process of self-reflection that continues today.

The specific content of the HILS program is less significant than that it provides a space and time away from the business to reflect on one's own thoughts and feelings, to utilize the company of other business executives to give and receive feedback, and to see ourselves through others' eyes and experiences. It was an uncomfortable week of opening up to others, an animating week of realizing that a better understanding of self came through such openness and vulnerability.

Each member of our management team went through the HILS experience. We followed up on this program with a mutual feedback seminar lasting three intense days, focusing on the actions we needed to continue, start, and stop in order to be more effective, individually and collectively. These sessions were a turning point for us as a company, enabling us to begin a process of Five Whys dialogues with one another and fostering an atmosphere of more direct and honest engagement. Those sessions also resulted in having to part company with our COO. After much individual and collective soul searching, it was clear that he was not aligned with the direction we were taking.

Since those self-reflective sessions, our company has instituted a semiformal system of coaching for one another, practicing an ethos of straight talk. Each member of our management team undergoes a HILS seminar at some stage, enduring the gallows humor associated with the suggestion that it's time to do a little "head shrinking." Several of us undergo formal executive coaching on a regular basis. We pair staff members to provide coaching during the year, and our annual retreat usually includes a component of small group and collective exchanges. These have become approaches our company has used to ensure that the Five Whys dialogue is ongoing for each of us and among us all.

Take-Aways from the Five Whys Dialogue

I have a number of take-aways from the Five Whys exercise: (1) finding and trusting one's own voice, (2) learning to open oneself up to feedback, (3) facilitating a marketplace of ideas by sharing one's voice with others, (4) learning about leadership from the middle, and (5) learning the art of letting go. Let's discuss each takeaway in more detail.

Finding and trusting one's voice. A title (such as CEO) and stewardship are different things. Stewardship, for me, has a lot to do with digging down and finding your own voice before sharing it with others. I spent years with my senior management team, in the early part of my tenure, talking about our company's core competencies and what we wanted to be when we grew up. I needed those debates and discussions, needed to hear what others felt passionate about, if only to uncover what mattered most to me: working alongside others to realize our potential, linking that potential to a sense of shared purpose and meaning, leveraging that sense of shared purpose to restore the health of the land and community around us.

Then there's the issue of trusting your voice—quite a different matter from discovering it. For years while driving from the airport in Atlanta to our offices located in the northern part of the city I would feel uneasy as I passed mile after mile of look-alike office towers. For a long time I thought it was envy and ambition talking, the desire to be able to put our own company signage on similar marquee properties.[10] It took me even longer to realize that what I was feeling was more like dread, a deep-seated concern that I was being seduced by this "sign" of success, aspiring to be another marquee real-estate name. I had first forgotten—then later dismissed—an ideal I used to have about building community, something that I had been fascinated by and researched in college. *Utopian idealism,* I thought sardonically, *has nothing to do with business.*

For some—and certainly for me—it takes a considerable amount of time and effort to tunnel through this cynical voice in one's head. In the absence of trusting your own voice, you end up believing those of others. For a long time I believed that real estate was all about trying to replicate what I saw around me. Tall office towers with shimmering glass facades, lusciously landscaped grounds with exotic plants, enormous acreage devoted solely to industrial parks, corporate art collections, vast and meticulously kept parking surfaces: bigger, brighter, well-appointed, sculpted, single-use environments that look wonderful on the glossy covers of real estate portfolios but are out of place and context and are wasteful.

There are 4.6 million commercial buildings in the United States today, and our economy adds 170,000 more each year. We add 2 million new homes to the current stock of 103 million.[11] Between 1970 and 1990 we built approximately 25,000 shopping centers, or one every seven hours.[12] Development in the United States consumes a square mile of land every 2.5 hours.[13] From 1990 to 2004 we developed 25 percent of the total amount of land we had developed in the entire 225 years of the republic.[14] Experts project that 80 percent of the building inventory we will have twenty years from now has yet to be built.[15]

With that pace of development comes a host of problems we haven't begun to wrap our hands around. Every hour of the day more than forty-five acres of farmland in the United States are converted to development.[16] We are losing topsoil twenty to forty times faster than it can be replenished, a fact that has serious consequences for future food production and is resulting in the alteration and loss of our wetlands and marshlands to a degree few of us can fathom.[17] Building homes consumes 25 percent of all wood harvested.[18] Construction activity accounts for around 40 percent of our landfill content. Our sedentary, car-centric lives, a product of sprawl, are linked strongly to obesity rates.[19] The list goes on and on. I've tried trusting voices other than my own, voices that speak in glowing terms of the economic growth and aesthetic nourishment that real estate development provides. My judgment and trust have been misplaced. It hasn't worked. It's not working.

Opening oneself up to feedback. Of all the pieces of the puzzle involving the principle of restraint, this one looms as perhaps the most challenging and critical. There is first the issue of trust. It sometimes takes fortitude for a colleague to speak honestly to me when I ask for feedback, since there are natural concerns about what the consequences might be of being forthright with the head of a company. There is also the issue of self-trust in the face of feedback, which involves peeling away of layers of defensiveness.

While individual responses to feedback can vary widely, I'd offer up my own experience as an example of not-so-pretty behavior. There is often a first stage of overt, aggressive response to feedback, when you question and challenge and correct what you belief are inaccuracies and misimpressions. Then, once this overt level of defensiveness dissolves, it is sometimes followed by a desire to explain your position to others—simply a more subtle form of defensiveness. Then ensues a stage of puzzlement and frustration, first as you wrestle with the notion that others' perceptions of you constitute a reality and are valid, even if you disagree. Also it's necessary to recognize that your role in the give-and-take of feedback is that others give and you receive. Self-restraint is called for in true feedback. If you can transcend these initial barriers, what follows is the gift of having others provide honest perspectives that you may have been unwilling to consider, a step that leads to a more authentic engagement with self.

Sharing one's voice with others. Our staff meetings are marked by a certain irreverent chaos. Who's leading the meeting? How are decisions arrived at? Who gets to decide? I believe our meetings often evoke a sense of entitlement. The term is one I have some trouble with; to me *entitlement* has an old, somewhat negative connotation of medieval, seigniorial rights and all that such rights convey (noblesse oblige, decision by fiat, etc.). But the notion of entitlement works when I think of it as creating an environment that echoes the Platonic notion of a marketplace of ideas, where straight talk from each member of the company is freely forthcoming. There is sufficient trust among members of the organization such that ideas and opinions are openly shared with one another. It's a simple notion, so simple that it seems mundane. But a notion of entitlement is anything but ordinary and typical. It goes a long way toward creating a culture of leading from the middle.

Leading from the middle. My sister Tovah does not work at our company, though she is one of six shareholders and a member of our board. She comes to the company headquarters in Savannah for about six hours, four times a year. She's not making day-to-day managerial decisions, and she's not even up to speed on most things that engage our senior management team. She doesn't own enough of the company stock to force decisions to go her way. She's not the de facto matriarch of the family, someone to whom everyone goes for guidance and advice.[20] In fact, more often times than not Tovah's take on a given situation is the minority view among family members. And yet she, more than anyone involved with the company, changed the course of the way we view and conduct our business.

How? Authenticity and passion.[21]

Tovah, I think, found her internal voice long before I did, perhaps because she wasn't involved in the day-to-day operations as I was and so was less invested in a business-as-usual approach to managing the company. Her distance allowed her to view our actions through a different lens. She read books and sought out information that was more about social and environmental justice issues, not the business books I was reading. People she came into contact with and shaped her thinking comprised a different social network than my own circle.

Tovah did not have a vision of what Melaver, Inc., should become. She simply had a clear conviction of what it should not be. It should not contribute to sprawl. It should not impact negatively on the environment. It should not be disrespectful of people and place. She left it up to the staff to figure out how to accomplish this.

I have immense respect for Tovah's passion, even if I don't always agree with her. Once I reported to our board that we had just received a gold LEED certification on a McDonald's we had developed, the first and only LEED McDonald's anywhere. "Should we," she asked, "even be engaged in building a McDonald's? Doesn't that seem counter to what we're about?" And more recently, as we considered taking on GE as a capital investor, Tovah felt strongly about not partnering with a company that had taken little responsibility for the cleanup of some eighty-seven Superfund sites, the largest environmental degradations by any corporation on the planet. When Tovah is not around—all but four days a year—our management team has learned to look at things from what would likely be Tovah's perspective.

Companies ranging from small to large all have their Tovahs, if they are fortunate. Ray Anderson, founder of Interface, Inc., began his own journey toward sustainability because a colleague sent him a Paul Hawken's book *The Ecology of Commerce*. Yvon Chouinard, founder of Patagonia, got a kick in the head from an outside consultant, Dr. Michael Kami, who challenged Chouinard about why he was in business. Max De Pree, former CEO of Herman Miller, acknowledges the leadership roles played by model maker Pep Nagelkirk and department supervisor Howard Redder. Hewlett-Packard has benefited from the gadfly role played by Barbara Waugh, Costco by Sheri Flies.[22]

The strategies for cultivating leadership from the middle are as wide-ranging as the examples. A company could create a "spiritual ombudsman" who is charged with providing a critical eye on a business's activities. Cross-functional teams also seem to foster middle leadership, such as that provided by Jon Ratner and his sustainability team within the Forest City development company. Xerox, Alcoa, BP, GE, and Wal-Mart—a list that raises skepticism when it comes to these companies' depth and authenticity of commitment to sustainability—have all been profiled for their efforts to nurture a broad network of green leaders both internally and with other corporate partners.[23] Some organizations find and/or cultivate a so-called champion or group of champions in-house that then provide the nucleus for creating change within the company.[24]

Finding and trusting one's own voice, opening oneself up to feedback, sharing one's voice with others, embracing leadership from the middle: These lessons learned from the mirror dialogue involve melding the practice of stewardship with the principle of restraint. Stewardship of a company is not about imposing one's own personal desires and control on a business but about learning to restrain such desires, which are often fueled by the drive for esteem. Stewardship involves restraining those externalized voices that seem to define success in the interest of realizing one's own highest potential. And stewardship entails connecting the drive to realize one's own highest potential to similar drives among the members of a group. Stewardship, in short, links the act of self-restraint to a mind-set of letting go, trusting in oneself and in the capacity of the group to make the right things happen.[25] One key obstacle standing in the way of stewardship and shared leadership is the challenge of silos.

The Challenge of Silos

The tendency of a group of people to be divorced from its sense of place, the tendency of a business to segment its workforce into one of four distinct roles: These are examples of silos, where parts of a system are removed and isolated from a more holistic sensibility. In the upcoming chapters, we will constantly return to the challenge of silos in various guises: the tendency of a company to wall itself off from competitors, the inclination of a company to stay removed from the needs of a community, the reluctance of the business community to integrate itself into the workings of the other major sectors of society. The road toward becoming a sustainable business is hindered by the tendency of a business group to insulate itself. Finding ways to overcome the challenge of silos at the company level becomes a critical step toward fostering a sustainable ethos in the larger context of land and community.

Silos challenge a culture of Five Whys dialogue generally, and the practice of leading from the middle more particularly. In a restorative business, middle leadership suffuses the organization such that everyone takes responsibility for a company's raison d'être. In a siloed organization, however, there is a strong tendency to restrict work to autonomous functional disciplines, where few people have a view of, much less a say-so in, the whole picture. A siloed structure is one whereby only a few are afforded the opportunity to monitor, question, provide feedback, and make suggestions as to what a company does or should do. Such an approach squanders a golden opportunity to enable the entire staff to maximize its potential.

Not seeing the whole picture is hardly a new problem. As Rachel Carson noted decades ago, "this is an era of specialists, each of whom sees his own problem and is unaware of or intolerant of the larger frame into which it fits."[26] Ralph Waldo Emerson, in his *American Scholar Address*, bemoans the state of society in which humankind is minutely subdivided into functions and thus lacks a certain wholeness or completeness:

> Man is thus metamorphosed into a thing, into many things. The planter, who is Man sent out into the field to gather food, is seldom cheered by any idea of the true dignity of his ministry. He sees his bushel and his cart, and nothing beyond, and sinks into the farmer, instead of Man on the farm. The tradesman scarcely ever gives an ideal worth to his work, but is ridden by the routine of his craft, and the soul is subject to dollars. The priest becomes a form; the attorney, a statute-book; the mechanic, a machine; the sailor, a rope of a ship.

This sense of fragmentation, dehumanization, and lack of social coherence is one numerous writers have focused on as a challenge to restoring land and community to a healthy, symbiotic relationship.[27] The challenge is compounded by the fact that typically those few individuals who are best placed to see the larger picture—CEOs among others—are least likely to be motivated to see beyond their own frame of reference. As the writer and social critic Upton Sinclair noted, "It is difficult to get a man to understand something when his salary depends upon his not understanding it."[28]

In 1996 the Drucker Foundation published a volume of essays by business leaders and teachers titled *The Leader of the Future*. The insights and advice provided by these thirty-one essays comprise an intimidating list of expectations regarding leadership, ranging from demonstrating the capacity to follow and delegate as well as lead, to manifesting various types of understanding and knowledge of self and others, and shaping an environment of ongoing learning.[29]

Impossible? Certainly, as long as the expectation is that all these characteristics need to reside in a single individual. However, if we take the viewpoint that one of us is not as smart as all of us, a paradigm shift occurs. As Edgar Schein, in his essay "Leadership and Organizational Culture," notes:

Perhaps the most salient aspect of future leadership will be that these characteristics will not be present in a few people all the time but will be present in many people some of the time, as circumstances change and as different people develop the insight to move into leadership roles. Leadership will then increasingly be an emergent function rather than a property of people appointed to formal roles.[30]

We would do well to view leadership as a set of functions manifested in a variety of people and occurring across functional lines, to foster stewardship by transcending mental and structural silos.

Providing an Alternative to the Silo

From its inception Melaver, Inc., has had a flat, horizontal structure. Everyone wore a number of hats, we communicated incessantly with one another, and job assignments were often a matter of who had excess capacity at any given moment. Chaotic it was, but in our small, entrepreneurial environment, it worked. As we added more people, however, the confusion began to mount. So too did a desire among some of our new hires for an organizational chart, titles on business cards, and direct reporting relationships. I can't say that I was thrilled with the prospect, but nevertheless acknowledged that greater order was needed. We spent the several months working to devise a more formal company architecture, one we could all live with and support. The results surprised me as much as anyone else.

The organizational chart we developed (Figure 2-1), is best viewed through 3-D glasses. That already says a lot. I have to laugh when, as part of a formal presentation to a financial institution, someone requests our org chart and this 3-D diagram is passed around, along with pairs of those old-fashioned red and green paper-framed glasses. It's quite a sight to see a collection of suits sitting around a conference table, wearing those things. The rest of my senior management team, somewhat chagrined by the outlandishness and apparent unprofessionalism of what we designed, inevitably tries to substitute a more traditional, formal tree-shaped hierarchy. But the real org chart is the one provided

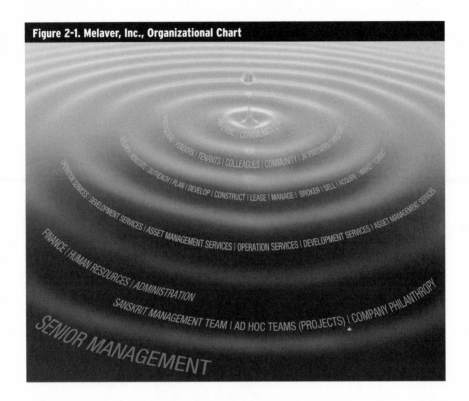

Figure 2-1. Melaver, Inc., Organizational Chart

here. It has been updated from the original version, to reflect the growing complexity of stakeholder relations.

Our org chart is comprised of a series of concentric rings, with our core values at the very center. That's our true center, our purpose, the "thing" we all report to. Our core values inform our land-community ethic, which we view most immediately in terms of a close ring of stakeholders: tenants, vendors, colleagues, shareholders and board members, key trade associations, and the community at large. Just beyond are our activities that provide services to our stakeholders. And just beyond this orbit are our business units, then the administrative divisions that serve those units, and then our management team and senior managers. The leadership and reporting relationships emanate from the values we provide (the smallest of the circles first), not from senior management.

A gimmick? Perhaps. But we don't share this org chart with people outside the organization unless it's requested. Our own board isn't particularly aware of it. But my colleagues know it, and they quietly compare our actions every day with the value chain expressed in the chart. Do they know who our CEO and COO and CFO are and what they do? Sure. But they also know decisions are arrived at through a process of constant questioning and debate and that those who are closest to the action are often called upon to make critical assessments and value judgments. They know that all decisions must be consonant with our core values and that anyone in the company can question an approach or decision based on a sense that we are deviating from our true center.

All of us are leaders in the middle—or at least potentially leaders in the middle, if we would but realize it.

I'm CEO of a company, but I report to my board of directors, who in turn are accountable to the stakeholders in the communities we serve. Those stakeholders—businesspeople, educators, the media, those involved in the day-to-day running of our civic institutions, nonprofit professionals—have their own mandates. Facility managers on university campuses are leaders in the middle, capable of bringing together students and faculty and administrators to shape the way our buildings can teach us. Bank and insurance underwriters can lead us in innovative ways by bringing catalytic capital to underserved areas. Purchasing agents for retailers can shape the buying habits of consumers downstream and the manufacturing practices of suppliers upstream. City planners can design the places where we work and live and play in ways that reduce waste, cause us to spend less time in solo transit, and enhance community. Academics have the capacity to link fragmented knowledge across disciplines so that our understanding of the workings of the natural world becomes more synthesized and complete. Environmental advocates have the passion and ability to be the voice of those who too often are ignored. Government workers have an understanding of the workings of civic organizations that can translate into powerful change. The list goes on and on.

Tovah's underlying message is clear. We each have a role to play—a responsibility—in utilizing our own understanding of a system in order to restore that system. The question then becomes, How does that happen?

Mapping a Dialectic

The intention behind Melaver, Inc.'s, organizational chart informs everything we do. When we hire someone, it is after a lengthy interview process to determine the degree to which we collectively believe this person will challenge, sharpen, and enhance our sense of community. When we decide to acquire a property or evaluate a development deal, many of us participate in the decision making. When we establish policies—both small and broad in scope—my colleagues all weigh in.

Do we agree with each other, at least most of the time? Hardly. Creating and nurturing a culture in which everyone is encouraged to weigh in with an opinion is reminiscent of social critic H. L. Mencken's description of living with a dog or an idealist—it's messy. While this messiness might have its own entrepreneurial charm at times, we still have a business to run, a business that calls for efficient decision making and execution. And while our organizational chart describes how we are *structured* and our Five Whys dialogue describes how we *engage* with one another, we still need a methodology that facilitates decision making. For that we need to consider a conventional business tool called force-field analysis as well as our own unconventional reworking of this tool.

Force-field analysis was developed to help business leaders manage change in an organization. Typically, force-field analysis takes a decision that management has *already decided to implement* and looks at the various components of a company—its stakeholders, internal systems, and market situation—in terms of whether they are either drivers or resistors to the change being promoted. There are a few things worth emphasizing about this business tool: (1) a decision to change the company in some way has already been made; (2) the decision has been made by leadership and will be imposed (more or less) on the rest of the organization; (3) the implementation of the decision has been framed in an adversarial manner, dividing the company into those who favor it (drivers) and those who are likely to resist it (resistors), without any space in the equation for a middle ground.

Interestingly, variations on this type of conventional business tool are used by environmental advocacy organizations such as The Natural Step as well as by more mainstream business consultants, to assist organizations in implementing sustainability into the work place. The approach begins with a *champion* or *group of champions*—people who feel passionate about instituting change within an organization. The champions are tasked with pulling together a group of *early adopters,* oftentimes a cross-functional team that has buy-in from senior leadership. This cross-functional team of champions first assesses current practices and then establishes objectives or goals for moving the organization in a particular direction. The change management group focuses first on low-hanging fruit—easy victories that demonstrate the overarching vision is reachable through a series of clear, deliberate steps. The early victories serve to attract others: first *brokers* who use their broad networks to get the organization buzzing about positive changes in the works, then *early majority participants* who support the pioneering change-management team. Eventually a tipping point is reached, whereby the notable resistors in an organization get on the bandwagon.[31]

There is nothing innately wrong with such an approach. In fact, it may be how some businesses and organizations change, particularly where change is a dogfight that calls for stealth tactics from within. But this approach frames change as a competition, with proponents of change squaring off against those who resist it. Such contentious business climates certainly exist.

I wonder, though, whether it's a situation of reaping what you sow: If you view change within a company as a battle of opposing forces, a battle is what you will get. But a company that lives by contentious approaches to change also dies by them. Change instituted by contentious means will not sustain itself over the long haul. Any policy executed in this fashion is vulnerable to the next winds of change blowing through an organization, which are likely to use the same force-field tactics to oust what had just been implemented.

How sustainable practices are introduced in an organization is integral to the practices themselves. Managing a sustainable business calls for tools and processes that build foundations for the long term, not for tactics that lead to adjustments with a short shelf life. Sustainable management calls for mechanisms that validate and engage diverse viewpoints.

In lieu of force-field analysis, a process for managing dialectical discourse and shaping alignment from that discourse is needed.

Let's take, for instance, a set of guidelines we use called the Five Restraints. The guidelines evolved from a belief that we needed to be clear about what types of business practices we would *not* engage in. Those Five Restraints are:

1. We will not develop in greenfield areas.
2. We will not develop projects that focus primarily on second-home users and/or cater to land speculation.
3. We will not acquire a property without committing to a program that upgrades the acquisition to criteria established by the U.S. Green Building Council (LEED guidelines).
4. We will not take on a property management assignment without the commitment of the owner/asset manager to sustainable management practices.
5. We will not broker a real estate transaction without presenting to the client the benefits of sustainable practices.

Let's focus on the first restraint, greenfield development. It is a complex issue within our company. My colleagues and I face definitional and philosophical differences on this topic. Does greenfield include a parcel of land located within an urban core with a small stand of trees on it? How about a tract placed on the market by a paper manufacturer that consists of fast-growing slash pines intended for the pulp mill—is that really greenfield? What if we purchase an office complex that includes undeveloped land that most developers would slate for future development? Is it OK to sell off that greenfield site to someone else who would then develop it, essentially sloughing off our dilemma to someone else? What about a more fragile habitat, such as a barrier island, that had been developed previously and is being considered for redevelopment? Should we consider bidding on being the master developer for that island, knowing that even if we engaged in restorative practices, we would still be part of the chain of title on an ecosystem that should never have been built on in the first place?

And then there are the philosophical differences. What if a piece of greenfield were on the market and we knew someone was going to develop it; wouldn't it be better if we developed it rather than some less sensitive operator? What about a poor agrarian community, consisting mostly of farmers; wouldn't our development in this community serve as a catalyst for positive, social transformation? How about a rural area pinched between two rapidly expanding metropolitan areas and clearly in the direction of economic growth? It's going to be swallowed up anyhow. Why should we handicap ourselves by not competing for the development? And what do we do in the case of a community that approaches us, because of our sustainable track record, to do a master planned development in a bedroom suburban community? Is there anything wrong with that? I raise these issues not because I don't have opinions on each one (I do), but because we don't have univocal agreement within our company.

Some of our staff members are concerned about the "limits to growth" value system embedded in our Five Restraints. They feel that it makes it more time-consuming for us to find deals. And they feel that we lose some of our ability to demonstrate a different approach to design and construction by shying away from more conventional projects and locations. If advocacy and outreach are a key part of what we're about (they are), are we not dampening our influence by resisting development in some situations and locales? Finally, the guidelines can seem rigid and holier-than-thou to those around us, conveying a sense that we are hard to deal with or that we are more akin to idealistic dreamers than pragmatic businesspeople.

Were we to approach this issue of greenfield development from a more conventional change-management approach, we might proceed in this way: Our senior management team mandates that we utilize a strict interpretation of greenfield. We then conduct a force-field analysis, identifying drivers and resistors. Finally we adopt tactics that would "sell" the idea to the unconvinced, until we had broad "buy-in" for the new policy. Top-down policy, change viewed as contentious, the process of managing change informed by a marketing strategy built around consumption ("buying in"): That's the more conventional approach to change management.

Contrast this approach—which divides the company into two opposing camps, drivers and resistors— with the Dialectical Process Map (Figure 2-2), a tool that has evolved from numerous debates and questioning on issues such as greenfield development. In lieu of positions for or against change, this map lays out arguments along a spectrum from narrow to loose interpretations. Instead of starting out from the perspective of having a specific end goal in mind (a mandated change, for instance), this map poses a question ("What's your thought on greenfield development?") and engages the company to help collectively shape an end goal.

Granted, this Dialectical Process Map is more complex than forcefield analysis. But what is lost in simple, neat appearance is made up for in content. The difference between the two is like taking a straw vote by raising hands versus engaging in debate. As one can see from Figure 2-2, structuring the issue of greenfield development in this way highlights creative tensions within the company. It's no longer a question of dividing the company into those promoting change and those resisting. It is also no longer a question of power and prestige, of who holds what position on a given issue, that determines how a decision is made. Instead the focus becomes the issue itself, and the rationale used to support a particular position.

Although skeptics might wonder if such a map inhibits clarity of thought and execution, I believe it facilitates good decision making. Everyone in the company has been heard. Everyone's point of view has been validated, irrespective of the outcome. Moreover this approach emphasizes the thought process informing a decision rather than the decision itself. This approach weaves together two critical strands of a collaborative culture together: (1) a marketplace of ideas approach to decision making in which the most compelling ideas are selected, and (2) democratic access to this marketplace such that all staff members feel they are engaged and valued participants in the discourse. We agree and feel passionate about a process of critical inquiry and debate, even if we struggle to find consensus.

The key is managing a process that balances alignment and misalignment. Too much alignment and a business contends with the problem

Figure 2-2: Dialectical Process Map

TOPIC: GREENFIELD DEVELOPMENT

	Thesis (narrow interpretation)	Antithesis (loose interpretation)
Stakeholders		
Shareholders	Divided: Worry about lost revenue from avoiding more conventional deals but are mission-driven when it comes to sustainability.	
Board Members	Divided, similar to Shareholders.	
CEO	Believes there are enough projects out there to work with existing infrastructure.	
Senior Management Team	Looser. More focused on strong financial returns but not at expense of company brand.	
Staff		Believe that we can teach others how to develop better.
Systems		
Structure	We're set up more to manage smaller urban core type projects.	
Culture	Entrepreneurial spirit favors keeping our options open, but triple bottom line ethos favors more restraint.	
Controls	We're better suited to manage smaller-scale or urban projects.	
Operations	We're better suited to manage smaller-scale or urban projects.	
Business Model	Designed for more restrained growth.	
Recruitment & Hiring	Mixed. Personnel attracted to entrepreneurship but also sustainable ethos.	
Work Environment		Entrepreneurial, fast-paced, moderated by sustainable ethos.
Situation		
Market Performance		Company performance would warrant more deal flow and, as such, looser interpretation.
Competition	Mixed. Market pushing us to be thought and product leader, but what does that mean?	
Technological Change		Sustainable building features declining in price making it easier to apply more broadly.
Critical Events	Top of mind awareness of global warming calls for working with existing infrastructure.	
Competing Initiatives		Lots of urban-edge locations out there looking to be done more sustainably.
Organizational Morale		Built for strong, fast growth that would push for looser interpretation.
Information & Knowledge	Market information augurs for looser interpretation while knowledge about the environment calls for greater restraint.	

of groupthink: There is lack of diversity necessary for good decision making, or fear within a workforce of articulating a dissenting opinion.[32] Too much misalignment and a business falls into dysfunction. Creative tension or "creative abrasion"[33] engenders good decision making, providing a critical foundation for a sustainable business. Rather than winners and losers, a situation is fostered where all viewpoints are validated.

So where is Melaver, Inc., on the issue of greenfield development? At the moment ours is a narrow interpretation. We focus our attention on urban core areas, largely in-fill or redevelopment work. But that could change, depending on circumstances such as where affordable housing is needed or where a particular brownfield (i.e., environmentally degraded) site outside an urban core area seems to call for remediation or where, by working in an area outside of an urban core area, we might be able to set aside significant acreage for permanent conservation easement. For now we're not struggling to find work by limiting our activity to urban core areas. I doubt we will for many years to come. Exercising restraint over where we build fits in with a collective sense of who we are and the positive impact we hope to have on the overall health of our land and community.

Having said this, we are constantly pitched potential development deals that are located on the urban fringe. And we are constantly reminded that, because the urban fringe is where most development work is taking place these days in the United States, if we wish to raise the bar on developing more sustainably we need to consider such projects. And we do. Each time a deal comes our way, we draw upon our Dialectical Process Map. Groundhog Day at our company once again? Perhaps. But each time we revisit an issue such as greenfield development it looks slightly different and the arguments have shifted.

What hasn't changed is the process of engaging all within the company in debates. Moreover, as we continue to add new people to our company and as we continue to broaden the scope of our activities to include a wider circle of engaged stakeholders, those new people, much like Frank Kermode's notion of a classic, shift our collective thinking.

This type of decision-making process is emblematic of a company that matures alongside a workforce that similarly matures. A company that matures alongside its workforce does not engage in what economist Joseph Schumpeter famously termed acts of "creative destruction" (where the new rises out of the ashes it has precipitated) but instead engenders evolutionary succession. Most of us in the business world today have a sense of what creative destruction feels like: It is the experience of continual change, whereby a company barely seems to get comfortable with a strategic direction before it abandons that approach in lieu of the next strategic move. In companies where this works poorly the experience is one of lurching from one business trend (e.g., reengineering or Six Sigma operational efficiencies) to the next. Even in companies where transitions are executed fluidly there is still a sense of discontinuity between the new system and the older one.

What is needed is an approach where individual and collective growth move in tandem with one another and where there is continuity between current and prior ways of addressing problems and solutions. As opposed to creative destruction, a culture of dialectical give-and-take uses different viewpoints and approaches creatively to foster evolutionary change. The analogies between a company that fosters a culture of evolutionary change and an ecosystem that grows naturally through a complex system of diverse parts are apt.

But what about the negative effects of this dialectic, especially the fact that it is likely to slow decision making? And what happens in the absence of consensual agreement? Doesn't a company's senior leadership make the key decisions anyway? Isn't this an elaborate dissimulation, an old autocratic model costuming itself in the guise of participative leadership?

Using the Precautionary Principle

As a company we've never formalized how we handle issues when we are deadlocked. However, we do have an unwritten guideline much like what is referred to as the precautionary principle. This principle, adopted by the United Nations General Assembly in 1982 in its World Charter for Nature,[34] holds the following: "When an activity raises threats of harm to human health or the environment, precautionary measures should be taken even if some cause and effect relationships are not fully established scientifically."

The precautionary principle epitomizes seven basic tenets:

1. A long-term perspective
2. An integrated view of the world
3. Empowering the public through transparent communication of information
4. Recognition that our future could very well be impaired
5. Belief that science is an uncertain discipline
6. Recognition of success, when it occurs
7. Open discussion of strategies and alternatives[35]

All these elements come into play in our decision-making process. Our analysis takes a long-term perspective, whether it's a hiring decision, consideration of with whom to partner on a potential deal, or a prospective development project. Whenever our group is uncertain about which direction to take, we act cautiously. When an issue seems potentially damaging to the human or natural environment, we hold off moving forward until we feel comfortable as a group that damage will not occur. Assessment of potential damage is, of course, a judgment call, but we prefer to be on the side of caution, accepting as much as we can the so-called law of unintended consequences and understanding that nature is complex, integrated in ways of which we are barely aware, and that we often have but a vague understanding of the results of what we undertake.[36] While all perspectives on a potential project may be helpful, none—even a scientific perspective—is infallible. Hence the need to communicate information transparently throughout the organization and rely on multiple perspectives to vet the information as best we can. These seven elements of the precautionary principle epitomize the ways in which a culture of restraint complements a culture of dialectical engagement.

A corollary practice often associated with the precautionary principle is adaptive management. Used in a number of fields,[37] adaptive management is applied in conservation project and ecosystem management to research practices systematically through a deliberate, trial-and-error process. As a company we more or less stumbled upon the practice of adaptive management. Once we made the decision, for instance, to build according to LEED standards, we tested those practices in several of our developments, comfortable that we could deliver a better building for equivalent market returns before committing all our projects to a minimum of LEED standards. That same process of cautiously testing our evolving notion of sustainability—where we build, where we don't build, what degree of high-performance building will we commit to, how we reduce our carbon footprint—has become an integral part of how we manage our business.

These approaches—use of the precautionary principle and adaptive management—result in a more protracted decision-making process. Should we provide consultancy services to third-party developers who, although they intend their projects to be "green," are working in areas where we ourselves would not develop? The question is an ongoing challenge for us, pitting an absolutist ethical position (we only consult on projects we ourselves would do) against a more utilitarian position (by teaching others what we know, we create greater good for a greater number of people). Should we accept third-party property management assignments where the potential client seems to be willing to accept only minimal sustainable practices? These are issues we struggle with, issues that cause us to proceed slowly and with caution.

Our brokerage division finds our protracted debates on potential deals frustrating. We have devoted considerable time to learning how to provide our brokers with sufficient clarity for their sakes, since we don't want to waste their time pitching us deals we are wary of. By the same token we don't wish to compromise our need to be as deliberative as we need to be. Over time our brokerage arm has learned to be less focused on deal-churn pace, while our development and acquisition teams have learned to communicate more clearly upfront about issues that cause us to hesitate before moving forward. It has taken us years, however, to find a modus vivendi that straddles our need to be cautious when we are uncertain of possible consequences of a decision, while also addressing the need to communicate clear and decisive direction to our stakeholders. It is not an easy balance to maintain.

But use of the precautionary principle seems critical to running a

sustainable business, especially after almost four centuries of full-throt-
tle consumptive practices. We have focused on maximizing throughput
(faster, more efficient delivery of goods) rather than focusing on optimization of effort.[38] We have embraced a master narrative about being
given dominion by God over all things and have taken it as license to
subdue the earth.[39] We have lost large animals, entire ecological communities, complete landscapes, and along with those losses, a "considerable
range of human feelings."[40] In one of the most eloquent passages in
environmental literature, Rachel Carson notes the hubris of such blow-
and-go behavior on the part of humankind:

> In each of these situations, one turns away to ponder the ques-
> tion: Who has made the decision that sets in motion these chains
> of poisonings, this ever-widening wave of death that spreads out,
> like ripples when a pebble is dropped into a still pond? . . . Who
> has decided—who has the *right* to decide—for the countless
> legions of people who were not consulted that the supreme value
> is a world without insects, even though it be also a sterile world
> ungraced by the curving wing of a bird in flight? The decision is
> that of the authoritarian temporarily entrusted with power; he
> has made it during a moment of inattention by millions to whom
> beauty and the ordered world of nature still have a meaning that
> is deep and imperative.[41]

Use of the precautionary principle means speaking on behalf of others
whose voice perhaps is not heard. Use of the precautionary principle is
about setting in motion a different, more life-affirming series of ripples
than the one Carson decries.

Limiting Growth

As a company we have forged a set of practices that suggest a go-slow
business of restraint. We devote considerable time to fostering a bottom-
up culture, built on the needs of each staff member and radiating outward.

We take time hiring, using consensual processes to add folks who will be new classics on the bookshelf, serving to sharpen our own sensibilities and renewing our sense of collective purpose. We engage with one another Socratically, drawing on our Five Whys to provide mutual feedback for personal and professional growth. We leverage leadership from all tiers, taking counsel from wherever it comes. We utilize a Dialectical Process Map to give voice to all opinions. In the face of deadlock, uncertainty, or lack of consensus, we lean in the direction of restraint, drawing on the wisdom of the precautionary principle. These tools and management practices are informed by a set of core values embedded at the very center of our organizational chart, core values focused on the health and well-being of both our land and community.

But this set of go-slow tools and management practices begs the question of growth. Can we grow as a company with such (seemingly) painstaking processes embedded in the company culture? Are we, to use business shorthand, scalable, meaning, Can we use our business model to grow efficiently and effectively?

It's not an academic question. Our business is real estate, with a significant portion devoted to development. We can always develop more projects than we do. From time to time, we are approached by large investment firms interested in providing additional capital to develop green buildings. These firms wish to know how scalable we are. Can we handle the additional project load? Can we develop and replicate *each year* a quantity of projects equal to our total current inventory? Can we take a boatload of cash from these investment houses and put it into play for them in the form of financially performing, green development projects?

The answer is sure, we are scalable. We would need to hire additional project managers to oversee the additional work, but our core group could handle a good deal more product than we are currently managing. The tools and management practices we have discussed thus far lend themselves to speed and scalability, largely by building foundations that, once laid, can facilitate speed by unleashing the energy and passion that comes from having a shared sense of meaning, purpose, and realizing our highest potential. But just because we are built for speed, does that mean we go full throttle? Just because we can scale up rapidly, do we wish to do so? It depends upon whom you ask.

There are some within our company who would prefer to ramp up our development production so that we mimic the scale of a publicly traded real estate company, utilizing sizeable amounts of outside investor capital to fuel that growth. There are others within the company, however, who are fearful of both the pace of such growth and the loss of company vision, culture, and control that would likely come from the active involvement of outside capital partners. It's an ongoing internal debate, one that lends itself well to our dialectical mapping process. Rather than view those viewpoints as oppositional, we try to hold the two in tension with one another, in large part because there are underlying elements of both positions we need in order to keep the company dynamic. Such a tension is not easy to maintain, and it's sometimes hard on my colleagues who desire closure.

The question is not *could* we grow or do we *want* to grow, but rather *should* we grow (and why or why not)? The answer becomes clearer when it's reframed around the issue of quality rather than quantity—the quality of growth of the individuals who make up our company as well as the quality of the products we develop. We are not interested in simply adding {x} more buildings to the more than 4.6 million commercial buildings in the United States, green or not. We want more cogent reasons for putting up a building than the availability of capital and our capacity for doing so. Our business philosophy calls for restrained building and management practices that emphasize nurture over churn. Our business philosophy and management practices reinforce one another. We are indeed scalable, but we try to grow at a pace that meshes with our sense of purpose.

We use our management practices as a mechanism for both reinforcing our business philosophy and providing a brake. We know that if we start adding people in droves and make decisions through top-down fiat, ignoring the wealth of leadership in the middle, our collective sense of purpose will attenuate. Perhaps it will do so imperceptibly at first. But over time we will have killed off something that is precious to us all. As Mitchell Kapor, founder of Lotus Development Corporation has noted:

Every new employee who is hired has to be integrated into the organization. . . . The extremely rapid hiring which characterizes high-growth start-ups can ultimately overwhelm the corporate immune system, leading to breakdowns in function.[42]

It's a sentiment shared by numerous other small businesses that have a social mission, such as Anchor Brewing (San Francisco), W. L. Butler Construction (Redwood City, California), New Hope Contracting (Dorchester, Massachusetts), and Rhythm and Hues Studio (Los Angeles).[43] Each of these companies is determined to be the best at what they do, providing exemplary service to customers, having great relationships with their vendors, and making significant contributions to the communities in which they are located. They are also willing to forgo economic and geographical growth in order to achieve their value-centric ends.[44]

From BAUhouse to NAUhouse

Our use of management practices structured around restraint has helped bring us together as a company. It has helped us answer positively a key question Max De Pree feels a company should enable its employees to ask: "Is this a place where they will let me do my best?"[45] It has fostered a learning dynamic that has ratcheted up our notion of what a sustainable business should be about.

When we first began our journey as a real estate company in the mid-1980s, we were simply doing Business as Usual—BAUhouse. Our focus was primarily on an economic bottom line. Over time we began to draw upon leaders in the middle, Tovah among others, to "green" our practices, constantly raising the bar on what that means. Soon other leaders from the middle of the company began to voice concerns over the social impacts of our practices. While it is important to develop a building that uses less energy, it seems similarly important to construct green buildings for people who can least afford the monthly utility and water bills. It's even more important to locate green, affordable housing in urban core areas adjacent to efficient transportation systems. In thinking through our own practices, particularly what we are dissatisfied with, we began to draw on what Badaracco refers to as "carefully targeted doses of misalignment" in the organization to focus more attention on the social consequences of our practices.

More recently we have begun to draw on internal company debates to think soberly about the nature of growth. The U.S. Green Building Council, brilliantly successful at fostering widespread awareness and adoption of LEED, has been adept at teaching the industry *how* to build differently. But it has remained relatively quiet on the issue of limiting *where* we build and even *if* we build at all. As the renowned architect Bob Berkebile has noted, even if we were to build every building to Platinum LEED standards (the highest certification level), we would still be degrading the planet; we would simply be degrading it more slowly.[46] With that critique in mind, we have begun to articulate a philosophy having to do as much with conservation as sustainability.

Over the past twenty years, we have utilized the dialectics of alignment to go from a Business as Usual company to a green company to a triple-bottom-line company to, at this point, a company trying to live up to the ideals espoused by forester and ecologist Aldo Leopold about nurturing the health of both land and community. Our company's evolution toward Leopold's land-community ethic can be summarized in the Sustainability Pyramid (Figure 2-3).

Will we complete the journey from BAUhouse to NAUhouse, from Business as Usual to Nature as Usual?[47] No. Will we draw upon the dialectics of alignment to move in that direction? I hope so.

From an ethical perspective, we are moving from an anthropocentric orientation to one that is more ecocentric, widening our focus to consider consequences that affect all of nature, not simply human concerns. Granted, I'm not convinced it's possible to step outside an anthropocentric perspective entirely, but that's a question better left to philosophers and ethicists. I do feel comfortable saying that our current company orientation is that we don't assume nature is there for our taking. We are beginning to shy away from a terminology of *natural resources,* with all that the phrase implies about nature being a commodity at humans' behest.

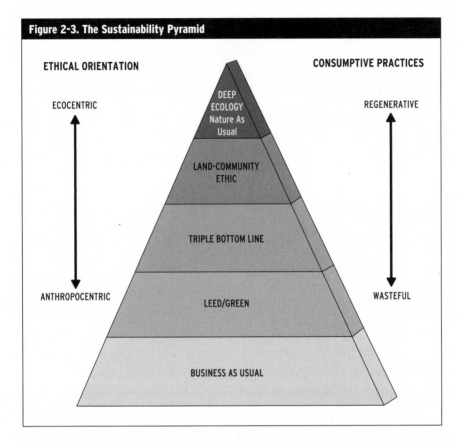

Figure 2-3. The Sustainability Pyramid

ETHICAL ORIENTATION   CONSUMPTIVE PRACTICES

ECOCENTRIC   REGENERATIVE

ANTHROPOCENTRIC   WASTEFUL

DEEP ECOLOGY Nature As Usual

LAND-COMMUNITY ETHIC

TRIPLE BOTTOM LINE

LEED/GREEN

BUSINESS AS USUAL

As a company we are starting to wrap our heads around the sense that we don't know as much as we thought we did—and that is a good thing. And while we still have staff members who worry about being thought of by others as starry-eyed idealists, my colleagues and I are more comfortable with the notion that a sustainable business inherently carries with it an emotional component. As biologist Stephen Jay Gould eloquently put it: "We cannot win this battle to save species and environments without forging an emotional bond between ourselves and nature as well—for we will not fight to save what we do not love."[48] Managing a sustainable business is dependent on fostering a company culture in which voices of emotion are as valid (and as validated) as voices of rational discourse.

From the perspective of consumption, we are moving away from our earlier, more wasteful practices. We do the usual things environmentally oriented companies do: recycle, purchase recycled products, carpool, provide financial incentives for hybrid vehicles, purchase green tags for energy that help offset our carbon emissions and promote alternative energy, create programs for reducing our overall environmental footprint, and so forth. But we are also beginning to take a deeper look at the deployment of ourselves in the context of community health, developing strategies not only to give back to community but also immerse ourselves in the overall health of where we live and work and play.

Coda

At the end of the day, the creative tension of alignment/misalignment is about maturation at both the individual and company level. This tension is the energy driving our company. And so the question then becomes, How does this energy come together synergistically rather than dissipate? How does a sustainable business pull these disparate voices together? How do the dialectics at work within a company evolve into synthesis? These questions will be the focus of the next chapter.

Before beginning chapter three, let's revisit our Restorative Process Map. Shaping a sustainable business involves the principle of recovery, a deliberate effort at greater self-awareness through a thoughtful exploration of one's context—place and people. Recovery also entails a dialogue with oneself—the "dialogue with a mirror"—that serves as a segue into the principle of restraint. Recovering a more authentic sense of self carries with it a greater awareness of those externalities (esteem from others, for example) that inhibit personal development. Recovering a more authentic sense of self also fosters a greater awareness of how the society of others, particularly critical engagement with others, can facilitate personal development. Disagreement and debate, horizontal leadership from the middle, consensual decision making: These are elements of a business culture that link elements of (personal and companywide) restraint to elements of (personal and companywide) growth, enabling us to reach our highest potential individually and as a company. In the process, meaning for the individual and purpose for the company become intertwined. The basic components of this process are captured in our updated Restorative Process Map (Figure 2-4).

In chapter three we turn our attention to the third box in our map and look at synthesizing the disparate voices and values within a company into a shared sense of community.

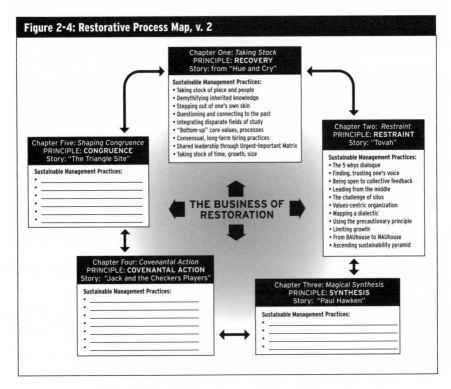

Figure 2-4: Restorative Process Map, v. 2

Chapter One: *Taking Stock*
PRINCIPLE: **RECOVERY**
Story: from "Hue and Cry"

Sustainable Management Practices:
• Taking stock of place and people
• Demythifying inherited knowledge
• Stepping out of one's own skin
• Questioning and connecting to the past
• Integrating disparate fields of study
• "Bottom-up" core values, processes
• Consensual, long-term hiring practices
• Shared leadership through Urgent-Important Matrix
• Taking stock of time, growth, size

Chapter Two: *Restraint*
PRINCIPLE: **RESTRAINT**
Story: "Tovah"

Sustainable Management Practices:
• The 5 whys dialogue
• Finding, trusting one's voice
• Being open to collective feedback
• Leading from the middle
• The challenge of silos
• Values-centric organization
• Mapping a dialectic
• Using the precautionary principle
• Limiting growth
• From BAUhouse to NAUhouse
• Ascending sustainability pyramid

Chapter Five: *Shaping Congruence*
PRINCIPLE: **CONGRUENCE**
Story: "The Triangle Site"

Sustainable Management Practices:
• _____
• _____
• _____
• _____
•

THE BUSINESS OF RESTORATION

Chapter Four: *Covenantal Action*
PRINCIPLE: **COVENANTAL ACTION**
Story: "Jack and the Checkers Players"

Sustainable Management Practices:
• _____
• _____
• _____
• _____
• _____

Chapter Three: *Magical Synthesis*
PRINCIPLE: **SYNTHESIS**
Story: "Paul Hawken"

Sustainable Management Practices:
• _____
• _____
• _____
•

MAGICAL SYNTHESIS

The garden taught me that not only wasn't I all-know-ing or all-powerful, but that it was a mistake to try to be. I could put the seeds into the ground. I could water. I could fertilize. I could grate. I could weed. But that was about it. The rest was up to them. Sometimes that was hard to accept. I had to be constantly doing some-thing for, or to, my plants. I couldn't accept the idea that every bit of progress wasn't in some small measure due to me. Or to put it another way, I couldn't believe that my plants could, for long stretches at a time, do without me. And very well. I have seen meddling parents behave much the same way toward their children. Sometimes you have to let go.

—Richard Goodman, *French Dirt*[1]

Sometimes you have to let go. This statement from Richard Goodman may be appropriate for gardening,[2] but in the context of managing a business? You've got to be kidding. Especially in light of this play of dialectical voices in a company that's kicking up a cacophony of dispa-rate opinions. What seems to be called for instead is a strong leadership hand, a hand that will synthesize all these various voices into a coherent vision. This seems to make perfect sense, right? Synthesis follows from dialectical debate. From a managerial perspective, linking the notion of synthesis, the focus of our attention in this chapter, to an act of letting go[3] seems counterintuitive.

Managing a sustainable business, after all, is about the management of change. The literature on change management sounds neat and simple and, above all, beautifully orchestrated: You *storm* (brainstorm ideas and vision for the future), you *form* (begin to shape these ideas into a system), you *norm* (things become more routine and less chaotic), and then you *perform*. While there's a clear process of synthesis involved in these four steps, there doesn't seem to be much room for the act of letting go. Change management, in this conventional scenario, is about an implicit agency of leadership creating order, not letting go. Couldn't be simpler.

I wish managing my own business—or any business, for that matter—were so clear-cut, neat, and linear.

But the changes we underwent as a company were anything but clear-cut and linear. They were messy and chaotic. Ideas we played with for a while were set aside, only to be picked up again later. Debates about whether our value proposition—a term used to categorize the type of business one excels at—was that of service or innovative practice kept resurfacing.[4] For example, our long-term emphasis on property management and staying close to our tenants seemed to suggest that we provided value through service. On the other hand, our focus on high-performance, green development practices suggested that we provided value through innovation. It seemed we would never get our hands around that issue. We added staff members, certain they were what we needed, and held on to them way beyond their own happiness and ours. We felt we were doing real estate in a very different way but could never quite put our finger on what that difference entailed.

We actively debated a number of issues over an extended period of years. The dynamic of dialectical play was very much with us in those days, but we didn't recognize it because we lacked the context. In a nutshell, we were building a culture of process and values without having an overarching purpose—contrary to what the business literature says is supposed to happen. For a while, the culture of the company—nonhierarchical, respectful of person, focused on our core values of learning and serving and growing and doing the right thing—was itself the purpose.

The big challenge facing the company in the early to mid-nineties was that the sum of the parts of the culture did not constitute a whole, for one simple reason. We lacked a unifying purpose around which those parts of a culture could coalesce. We lacked an overarching philosophy. It wasn't just staff members who felt a bit adrift; family shareholders were still very much divided about the notion of a more "environmentally friendly" set of real estate practices. There was even talk of selling the business.

THE STORY

Against the backdrop of constant debate about real estate development, family and staff members decided to hold a one-day, in-house symposium on sustainable real estate. Environmental author and activist Paul Hawken; John Knott , a well-regarded developer out of Charleston, South Carolina, who later became a member of our board; and Jason McLennan, a protégé of the architect Bob Berkebile from Kansas City, were asked to join us in a conversation regarding the future of our company.

I remember that day well. Jason spoke first, talking about his roots growing up in the town of Sudbury, Canada, breathing in the air of the local coal refinery, some of the worst air in the entire country. He went on to trace his own journey into green architecture before launching in to a discussion of the U.S. Green Building Council's nascent LEED program. John Knott spoke next. He too began with his roots, as part of the fourth generation in a family of master craftsmen living in Baltimore, whose father was the type of meticulous builder who guaranteed his company's work even when problems were not the result of his handiwork. John then described several cutting-edge development projects with which he was involved.

Finally Paul Hawken got up to speak, without notes or PowerPoint. Paul's talk ranged a good bit and drew significantly from his chapter on Curitiba, Brazil, in *Natural Capitalism,* then just recently published. I had read the book quickly in anticipation of Paul's visit. It's a strange mélange of despair and hope, a rapid-fire assault on our wasteful practices, and a mix of pragmatic, on-the-ground solutions for turning things around. Curitiba is presented as a city that "gets it." Paul's voice that day conveyed the same sense of despair-hope, a softly ironic tone that suggested wistfulness. His voice, in addition to his message, had us hooked.

We took a break in the action, began asking a series of polite, academic questions about points the speakers had made. And then John, with a characteristic bull-in-the-china-shop bluntness I have come to know well at board meetings, blurted out, "So why are we here?" Everyone froze. All social conviviality was gone. And everyone was staring at me.

I managed to stammer something to the effect that we were at a crossroads as a family business. Some of us cared very deeply about doing real estate in a different way. And some of us felt that as long as we gave back to the community, it didn't matter what we did. We were divided as a family, and there was serious thought to selling our real estate holdings—a portfolio of shopping centers, warehouses, and office buildings—and investing the proceeds in a socially responsible investment (SRI) fund such as Calvert or Domini.

At that juncture Paul stepped in. "Why," he said, "would you take the values that you have developed over three generations and simply hand them over to someone else?"

The thoughtful silence that ensued seemed to go on indefinitely. You could see subtle smiles of relief and dawning comprehension around the room. It was a magical moment, one that pulled it all together for us. We left that conference room at the end of the day unified in the conviction that everything we would do as a real estate company we would do sustainably.

I've done a good bit of reflecting about that moment. It's not that things just came together for us out of nowhere. There was a tremendous amount of spadework involved. We had spent more than a decade, from the late 1980s to the late 1990s, talking as a family and as a company about our past history, about our core values, about what gave each of us meaning in life. But in that magical moment all of the spadework came together, synthesized into a clear vision.

Think about it: We could have done all the hard work and yet never pulled it together. Or we could have experienced that encounter with Paul Hawken and walked on by, missing the magical moment without realizing it. How does it happen, this bubbling up of effort that has occurred over many years, timed with something catalytic that converts that work and energy into a clear and compelling vision?

Synthesizing the Hedgehog and the Scorpion

Why would you take the values that you have developed over three generations and simply hand them over to someone else? The power of Hawken's question rests primarily on two rhetorical moves: a linguistic play and an inversion.

The linguistic play is fairly obvious and wasn't missed by anyone around the conference table that day. For the monetary notion of "value," Hawken substituted a far-reaching definition having to do with our past history and actions, the time spent living in community with others, our ethical beliefs and practices, our sense of purpose. This resonated with family and staff. I know it resonated with me, linking me and that instant in time to a storehouse of memories of growing up in a family business, living (at least virtually) above the family store. Selling our family grocery business in the 1980s had left intact our company and our family and what that stood for. Dismantling things now would have meant parting with values that had been with us for generations. It's no wonder the term *selling out* is fraught with emotional and value-laden content.

But there was also a subtler aspect to Hawken's comment, one that inverts the conventional view of classical economics. In today's business context one *realizes value* when one sells something. When we develop land into a building, we purchase the land, contract with experts to help with the project, purchase material and labor to build the structure, devote time to leasing it up. The sum of those activities and materials comprises our cost. We sell the building at some amount above our initial cost (hopefully) to make a profit. In doing so, we are said to have realized the value of the project. That difference between what the market is willing to pay for the building and what our costs are is the so-called value we have created, through our ingenuity and creativity and luck provided by external influences. Value realization, in an economic sense, is making concrete and tangible what had before been intangible and uncertain.

What Hawken was drawing our attention to that day—though it would be a long time before I understood it—was this: In a market economy, what we take for granted as the realizing of value, exchanging something abstract for something concrete, is actually taking something real and vital (our creativity, our collective work, the results of our efforts) and converting it into an abstraction. Moreover, handing over the values we had created to some other party fundamentally diminished the original effort in the exchange. Why indeed would we hand over values we created across three generations to someone else? If we did, would we facilitate future value creation through investment or kissing those values good-bye? Would we be realizing value or *not* realizing fundamentally what we'd been about?

Businesspeople often speak of a company's "exit strategy"; a business's very inception often entails serious consideration as to how its founders will exit the company, by selling out to other investors, going public, or being absorbed by a larger corporation. But properly speaking, there is no exit out there. When we produce, consume, and discard our waste, there is no place outside nature's system where we can throw things away. Similarly, in a business context a company doesn't exit the system when it sells out to others. Its capital (financial, intellectual, human capital) is simply redeployed elsewhere. In the process of being sold, in the process of having its capital converted from something concrete into something more abstract (the sales price), a business deludes itself that it is exiting the picture. It is actually discarding what it perceives is of lesser value while making an entrance strategy into a new endeavor with the values (potentially) left behind. Hawken's comment leads us to this challenge: How does a company change, evolving into realizing its potential, while still holding true to the values that served it well thus far?

In *Good to Great*, James Collins identifies a critical feature of great companies, something he calls the Hedgehog Concept:

> A Hedgehog Concept is not a goal to be the best, a strategy to be the best, an intention to be the best, a plan to be the best. It is an understanding of what you can be the best at. The distinction is absolutely crucial.[5]

It's a forward-looking concept: *Understanding what you can be the best at* calls for having a vision way down the road of what a company has the innate capacity to evolve into. The vision may not necessarily be attainable, but it is one that a company can aspire to. The Hedgehog Concept is about evolving to realize a company's highest potential. But what about looking backward to consider what a company has been the best at throughout its history? What about the issue of continuity as well as change?

One of my kids' favorite stories is the fable about the frog and the scorpion. A frog and a scorpion have arrived at the bank of a swift river. The scorpion says to the frog, "I need your help to get across. I'll climb on your back and you can carry us both across the river." To which the frog replies, "What do you think I am, an idiot? How do I know that you won't sting me once we begin our journey?" And so the scorpion answers, "That would be crazy. If I did that, we would both die in the river." So the frog agrees and allows the scorpion to climb on his back, and they begin their traverse. Midway across the river, the scorpion, sure enough, stings the frog, who quickly starts to die. "Scorpion," says the frog, "why did you do this?" To which the scorpion replies, "I'm a scorpion. It's my nature."

I've never figured out why a good swimmer like the frog agrees to such a one-sided bargain in the first place. Maybe it's his nature. My point in drawing on this story is this: As a company, it's not enough to understand what you can be the best at, to identify your Hedgehog Concept. It's also critical to identify your Scorpion Concept, to understand your fundamental nature, what you *are* by virtue of what you *have been*, and *connect the two*. It's important to ask, What, fundamentally, is the underlying nature of the company? What has it always been?

In a global economy, this reflection upon roots and core nature surely seems antiquated, harking back more to the economist E. F. Schumacher rather than a contemporary writer such as Thomas Friedman. Friedman notes: "When memories exceed dreams, the end is near. The hallmark of a truly successful organization is the willingness to abandon what made it successful and start fresh."[6] Contrast this with Schumacher's notion of the "economics of permanence," which he associates with wisdom:

> We must study the economics of permanence. Nothing makes sense unless its continuance for a long time can be projected without running into absurdities. There can be "growth" towards a limited objective, but there cannot be unlimited, generalized growth. It is more likely, as Gandhi said, that "Earth provides enough to satisfy every man's need, but not every man's greed."[7]

Is there a way in which the two might be synthesized, integrated? Our encounter with Paul Hawken suggested that there is a point of convergence between realizing our highest potential and staying within our essential nature.

Hawken's comment to our group brought us face to face with synthesizing hedgehog and scorpion, future and past, growth and restraint, the changes we were considering adopting as a company in light of an ethos of continuity. And at the juncture of these tensions, we realized a sense of shared values centered on land and community.

We came to realize our nature was all about place and people, and that what we would be best at going forward was what we had been good at all along: fostering and nurturing the overall health and well-being of our land and community. We weren't using the term *triple bottom line* back then. But the notion of running a business with deep ties to the social community and a deep commitment to the natural environment made complete, intuitive sense. No surprise, in retrospect, that we were off and running after that one-day symposium, with a vision that would facilitate the synthesis of disparate voices and opinions throughout the company.

Synthesizing Sociability, Solidarity, and Value Realization

Our company's strong, longstanding emphasis on community contributed significantly to the magical synthesis occurring that day. But that begs the question: What does a business culture based on a sense of community entail?

Most of us have at a vague awareness that a business provides a sense of community for its workforce. Rob Goffee and Gareth Jones, in an article on "E" cultures (those that focus on efficiencies and an economic bottom line) and "O" cultures (businesses that focus on their "softer" organizational aspects),[8] have developed a helpful matrix for analyzing community in a business culture. Goffee and Jones use a *sociability index* to examine the degree to which those in a company exhibit personal connections to one another. Traits measured include the degree of sincere friendliness among staff members, socializing outside the office, confiding in personal matters, and so forth. A second index, the *solidarity index*, is used to measure organizational effectiveness. It includes sharing the same business objectives, getting work done effectively, a collective desire to win and ability to capitalize quickly on competitive advantages, sharing the same strategic goals, and the like. A company such as the privately held software company SAS is viewed as being strong on sociability, while a company such as GE is perceived to be strong on solidarity. Goffee and Jones' work is captured in Figure 3-1.

It's a helpful matrix, but it doesn't go far enough. The quadrant labeled *communal,* where there is strong solidarity and strong sociability, doesn't exactly equate to community. Yes, there is a sense that in a communal type of organization staff members get along with each other

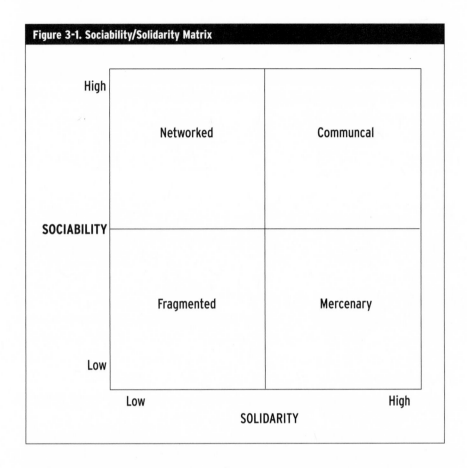

Figure 3-1. Sociability/Solidarity Matrix

and work together well. But sports teams can do that. So too can voluntary organizations (e.g., Rotary) and quasi-governmental organizations (chamber of commerce), none of which we would refer to as communities so much as tightly knit organizations that perform well together. Something is missing.

To Goffee and Jones' sociability-solidarity matrix I would add a third axis, one featuring a shared sense of meaning and purpose—value realization. This third plane addresses questions such as: Does the organization not only meet a personal need to belong but also provide meaningful work and a sense of what is truly valuable?[9] Does it facilitate self-discovery, lifelong learning, personal growth, and the opportunity to reach one's full potential?[10] Does the culture foster a sense of moral obligation and provide a context for one's role in society and the larger world?[11] Does the organization serve as a vehicle for creative expression?[12] Does the environment facilitate joy?[13] And finally, and perhaps most important, to what extent does the company as a whole serve to synthesize individual staff members' sense of value realization into a collective sense of purpose and meaning?

Adding this third dimension enables a company to assess not only the degree to which its culture functions effectively (solidarity, noted on the horizontal or x-axis) and the degree to which its culture fosters personal cohesion (sociability, noted on the vertical or y-axis) but the degree to which its culture epitomizes a value-centric ethos.

Such a 3-D metric enables one to assess a company's overall level of community at discrete points in time. For instance, in the mid-nineties our company's degree of solidarity was fair, with each staff member functioning with a significant degree of autonomy and independence but not strong coordination (let's score it a 5 on a 10-point scale). Sociability was also fair, as staff members tended to socialize to a moderate degree with one another (again, let's say a 5). And our degree of value realization was relatively low, since we did not synthesize individuals' values into an overarching belief system (let's score it a 3).

By 2000 we were working hard on synthesizing our value system (value realization, the z-axis, had increased to a 5). As a result of that collective work our sociability index, the y-axis, had improved (call it a 6). But our capacity to work well together efficiently as a business was suffering somewhat as we struggled with how our shared value systems translated into a well-run company (let's score it as a 3).

By 2005, however, our overarching philosophy of sustainability was well formed and so value alignment was high (an 8). After years of awkward efforts to coordinate our sustainable work we had figured out how to make our sustainable management practices function effectively (solidarity score at a 7). And our overall camaraderie was also strong (sociability index at an 8). The numeric scores here are obviously subjective and are meant to demonstrate how this 3-D concept works. This picture of how community can be measured is provided in Figure 3-2.

A few comments about this approach: Evaluating the alignment of values within an organization is a critical, missing part of assessing

Figure 3-2. Measuring Community in 3-D

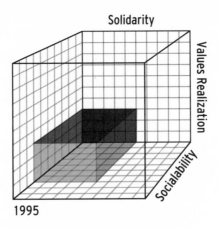

1995

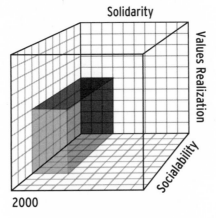

2000

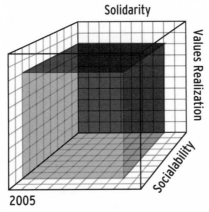

2005

community. It needs to be considered equally with the degree to which staff members work effectively with one another (solidarity) and the degree to which they interact with one another socially (sociability). The three criteria—solidarity, sociability, and value alignment—are correlated. A higher degree of value alignment within an organization is likely to result in a higher degree of solidarity and sociability. Having said that, there is no idealized version of community implied in this three-dimensional evaluation. The point is not to aim for a maximum score on each of the three axes. Each organization will decide for itself what its goal should be and assess the level and nature of community it actually fosters by using this goal as a benchmark for performance.

A sustainable business does indeed aspire to a high level of value alignment, where individuals live up to their highest potential and, simultaneously, are part of something larger than themselves. Steve Olson, associate director of the Center for Ethics and Corporate Responsibility at Georgia State University, refers to this duality in terms of a process that fosters both individuation and social integration:

> [This stage of development] focuses on renegotiating one's relation to the institutions in which one operates (family, work, government, community) while working out one's unique vocational contributions to those institutions. The major shift that occurs . . . is that the person comes to believe and act out of the awareness that the locus of control, responsibility, and authority is always internal to oneself. This move toward full "individuation" enables the person to operate in a fully cooperative and collaborative fashion for the first time, as it were, because one cannot be fully related unless one is, paradoxically, fully individuated.[14]

The individual's larger sense of purpose is not imposed by senior management. But the business culture provides fertile ground within which the individual's values can be realized.

The culture of a sustainable business serves to synthesize both greater individuation and social integration, fostering a sense of greater cohesion within a company that is shaped by diverse, individualized journeys of self-discovery. On the one hand, business fosters what scientist Lewis Thomas calls "the absolute unpredictability and total improbability of our connected minds."[15] On the other hand, business functions as something of a "social architect,"[16] providing spiritual building materials to facilitate self-construction and shared leadership. Biologist Janine Benyus captures this dynamic well:

> There exists a sweet spot between chaos and order, gas and crystal, wild and tame. In that spot lies the powerfully creative force of self-organization. . . . Tropical agroecologist Jack Ewel also alludes to this free ordering when he says, "Imitate the vegetative structure of an ecosystem, and you will be granted function."[17]

Imitate the vegetative structure of an ecosystem? A bit far-fetched, more the purview of a biologist such as Benyus than that of a businessperson, perhaps? Nevertheless, a number of authors, business leaders in their own right, make the strong connection between a business culture and an ecosystem.[18] A sustainable community, in a business context, is one in which the ground is fertile for individuals to grow and mature while also allowing for a business's similar drive toward fulfilling its purpose. It is, as Benyus suggests, a dance between chaos and order, where careful attention to nurturing the environment integrates with a willingness to let go and enable staff members to shape their course.

Synthesizing Values

Thus far, we have been discussing value realization at an abstract level. But what does this look like up close?

Our company was very fortunate, at one of its annual retreats, to have Steve Olson facilitate two days of discussion on values. Olson, in addition to being a scholar of ethics and business corporate responsibility, is an authority on the Hall-Tonna Values Inventory, which is particularly germane here.

The Hall-Tonna Values Inventory is a list of 125 values, some that are end points or goals (goals values), others that are means to achieve those goals (means values). These 125 values are divided into eight distinct stages, ranging from basic foundation values on the low end to visionary values on the high end. *Foundational values* are associated with safety, security, and family (stages one through three). *Focus values* are linked to one's institution and vocation (stages four and five). *Visionary values* are related to establishing a new order and wisdom, and improving world order (stages six through eight). Businesses, as well as individuals, evolve through these eight stages. Moreover, a distinct type of business leadership is associated with each value stage a company finds itself in. One of the many ideas behind this inventory is that a business (or individual) grows and matures over time through at least several of these stages. While Hall and Tonna have identified 125 values in all, they contend that a business or individual can prioritize only ten to twenty values at any given time.

The Hall-Tonna Values Inventory is poorly known within the business world, and that, I feel, is our loss. It is a diagnostic tool that, unlike any other I have encountered, facilitates the synthesis of values among individuals at a company. The tool enables assessment of where each person's value system is currently focused, presents aggregated results, and enables a company to determine whether there exists staff coalescence around certain values. It enables a company to determine how it is trending and to evaluate the counter-trends creating inherent tensions. Fundamentally it enables a company to answer a critical question: What is it we collectively care about?

And that is how we approached this tool. As a prelude to our company retreat, Olson had everyone respond to an online survey about values. The results of this survey are provided in Figure 3-3, with the number of times staff members showed a preference for a particular value indicated in parentheses. Stage one values, associated with the basic question of safety, and stage eight values, associated with the visionary goal of changing the world order, have been left off this chart, since our company has not collectively identified either stage as a current and collective priority.

The results captured in Figure 3-3 provide a gold mine of information on our company. I'd like to highlight just a few points. A casual

Table 3-3: Hall-Tonna Survey of Values at Melaver, Inc., 2007						
Stages	**2: SECURITY**	**3: FAMILY**	**4: INSTITUTION**	**5: VOCATION**	**6: NEW ORDER**	**7: WISDOM**
Goals Values	Security (28)	Family/ Belonging (70)	Belief/ Philosophy (82)	Equality/ Liberation (42)	Knowledge/ Insight (40)	Truth/Wisdom (25)
		Self Worth (48)	Play/Recreation (55)	Integration/ Wholeness (27)	Being Self (35)	
			Work//Wealth/ Value (53)	Self-Actualization (39)	Construction/ New Order (21)	
			Competence & Confidence (34)		Faith/Risk/ Vision (18)	
Means Values		Courtesy & Hospitality (40)	Responsibility (75)	Sharing/ Listening/Trust (59)	Accountability/ Ethics (66)	
		Social Affirmation (40)	Efficiency/ Planning (59)	Adaptability/ Flexibility (58)	Limitation/ Celebration (54)	
			Loyalty/Fidelity (59)	Quality/ Evaluation (45)	Detachment/ Solitude (48)	
			Productivity (54)	Search/ Meaning/Hope (44)		
			Duty/Obligation (47)	Relaxation (40)		
			Ownership (47)			
			Reason (46)			
			Achievement/ Success (43)			
Value Cluster	FOUNDATION		Focus		Vision	
Leadership Style	PATERNALIST	MANAGER	FACILITATOR	COLLABORATOR	SERVANT	VISIONARY

glance at this chart shows a clustering of values in stages four and five, with significant movement forward toward stage six. What this indicates is a company that has evolved largely beyond foundational values, is grounded in so-called focus values that move toward increasingly complex and holistic ways of thinking, and is aspiring to a form of self-knowledge and awareness that enables the company to serve as an instrument for social change. One of the aspirational values of the company (construction/new order, stage six) provides an indication of the direction we are moving:

> Developing and initiating a new institution or transforming the organization in which one works in order to prosper in the world of business, enhance the quality of life, create meaningful work for all employees, and develop an institution that benefits society.

One other important aspect of our Hall-Tonna survey is the pull back toward the value of family and belonging (stage three), which staff members rated second highest overall. Olson refers to this as a regressive pull back toward more fundamental values, in contrast to the progressive move toward later-stage values. It's worth examining this tension closely, since it captures a critical dilemma familiar to most of us: work-life balance.

Thus far we have focused on numerous sustainable management practices and principles that, while perhaps unconventional, are likely to seem compelling to many: work that has meaning and purpose; shared leadership in which purpose is built from the bottom up, collectively; core values that serve as the central focus for all activities; decisions that are made with caution and care in the long-term interest of land and community; focus on individuals realizing their own highest potential as well as a collective company focus on values that point to a new order. This portrait of a sustainable business is indeed compelling. And therein lies the rub.

A business, even a sustainable business cannot and should not substitute for the individual's need for a broader, integrated, communal life. It can and should be a contributing part. But not a substitute.

Our country is characterized as a skilled workforce of free agents, a transitory culture of creative, autonomous souls who seek out loose-tie associations.[19] We spend more and more time in our cars, with 25 percent of our waking hours devoted to activities linked to driving.[20] Meanwhile every ten minutes of commuting time translates into a 10

percent reduction in involvement in community affairs.[21] Our response
to commuting to work is telecommuting, a positive response to reducing
energy consumption but hardly a trend toward greater communal cohesiveness.[22] Instead of community, we often speak in terms of multiple
microcultures, many of them virtual.[23]

Amid this fragmentation is a yearning for something more, a connectedness that is both physical and spiritual, an antidote to fragmentation.
Many in our culture pin their hopes for this antidote on the workplace—
often with only a vague realization of doing so. As someone who grew up
in a family business, I feel deep ambivalence about the notion of community inhering primarily in a business context. There is gratification in
being part of a dynamic group that has a high degree of sociability and
solidarity and that also aspires to create a new order. Such a dynamic
community is a tonic to the general world of profound fragmentation.

But there are a number of concerns here. As we move, as a company,
up the Sustainability Pyramid (see Figure 2-3), each successive step takes
its toll on individuals. I'm not just talking about the long hours people
invest in aspiring to higher goals and values. More substantively, our
team is living constantly with subtle but demanding mental and metaphysical pressures of pushing beyond comfortable frontiers. I once
received an e-mail from someone who worked with us for a short time
before moving on to another position elsewhere. It's lovely for the willingness to provide honest feedback but somewhat painful in what it has
to say:

> I learned a lot in my . . . tenure at Melaver, Inc. . . . I learned
> about the challenges associated with running and being part of a
> values-based business. I truly appreciate the opportunity. [I also
> now recognize] that I was under stress, but did not realize how
> stressed out I was at Melaver until I began my current job at [X].
> I am no longer stressed and as a healthier person, I am more able
> to spend quality time with my family and friends and focus on
> the public work I do. I cannot even begin to describe how grate-
> ful I am for this change. It makes an enormous difference, and I
> believe, makes me a better person in all aspects of my life.

No doubt: Value-centric companies take their toll. A company that evolves through a strategy of adaptive capacity calls for time and patience and a willingness to move in a gyrelike spiraling fashion, ratcheting upward but in a gradual escalation of growth, so that we all move together. There are times when I feel that our own evolution through the latter value stages of the Hall-Tonna schema is happening a bit too intensively. I feel certain my colleagues share that concern. Dismissing this critique as something that simply comes with the territory of being a mission-driven company somehow leaves me a bit dissatisfied.

I am also uncomfortable with the idea of work serving as the primary context for fulfilling our yearning for community. Too often work is the simulacrum for other communal contexts in which personal growth traditionally has occurred: the family, the neighborhood, spiritual and civic activities, and civic and political engagement. For me, there are times when I find it satisfying to bury myself in the camaraderie and shared purpose of the workplace. My retreat is fueled by the positive sense of making a difference through work and also by a sense of feeling disenfranchised elsewhere. But that retreat, I think, shortchanges my own growth and also the role I have to play in other contexts. Growth within the workplace should not be a zero-sum-game proposition, where time and effort spent in the workplace occurs at the expense of time and effort devoted elsewhere.

The key here is to experience this work-life challenge as a creative tension and not a zero-sum-game proposition. The tension elicited in our Hall-Tonna survey—a tension between the aspiration of creating a new order and the desire to feel a sense of belonging linked to a familial environment—can be a positive one. It can also be a negative one, as the e-mail from my former colleague attests. It's a difficult tension to maintain, but it also makes perfect sense. It would be hard, perhaps impossible, to nurture a sense of communal belonging within a company without tapping into a more foundational sense of belonging provided by one's extended family. And in our case, certainly, it underscores our orientation as a family business. Synthesizing values within a business organization relies deeply upon such foundations.

How does a company nurture a culture in which individual staff members collectively aspire to more visionary values such as fostering a land-community ethic? It certainly helps to hire people from the get-go who are looking for a larger sense of meaning and purpose from work. Another part of the answer has to do with fostering bottom-up management practices that provide a sense of entitlement among staff members to give voice to their individual sensibilities. It helps too to have business practices that validate and manage this internal dialectic in constructive ways. Part of the answer has to do with providing a context within which to synthesize this dialectical play of voices. Part of the answer has to do with a culture that synthesizes scorpion (who we are) and hedgehog (what we hope to become). And finally part of the answer has to do with the ways in which leadership is shared throughout the organization.

Steve Olson characterizes this type of leadership as helping to move a company in the direction of shaping a new order:

> Cycle five leadership is intensively collaborative. Visionary and empathic, yet tough and independent, cycle five collaborative leaders facilitate the engagement of the organization's members with each other, with their organization's deeper purposes, and with their collective contributions to the persons and purposes which it serves.

How does a company evolve to the point of aspiring to create a new order? The answer hinges on the principle of synthesis. Synthesis calls for a business ethos and vision that realizes the value of fusing the dynamics of change with a sensibility for continuity. Synthesis calls for a business culture that cultivates disparate voices (the play of dialectics), but also a culture that integrates those voices into a shared sense of purpose. Synthesis calls for a leadership of collaboration, in which disparate skills, talents, and viewpoints are suffused. In a nutshell, managing a sustainable business calls for a synthesis of vision (what do we want to be), culture (how we function with one another), and stewardship (who is shepherding our direction and how that leadership structured).

Transforming Dangers into Opportunities

The opportunities for a company to be an agent of social change for a new order can be breathtaking. But these opportunities also present challenges, the most significant of which may be that of engendering a silolike, cliquish orientation toward the rest of the world. Synthesis, while providing the liberating power of integrating individual voices, sensibilities, skills, and needs, also carries with it the potential to draw firm boundaries between those who are part of the group and those who are not. The issue of cliquishness or boundary setting can also be extended to knowledge sharing and concepts such as the nature of competition.

A more conventional business approach would recognize the competitive advantage from having a sustainable business and thus would be inclined to put up proprietary boundaries around what it knows and how it is structured. With such an approach, the process of synthesis gets stopped in its tracks as walls are built around the company to insulate it from the competition.

A sustainable business, however, draws on the very strengths of its own integrated social order to break down potential barriers. Sustainable management practices challenge the siloed orientation of businesses, because they are fundamentally about fostering a paradigm change in business practices and systems.

Sustainability expert Donella Meadows, who was responsible for perhaps the most influential piece of writing on systemic change, noted that the single most critical leverage point is to change the mind-set or paradigm out of which the system arises:[24]

> So how do you change paradigms? . . . In a nutshell, you keep pointing at the anomalies and failures in the old paradigm, you come yourself, loudly, with assurance, from the new one, you insert people with the new paradigm in places of public visibility and power. You don't waste time with reactionaries; rather you work with active change agents and with the vast middle ground of people who are open-minded.[25]

Sage advice. In this context of managing a sustainable business, Meadows's advice might be: Reframe the paradigm of competition upon which business is based, share what one knows loudly with others, and extend the synthesis that has occurred within a company to include a broader group of like-minded stakeholders. Let's consider each of these critical moves in a little more detail.

Reframing Competition

You keep pointing at the anomalies and failures in the old paradigm. . . . Though Donella Meadows did not specifically have the notion of competition in mind while penning these words, she might very well have pointed to competition as a pivotal aspect of a paradigm that is failing us.

Michael Porter, considered by many to be the guru of competitive advantage, made famous the five forces analysis of competition. These five forces determine "the ability of firms in an industry to earn, on average, rates of return on investment in excess of cost of capital." The five forces are:

1. Bargaining power of buyers. This influences the prices firms can charge. For example, firms that sell to Wal-Mart have to contend with its formidable ability to set the price of goods.
2. Bargaining power of suppliers. This is when a supplier has a product of limited supply that is in hot demand by the marketplace. The limited number of suppliers for photovoltaic panels is one current example.
3. Potential threat of new entrants into the field. The decision of Amazon.com to sell electronic goods online would be an example of a bookseller becoming a new entrant into the field of selling computers, cameras, and so forth, thus competing with bricks-and-mortar retailers such as Best Buy.
4. Threat of substitute products or services. The development of quality conference calling and video phones is proving to

be a threat to the airline industry, as companies can effectively meet without traveling.

5. Presence of competitors within existing firms in an industry;[26] for example, McDonald's vs. Burger King.

This five forces analysis is the bible of strategic approaches to business today, an analysis of powerful, almost unquestioned influence. But what happens to this model if a company reframes the whole concept of competition? What happens if a company makes partnering decisions—whom it will buy from and sell to, how it approaches potential "threats" from new entrants and other competitors, how it deals with the "threat" of substitute products and services—with a different mindset?[27] What happens if a company takes more of a collaborative than a competitive approach, linking the word to its Latin root *competere* for "striving together"?[28] Does a company lose its competitive advantage? Or does it change the whole nature of the game? What happens if a company shifts the entire notion of competition from one business going toe to toe with other similar companies to that of a business contending with itself and its capacity to sustain itself? If you begin with botanist Paul Godfrey's observation that "Nature bats last," what does that do to a company's approach to strategy and competitive advantage? Given potential environmental collapse on a global scale, against whom are we really competing, and what should our strategic approach to competition be?

Let's begin with my particular company and who our competition is. You might say our company competes with other development companies for outside capital. But at the moment, we're in the fortunate position of having investment capital providers seeking us out, looking for ways to add green real estate to their conventional portfolios. Of course, this situation changes almost daily, as more green product and green developers come on the market and institutional capital has more options from which to pick. That's OK. Worst-case scenario, we have less capital available to us and build less—not really an issue for us. Unlike publicly held companies we aren't faced with the dilemma of trying to place large amounts of investment capital beyond our capacity.

Well, perhaps we compete with other developers for tenants. Sure, that's always an issue. But if we do our job competently and address real need as opposed to creating need (addressed in more detail in chapter four) that shouldn't be much of a problem. Moreover, our projects appeal to a certain type of user—people who understand the longer-term financial advantages of locating in green facilities. And there's not that much competitive product out there. And as more comes on? Our position is simply "great; the more the merrier." We need a sea change in the way real estate is done.

In short, we compete with ourselves,[29] a competition that entails two interwoven components and how we define them. We struggle with the very notion of progress, which has taken its toll on this Earth. And we struggle with the notion of self-esteem and the extent to which the esteem traditionally accorded to a business has a lot to do with the ostensible "progress" and growth a business demonstrates to the market. Our culture celebrates fast companies that go from $0 to $1 billion in value in short order, and rock star CEOs hobnobbing in Davos, Switzerland, with the political elite. Sorely lacking are exemplars of doing more by doing less.

What do we do with our struggles? I think, primarily, we confront them directly, make them public, and share them with others. Admitting these struggles to ourselves and others goes a long way toward transcending them. By the talks we give, the learning sessions we sponsor, the political positions we promote in the community, the papers we publish, the advocacy roles we play, we make our struggles—much more than our solutions—the provenance of a broader constituency. We work best by posing questions and looking to the larger community for restorative solutions, solutions that require us to synthesize the best thinking out there.

So, for us, it's not simply a question of how to build a LEED home or office building but how we create entire mixed-use communities according to LEED standards. It's not just a question of how to build mixed-use sustainable communities but how to make them affordable for the growing number of people who can no longer afford to own their own places. It's not just a question of creating mixed-used communities with affordable housing but also fostering regional planning along geological water-basin lines. And it's not just a question of regional planning along geological lines but how to create a statewide conservation plan that effectively preserves many of our fragile areas from any type of development. It's not just a question of creating a statewide conservation plan but of creating broad stretches of conservation areas that restore ecosystems and natural hydrology altered by past land use practices. And it's not just a question of creating broad stretches of conservation areas but of creating new ways of building that result in no net additional footprint on our environment. And it's not just a question of having no net additional footprint on our environment but of creating an ethos that reduces waste, pure and simple. And it's not just a question of creating an ethos that reduces waste but of adopting a new paradigm that recharges our water resources and recharges our air and recharges our souls.

It's a tall set of charges. To deliver upon this mandate calls for us to reach out to others in the industry and beyond who know more than we do, to share knowledge well beyond our company's borders. This charge also calls for us to partner with a much broader set of stakeholders. This mandate demands a new, broader synthesis built upon the foundations of synthesis within our own company. What is called for, in short, is replacing the traditional business emphasis on competition and competitive advantage with a concept of collaborative advancement.

Doesn't this fly in the face of the traditional role of the corporation, which is simply and clearly maximizing profit for shareholders? Yes, it does. It substitutes a focus on optimizing value for stakeholders by leveraging our company values to make broader moves beyond corporate boundaries. Such an approach, oddly enough, also flies in the face of recent studies that contend that businesses making the move toward sustainable practices will reap a competitive advantage.[30] Such a view—savvily perceiving that competitive advantage is likely to be the best way to sell sustainability to the business community—misses the larger picture.

Yvon Chouinard, founder of Patagonia, noted, "I learned at an early age that it's better to invent your own game; then you can always be a winner."[31] We want a new game, not a blue-ocean strategy in which a unique product offering makes the competition irrelevant.[32] The new game is one in which work itself is redefined so as to be more in harmony with the social and natural environment, and one in which such work requires a broad collaborative effort that makes competition itself irrelevant. After all, competition is irrelevant on a dead planet.

Reframing competition, then, entails a number of critical moves. It requires transcending our notions of perceived scarcity by recognizing that there is no shortage of work out there for all sustainable businesses to engage in. It involves dispensing with the drive to be number one, with the concomitant sense that one's success must come at the expense of others. It means affirming an alternative vision, one in which business strives to be more in harmony with both the natural and social environments, with place and people. It means asking "whether it is in our collective interest to keep competing" and "strengthen[ing] our resolve to work at the same time to create healthy, productive, cooperative alternatives."[33]

Reframing Proprietary Knowledge

"[Y]ou come yourself, loudly, with assurance, from the new one." Donella Meadows's words again. Displacing the old paradigm, according to Meadows, does not simply entail developing an alternative but loudly proclaiming that new paradigm. But this raises an interesting question: As a restorative company works to extend its sense of place and people by sharing what it knows with others, is it giving away its competitive advantage?

The notion of knowledge sharing is not easy. We struggle with it all the time. Should we share our sustainable property management practices with large corporate entities, as sometimes requested? Should we be concerned when we partner with a general contractor who is clearly going to be learning on our dime and could edge us out of development deals in the future? What about our consultancy work, where we essentially hand over what we know to others? And so on.

I think knowledge sharing is fundamentally an issue of ego and branding. There's not much that we as a company really know that no one else knows or couldn't learn almost immediately. If we have something that differentiates us, it is our willingness to use and share what we know.

That's an odd and apparently paradoxical statement: Our competitive advantage comes from our conviction that we need to share the essence of our competitive advantage with whomever is willing to listen. As the message and practice spreads, as the walls of our company become more and more permeable, we experience both a sense of gratification and concern. The gratification comes with the rippling effect of a movement in which we are playing a part. The concern comes in that as this diffusion of knowledge gathers momentum our own role will be forgotten.

It's easy to be dismissive of these concerns: to say, "Yes, but our own role in this movement is the result of standing on the shoulders of so many who came before us," or to say, "Yes, but consider the bigger picture and the good work we contribute to it." These are good and compelling arguments, but I don't think they touch on the emotional core of the issue, which is this: In mission-driven endeavors, folks often feel compensated by certain intangibles, not the least of which is the credit that comes from taking chances, being visionary, and putting aside self-interest in the context of something larger. By sharing what we know with the outside world, do we in some way dilute—perhaps even undermine—the passion underlying our company's sense of mission and purpose?

A partial answer can be found, somewhat unfortunately, in viewing the hubris of others. We've seen a few visionary architects and developers, impressive, inspiring souls so caught up in their own press clippings that they belittle the efforts of others following in their footsteps. We've seen presentations at professional conferences in which speakers jostle one another to claim the prestige of being first on the sustainability scene. We've seen environmental groups trying to work collaboratively but bickering because of concerns over who gets top billing or who gets first claim on the limited supply of donor dollars. It's all too human. But as a company we don't want to be that way ourselves. We also can't. One of the redemptive aspects of being part of a small company looking to be an agent of social change is that we cannot be promulgators of a new order without the knowledge and assistance of others.

The only Hall-Tonna stage seven value that our company has collectively identified as a priority is that of truth/wisdom. The short synopsis of this value is telling:

Intense pursuit and discovery of ultimate truth above all other activities. This results in intimate knowledge of objective and subjective realities, which converges into the capacity to clearly comprehend people and systems and their inter-relationship.

As I read these words, I think what is called for is a deep commitment to what one knows is true, enveloped by an internal feeling of peace that, as long as the work gets done, it matters not at all who is credited for it. Framed in this way, the entire notion of proprietary knowledge is a fundamental contradiction in terms.

Reframing Partnering

"You don't waste time with reactionaries; rather you work with active change agents and with the vast middle ground of people who are open-minded." Once again, Donella Meadows. I would like to think that if I had read her work earlier in my career, I might have saved myself and my colleagues a lot of trouble. But I am probably deluding myself. The process involved in learning how and with whom to partner takes time and evolves as one's own capacity to place faith in the importance of one's work matures and takes hold.

The issue of reframing partnering differs from reframing sharing knowledge. With sharing knowledge the challenge is whether a company opens itself up and, if so, to what degree. But virtually every business these days at least speaks the language of partnering, and most engage a coterie of "outsiders" to assist with projects. The issue of partnering, then, is not so much one of inclusion, but the depth and the breadth of the inclusion: the degree to which one involves a set of outside partners in one's business affairs (depth) and the extent to which outside partners are involved (breadth).

We like to say we try to work with anyone. In our early projects we simply had to, because we were neophytes in a new approach to building. Our staff gets jazzed learning new techniques and bringing designers, public officials, leasing agents, potential tenants, contractors, and subcontractors along for the ride. It's part of who we are. We still hold to those learning/teaching ideals. While the notion of sustainable practices is actually quite old, its application in the real estate industry is fairly recent. It's foolish to discount anyone's intention from the get-go.

This general openness to partnering is also linked to our own experience of being mentored. We have been fortunate to have been guided by board members and others such as Paul Hawken and Bob Berkebile, who easily could have taken a high-handed approach with us, ridiculing our naive questions and approaches. I grimace a bit every time I think of some of the pronouncements I made in the early years; still grimace at my own basic lack of knowledge in so many areas. Those around me have graciously tolerated my ignorance and learning curve, perhaps in part because they understand what it takes to dismantle a lifetime of unquestioned assumptions and recover what one knows instinctively to be true.

The author Janisse Ray, who grew up in Baxley, Georgia, less than a hundred miles from my hometown, has written compellingly of this learning curve from being educated to becoming knowledgeable about one's environment:

> When I pick up my childhood like a picture and examine it really closely, I realize that I left home not knowing how to swim, not knowing the name of one wild bird except maybe crow, and that I couldn't identify wildflowers and trees. I knew the Dewey decimal system inside and out, could calculate the force of gravity on a ten-pound block sliding down an incline, had read Dumas and Chekhov and Brontë but couldn't tell a weasel from a warthog. I never knew a naturalist or that there was such a thing as an environmentalist.[34]

Her comments hit home. I left the comfort of living above the family store having little appreciation for the community of relationships developed by family members over half a century and having little sense of the place where I grew up. I knew street names but had little interest in their significance or the place names they supplanted. I knew few trees beyond the plentiful live oaks in town, didn't realize that they had not been there forever, didn't have a clue that a vast longleaf pine forest once thrived here. I could stock a grocery shelf with stacks of canned peas and thought taking stock was confined to the simple, tedious task of counting inventory. I wouldn't have known a barrier island from a barrio, though I played half-rubber on a barrier island beach each summer. I have so much to learn, so much to recover.

Because individually, collectively, and as a company my colleagues and I still have so much to learn, we try not to question the motives or intentions of others. We feel we should be as patient as others have been with us. Moreover, if we are to have any real chance as a species of stemming the geometric progression of environmental degradation, it's going to take all hands on deck to get the work done, irrespective of particular agendas and motivations.

Still, we have found that we function most effectively when we work, as Meadows suggests, with active change agents and the vast middle ground of open-minded folks. As Ray Anderson has trenchantly pointed out, once you adopt a conservation ethos you can't unlearn it. And that has proved true for our staff members, who are genuinely puzzled when others don't get the financial, environmental, and social rationale for conducting business sustainably. It seems so obvious and compelling, and thus frustrating when others don't get it.

Part of our own growth and cohesion as a company comes from not just sharing with others but also from the give-and-take of those relationships, the expectation that our partners will echo back to us their own thoughts. In a restorative business environment, information sharing and partnering dynamics are bivalent. We look to our partners to share their thoughts about how to develop a building more efficiently, how to structure a lease in creative ways that enable us to reduce waste, how to use more environmentally benign products.

Part of this collaborative ethos has to do with a sense of urgency that we cannot as human beings continue to waste our natural capital indefinitely. As we have grown as a company we feel an ever-greater urgency to partner as deeply as we can with as many professionals as will spread the word. Part of this collaborative ethos has to do with a sense of "paying it forward," of being as collaborative with our passion and knowledge as others have been with us.

The installation artist Michael Singer, whose own career has evolved and broadened over the past decade to include work on cutting-edge designs that integrate natural systems into the built environment, feels that it is only through partnering with a broad, diverse group of "brain trust" advisors that a truly restorative ethos can come about. In discussing with our company a project that is the subject of the following chapter (Sustainable Fellwood), Singer says:

> I'm suggesting a "team" process that engages an appropriate selection of folks who can contribute to the "new wisdom"; across disciplines, across cultures, people with specific expertise; an environmental ethicist, an artist/poet/dancer/writer, a social anthropologist, a communications-marketer, a historian, engineers, a philosopher, a medical professional, a community activist, an infrastructure specialist, a political analyst, a biologist, just to name a few. These consultants would work as a team closely interacting with the company's core colleagues. For lack of a better title call it a "brain trust" team.[35]

Singer views this brain trust of advisors as a natural extension of the sustainable business, serving to help identify and evaluate potential projects on the front end, working seamlessly as part of a larger team to implement the work, absorbing a business's shared values, perhaps even serving as the means by which those shared values are transformed to a higher point on the Hall-Tonna continuum.

It's not always easy to get this brain trust to work. For one thing, I often confront a criticism among colleagues that we rely too much on outside consultants—a criticism that is based at least in part on cost-containment concerns. For another, the use of such diffuse partnering is very nonlinear and seemingly chaotic, often at odds with the time-sensitive, goal-focused orientation of most business projects. Finally, the knowledge provided by an outside brain trust may seem superfluous, an unnecessary addition to competencies available within a company. In short, it is a struggle every time we consider bringing in outside expertise.

And yet just as we as a company aspire to work that cannot be accomplished without sharing knowledge with others, our collective effort to effect a new order cannot be realized without engaging and realizing the values of others around us. The positive experience of synthesizing the values immanent in our own business culture, rather than causing us to become insular and cliquish, has left us hungry for a broader notion of synthesis, incorporating outside partners, the community at large, and beyond that, all sectors of society.

Coda: Virtuous Returns

We began this chapter by discussing the struggle family and staff were having articulating a shared vision. It was a struggle that Paul Hawken magically helped resolve though a notion of realizing values. This entails the synthesis of continuity and change, of being and becoming. This moment of magical synthesis radiates outward, combining elements of sociability, solidarity, and value realization among staff members, and synthesizing various values through use of the Hall-Tonna Values Inventory. The upshot of these disparate elements coming together is movement toward a paradigm change, with specific application to competition, knowledge sharing, and partnering. We can see this general movement in greater detail by revisiting the Restorative Process Map (Figure 3-4).

Ray Anderson likes to say that a business can do well (financially) by doing good (morally). I would like to suggest a corollary. Economic experts on monetary supply like to discuss the multiplier effect, whereby every additional dollar added to the supply of money creates a much greater increase in economic activity. The same could be said of the activities of a sustainable business: Its often small acts of doing good become amplified in the general community. It creates what Anderson likes to call the "virtuous cycle."

A funny thing happens when you begin to promote a new paradigm, when you begin to reframe issues such as competition, proprietary knowledge, and partnering. First, as a result of looking at things

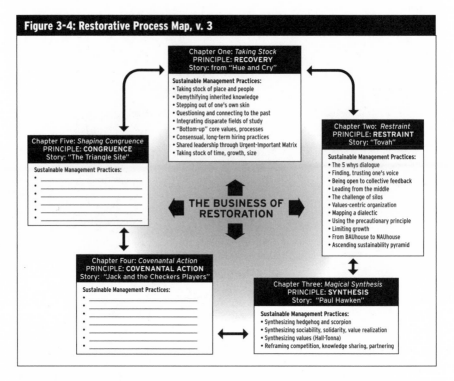

Figure 3-4: Restorative Process Map, v. 3

differently there's an outward rippling effect. The ripple effect serves as a sort of eco-locution, bouncing off "out there," rebounding back toward the source, and subsequently affecting it. The dynamic is akin to a forceful exhalation followed by an equally powerful inhalation: ripple out, ripple back in, influencer becoming the influenced, the dancer (as Yeats put it) becoming the dance.[36] The ripple-out effect and the return tidal wash are both critical components of managing a sustainable business.

Like our three-dimensional organizational chart (Figure 2-1), much of the work of a sustainable business mimics a series of concentric circles radiating outward. Our core values inform our sense of people and place, which influences a process of dialectical engagement within our company, which results in a synthesis of values, which broadens outward to affect our approach to competition, knowledge sharing, and partnering.

But if a sustainable business helps set in motion an outward rippling effect into the general community, it is also the beneficiary of this activity. Our own sense of purpose and meaning as a company becomes ever more validated as these ripples move outward. Our own sense of cohesiveness as a company becomes greater. Our movement toward the more visionary stages of the value spectrum becomes clearer, more distinct, more assured. It is a sense of taking our game to a different plane.

Bill Russell, legendary center of the famous Boston Celtics basketball team, has captured this sense about as well as anyone:

> Every so often, a Celtics game would heat up so that it became more than a physical or even mental game and would be magical. The feeling is difficult to describe, and I certainly never talked about it when I was playing. When it happened I could feel my play rise to a new level. . . . It would surround not only me and the other Celtics but also the players on the other team and even the referees.[37]

The magical flow comes when all parts cohere. The question, then, is how to reach that next level of play by involving not only other players, our competition, and the referee, but also other teams in the league, the sponsors, and the viewing audience ostensibly sitting idly on the sidelines. The next steps—broadening the focus to foster synthesis with a wider group of business stakeholders and shaping a sense of congruence in the larger community—are addressed in the following two chapters.

CHAPTER FOUR

COVENANTAL ACTION

When you speak of adopting a wider perspective this includes working cooperatively with other people. When you have crises which are global by nature for instance, such as the environment or problems of modern economic structure, this calls for a coordinated and concerted effort among many people, with a sense of responsibility and commitment. This is more encompassing than an individual or personal issue.
　　　　　—Dalai Lama, *The Art of Happiness*[1]

I weep for Narcissus, but I never noticed that Narcissus was beautiful. I weep because, each time he knelt beside my banks, I could see, in the depths of his eyes, my own beauty reflected.
　　　　　—Tale of Narcissus, told from the lake's point of view,
　　　　　　by Paul Coelho, *The Alchemist*[2]

So far we have discussed managing a sustainable business in the context of three fundamental principles: recovery, restraint, and synthesis. These three principles help a company transcend silos typically found in an organization.But our context is still writ small, limited to the community within a company. What about the larger community of which we are a part? Can we engage in restorative practices if we don't link our business's sense of a land-community ethic to a broader social context? The epigram by the Dalai Lama that opens this chapter suggests that a broader coalition is needed. If so, how is it shaped? How does one take the dialectical play and synthesis of values from *within* a business organization and amplify that dynamic to incorporate a larger constituency? It is one thing for a business to take stock of people and place. It is quite another challenge for a business to shape a more formal covenant with nature and community. This chapter focuses on the principle of covenantal action.

The term *covenant*, usually a binding agreement between two parties, carries biblical resonances of a spiritual compact, a commitment to adhere to expectations of thought and action. A legal definition of covenant is more of a pledge to do something, as well as a stipulation to the accuracy of certain claims. In the more restricted context of real estate, a covenant ensures a certain state of being, such as warranting "quiet enjoyment." But a broader and more compelling use of the term, also found in real estate, is a *covenant running with the land*, which means a "commitment binding all future owners of a property."[3] Covenantal action encompasses all these definitions.

TWO STORIES

A photograph (see Figure 4-1) hangs on the wall opposite my desk. I stare at it often. It depicts a street scene in my hometown, with some folks clustered around two people playing checkers.

It is the work of Jack Leigh, a Savannah photographer who died a few years back. His photographs are now collected by major museums, and many of his street scenes were taken not too far from where I live. His best-known piece is the image of the bird-girl statue that graces the cover of John Berendt's *Midnight in the Garden of Good and Evil*. I especially like the checkers players photograph, perhaps because of the story behind the picture.

Figure 4-1: *Checker Players*, 1977

Jack was walking along the streets of Savannah one morning when he saw a group of men playing checkers. He asked the men if he could take their picture. "No," was the quick reply. So Jack pulled up a chair and proceeded to watch. He engaged the men in conversation. I don't know how long he sat there. It might have been an hour; it might have been the whole day. But eventually one of the men turned to Jack and said, "OK, you can shoot us."

A simple reading of the story goes like this: The checkers players did not know Jack, and they probably did not know his work. Certainly there was initial distrust. What did this stranger want from them? Who would see the photo? Was he out to make a buck at their expense? How would he make them look? What use would he make of the picture? And so on. But Jack stayed around long enough to establish rapport and trust between him and his subjects.

What did Jack say to put the men at ease? How did he act? We don't know precisely, although local folklore holds that a covenant of understanding and trust was created. Jack offered assurances that his photograph would treat the men with dignity and respect. The men, as a result, gave their permission to be photographed. And Jack kept up his end of the deal, never violating (as far as we know) that trust, which was the basis for permission.

There is a second story I would like to juxtapose to this story of the checkers players, involving a friend of mine—let's call him Adrian—who specializes in real estate law. Adrian once told me about a land assemblage deal he was working on for a large corporate client. Land assemblage deals are tricky because once parcels of land begin to be purchased for development, the prices of remaining parcels skyrocket (even more so if the purchaser's identity becomes known). Oftentimes in assemblage work, both the nature of the project and the identities of the players are veiled. This is what Adrian did. Instead of writing a letter on company stationery indicating his client's desire to buy up the tracts of agricultural land, he went out and bought very simple, inexpensive paper and handwrote crude notes to the individual property owners, saying he wanted to purchase their property. As Adrian gleefully tells the story, the subterfuge worked. People thought he was a humble young student looking for a cheap place to build a home instead of assembling land for a commercial development. In this way Adrian was able to buy a bunch of land for his corporate client at attractive prices.

While it's easy to feel indignant about the questionable

actions of others, it's a bit more problematic when the actions are closer to home. Early in my own career, during assemblage work similar to Adrian's, I brought in an outside person who fronted for me in tying up parcels of land. At some point in the process we abandoned this tactic, feeling that the lack of transparency was inconsistent with our company and what we stood for. We've stuck to this commitment to transparency ever since. But I've never forgotten this lapse in my own actions.

Let's compare the stories of Jack and Adrian. Some of the dynamics at work in Jack Leigh's photograph are at work in Adrian's letter-writing ploy, with similar results. Jack got his photograph; Adrian got his parcels of land. Jack figured out a way to earn his subjects' trust. So too did Adrian. Each received permission to conduct a transaction. Each profited. But the differences in their tactics illustrate that there are uses and abuses of permission. Some people, like Jack, honestly create and fulfill a covenant. Others, like Adrian, create the semblance of a covenant—a false covenant—and then run roughshod over it. Assembling a parcel of land under false pretenses may be someone's idea of good business. But it's not sustainable, as it fosters a general spirit of mistrust within a community. When covenants are broken, the narrow self-interests of various constituencies square off against one another.

This raises a number of questions. What makes a covenant false—veiled intention? The lack of full disclosure? Should a business feel compelled to reveal its strategic intentions? Many, including Adrian, would say no. Part of a business's competitive advantage is keeping close wraps on its proprietary knowledge and purposes. Adrian's stratagem was legal. Even the vast body of business law regarding disclosure doesn't compel a business to be forthcoming in revealing business strategies. In addition to the degree of disclosure there's the question "To whom?" Jack Leigh needed the permission of the checkers players to snap their picture. But to whom is Adrian accountable? The land owners? The larger community? Himself? Who should provide or withhold permission? And on what basis? Larger questions loom here as well: What is the connection between managing a sustainable business and committing to covenantal action? Does one necessarily entail the other?

The story of Jack and the checkers players helps set the stage for some provisional answers to these questions. It is a story about transparency. It is a story in which the values involved in the process of taking the photograph (the means) are as important as the values involved in the ultimate goal (the ends); trust and intention intertwined. It is a story that addresses mutual needs, and it has a certain bilateral, contractual nature to the interaction. It's a story that "runs with the land," living on in the photograph itself as well as in this retelling.

Sustainable Fellwood

The story of Jack and the checkers players epitomizes how I would like our company to function and helps elucidate nuances and management practices embedded in the principle of covenantal action. Let's consider some of these nuances in the context of Sustainable Fellwood, a project in Savannah on which our company has served as the master developer. It's a story with a beginning and a middle, but one whose ending hasn't yet been written.

The Fellwood project is part of Westside Savannah, one of the poorest sections in the city. The general area, a 275-acre collection of neighborhoods just west of Savannah's tony historic downtown, had undergone a yearlong master-planning process in 2005 commissioned by the mayor. The need for regenerating the west side was clear. So too were the challenges. Much of the west side consists of numerous small plots of single-family homes, some boarded up and abandoned, making it challenging to create catalytic development through any one project. There were also political minefields that ran the gamut from concerns over gentrification to issues relating to minority contracting and job training. There is a tendency among development companies, including ours, to avoid such complicated projects because they involve so many uncertain (and politically explosive) moving parts. But covenantal action, as we will see, calls for engaging with the community at large, not running from it.

The potential jewel in Westside Savannah, a twenty-seven acre local housing project called Fellwood, was one of the first affordable housing projects ever built in the nation. Constructed in 1940 and owned by the Housing Authority of Savannah (HAS), Fellwood was carved out of the city's overall master plan for the west side because of HAS's control over that particular property. It wasn't clear to the city what plans, if any, the HAS had for this location. Moreover the HAS and the city had long been wary of one another, making it politically dicey to include Fellwood in the city's master plan.

Nevertheless shortly after the city's master plan was complete, the HAS issued a Request for Qualifications (RFQ) for a master developer to oversee planning and development of its site. Various community leaders were pushing us to compete for the project, assuring us that the political infighting between the HAS and the city would subside. The mayor was betting his legacy on the successful revitalization of the area, where he and other city council members had grown up. The city had already budgeted $4.5 million for infrastructure improvements for revitalizing the Fellwood project. The head of the HAS, soon to retire after twenty-six years on the job, also wanted this project as part of his own legacy. The new head of the HAS wanted Fellwood, her first project, to establish her bona fides. These various arguments persuaded us to compete for the project, which we were subsequently awarded.

When it's complete, Sustainable Fellwood will be an innovative, sustainable, mixed-use neighborhood development,[4] containing about 220 affordable multifamily housing units; a smattering of first-home, affordable, stand-alone residences (financed by Dream-Maker, the city's home-buyer assistance program); 100 senior housing units; four dozen market-rate town homes; a community center; 40,000 square feet of small retail establishments, and an area for job training and other civic-oriented functions. As part of the U.S. Green Building Council's pilot program for LEED for Neighborhood Development (LEED-ND),

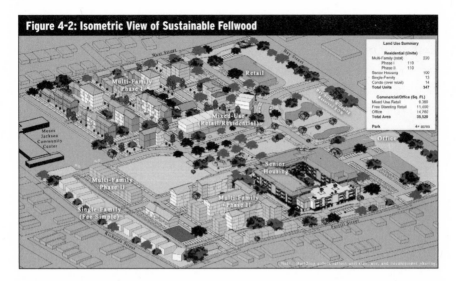

Figure 4-2: Isometric View of Sustainable Fellwood

Sustainable Fellwood looks to become one of the first LEED affordable neighborhood development projects in the nation. An isometric design is provided in Figure 4-2.

Sustainable Fellwood exhibits management practices discussed in this book. The project began by taking stock of people and place, largely through a series of neighborhood charettes, collaborative design sessions that brought together local residents, city stakeholders, and members of our development team. Those early sessions gave us all a feel for the history of Westside Savannah and Fellwood and a deeper comprehension of the passion residents felt for their neighborhood, and influenced our iterative designing and redesigning of the project. The selection of partners for our Sustainable Fellwood team—architect, urban planner, landscape designer, energy and water-management engineering, construction and legal expertise in affordable housing, general contracting, social programming—mimicked our company's deliberative hiring practices. We identified a coterie of principals who felt as passionately as our company does about fostering social change.

Our discussions within the Sustainable Fellwood team were bottom-up driven, with opinions weighing in from all sides on all aspects of the development. That same open-ended, nonhierarchical, dialectical play of voices extended beyond our team to an extended group of stakeholders including members of the HAS, the city bureau chiefs, and the

Fellwood Neighborhood Association. We brainstormed together about draft designs; type of construction; cutting-edge sustainable technologies; financial pro forma; various social, educational, and economic programs that we would like to see included in the project—the list goes on and on. From that brainstorming has evolved a shared vision of which no one partner could have conceived independently.

Two aspects of that brainstorming are worth exploring since they provide a helpful segue into critical aspects of covenantal action. Those aspects have to do with some of the project's social programming as well as its cutting-edge sustainable features.

Social Programming. Our team's early concepts for Sustainable Fellwood were not limited to just the physical, built environment. We also included some elements of social programming: use of the construction project to conduct job training for sustainable development, a health clinic, an organic garden with an ongoing program for community gardening, and a recreational program to teach and promote golf among kids in the community (First Tee).

These concepts received a boost when first members of our team, then later other members of the community, visited a mixed-use affordable housing project in Atlanta called the Villages at East Lake. The partners of the East Lake project had given serious thought to how education, housing, and recreation needed to be integrated, and they were generous in sharing with us their experiences of developing these social programs.

Our own team, along with key community members (including the mayor), returned from several site visits at East Lake ready to apply what had been learned to the social programming for Sustainable Fellwood. A task force was created to oversee this work, now divided into six major components: economic/job training and creation, education, health, culture, recreation, and social programming. The task force was charged to work with the neighborhood to identify specific needs, implement programs in each of these six areas, and integrate all components so that every distinct phase of the residents' lives (infancy to senior living) is provided for. There have since been discussions with the superintendent of schools about building a charter school in the vicinity. We are in the process of partnering with a local high school to assist with vocational training. Discussions on building a public health clinic are moving forward. The city is partnering with our team on reusing an adjacent and defunct recreational center to provide a variety of programs for the community.

It is probably clear from my discussion that the social programs are just beginning to take shape, but it is hard to tell which programs will take off and which will be shelved. Two main points are worth making: The presence of a model elsewhere, developed by an erstwhile "competitor," served as an important, external source of knowledge and information for our team. Moreover, a broad and diverse talent pool has worked together on this social programming task force. Shared knowledge and an expanded partnership circle have been at the core of our efforts. Pushing the boundaries of a development project to include a social dimension has resulted in an expanded circle of engaged stakeholders shaping a broader vision for Sustainable Fellwood well beyond the scope of work expected by the HAS. It is covenantal action in motion.

Cutting-Edge Sustainable Features. Sustainable Fellwood will contain many of the sustainable features found in our other development work: A tight exterior shell (walls and windows), Energy Star appliances and high-efficiency lighting to improve energy efficiency, low-flow water fixtures to conserve water, carpets and paints and cabinetry with reduced amounts of volatile organic compounds to improve indoor air quality, and materials that are, for the most part, produced in our region, thus supporting the local economy as well as reducing energy costs associated transportation. But this project has a few unusual pieces as well.

As a result of bringing to our "brain trust" two ingenious engineers, our team is conducting three-way talks with the city and International Paper (successor to Union Camp, which was the focus of Fallows's 1970 report, *The Water Lords*, discussed in chapter one), regarding a complex water and energy management system. The plan calls for capturing both storm water and sewage on site, running it through small treatment facilities on site, providing the newly treated water to International Paper for various manufacturing uses, and receiving in exchange from International Paper some of its excess steam, to be converted to electricity and used to help manage Sustainable Fellwood's energy loads. The win-win-win nature of this design is a bit astounding. The city doesn't have to tax its aging storm and sewerage infrastructure by treating water coming off Fellwood, since the water never leaves the site. International Paper can reduce its daily draw of groundwater and surface water by a small percentage and has a taker for its excess steam. The residents of Sustainable Fellwood get reduced energy bills.

Initially our team feared the neighborhood association would reject the sewage treatment idea outright, because placing a treatment facility on the grounds of Sustainable Fellwood could be seen as a stigma. So we asked the residents point-blank if this was a concern, communicating that we would not pursue this initiative if they objected. But the residents supported the treatment facility, as long as it was aesthetically pleasing. They also liked the prospect of reduced energy bills. But deep down, I think the authentic gesture of asking the residents for permission led to permission being granted. It's the story of Jack and the checkers players revisited.

Much of the work I am describing here captures initiatives in motion, things we are hoping to accomplish but that might not materialize. I hope this will not be the case, but in our development work our reach sometimes exceeds our grasp. But even if we accomplish only some of our goals we have raised the bar on cooperative planning in our community: A private developer, a government entity, a neighborhood association, and a major paper manufacturer sat down together to find ways to improve their respective financial bottom lines *and* conserve resources at the same time. In that way, Sustainable Fellwood is as much about processes and intentions, a critical aspect of creating true covenants, as it is about results.

Despite my personal reservations about discussing a project in media res, I feel that Sustainable Fellwood nicely illustrates three aspects of covenantal action: 1) extending the circles of engagement, 2) addressing true needs, and 3) seeking permission:

- **Extending the circles of engagement.** Managing a sustainable business entails extending restorative values beyond a company's borders to include a broader, more diverse set of stakeholders in the community. It has caused a rippling-out effect from our company to a group of professionals comprising Team Fellwood; to the HAS, neighborhood association, and city; to key community organizers bringing in a host of others helping with social programming; to the countywide school system; to businesses such as International Paper. This project has been all about asking for help and permission from the community at large and fostering covenantal relationships well beyond a company's borders.

- **Addressing true needs.** Business literature on change management and organizational management often draws on verbiage such as *creating buy-in.* I've never been overly fond of this language, since *buy-in*, to me, connotes the idea of pitching an idea to others who need to be "sold." But the issue of need is different. When a business identifies and addresses true needs in a community, a community doesn't have to "buy in" to the idea or be "sold." Instead, the community feels its values have been promulgated to others. It's no surprise that Sustainable Fellwood has been the beneficiary of such circles of engagement, because the project taps into a need felt keenly by so many in the community. That need concerns providing affordable housing and revitalizing an underserved area of the city. But that need also touches on issues of self-respect and trust and historical continuity. Covenantal action is based on satisfying deeply felt needs.
- **Seeking permission** (from land and community). When we competed to be the master developer for Sustainable Fellwood, we deliberately shied away from promulgating a specific design, contending that the project would have to be shaped after considerable discussions with various stakeholders. And that is indeed how things played out. The neighborhood association helped shape our thinking about the mix of housing and green space, the ways in which densities should be shaped, and the location of our senior housing component. Local law enforcement professionals weighed in on how to make the design safer

for the residents. City officials helped shape the design of our internal parks so as to marry aesthetic considerations to maintenance issues. Moreover, our stakeholders in this project identified environmental issues they cared deeply about: conserving the existing tree canopy, reducing utility costs, strategies for limiting water consumption and waste, using products that would improve indoor air quality. Covenantal action entails attention to social and environmental issues as well as to financial ones.

The first aspect of covenantal action—extending the circles of a sustainable company—has already been addressed in our discussion of the broad stakeholder involvement in Sustainable Fellwood. The other two issues, addressing needs and seeking permission, warrant further discussion.

Addressing Needs: Learning to Be Pulled in a Push Economy

In 1987 the World Commission on Environment and Development, often referred to as the Brundtland Commission (in honor of former Norwegian Prime Minister Gro Harlan Brundtland, who chaired the group), defined *sustainable development* as "development that meets the needs of the present without compromising the ability of future generations to meet their needs." It's a controversial definition, but I happen to like it precisely because it draws attention to a problematic issue: What is a need? Do we need land mines? How about pet rocks or more electricity? It is because of such thorny questions of definition that the term *sustainable development* has been the subject of serious critique, the feeling being that in the twinning *development* will earn top billing, supporting an economic creed for continued unbridled growth, while *sustainable* trots along behind, complaining about the pace and nature of this economic growth.[5]

So what about this question of need? Are my needs equivalent to those of Bill Gates? To those of a migrant farm worker? It's a thorny problem, underscoring a sense that need is as much a question of ethics and virtue as it is of economics. David Orr, drawing upon the Latin and Greek uses of the term *virtue* to connote a "practice of restraint," argues that a sense of virtue is embedded in a sense of community.[6] I agree. Need is linked to virtue, and virtue should be linked to aspects of personal behavior that transcend the individual in the larger interests of society. Just like any human being on this planet I need access to a plentiful source of clean water. But as a landowner that does not mean that I own the water beneath my property, nor does it entitle me to engage in practices that would diminish the quality and supply of drinking water for my neighbors. That is the gist of the need-virtue-community equation. But completing the syllogism doesn't seem to work: Surely we can't define need solely or even fundamentally as what is in society's best interests. Or can we? Who determines what those social needs are and upon what basis are those judgments made? How do we get a better handle on the linkages among a sense of need, virtue, restraint, and community, particularly in the context of managing a sustainable business?

A step in the right direction is to rethink the traditional practice of business as a "push proposition"—the effort to push goods and services onto a consuming public, often through marketing practices that foster a *sense* of need (but are actually fueling feelings of want or desire). Rather than pushing goods and services upon the market, a business can instead be pulled by market demands. Reframing in this way how business is conducted has its compelling aspects. However, there are challenges to rethinking business as a pull proposition, including: (1) differentiating what is commonly referred to as a pull strategy from a truly authentic approach, (2) determining the true needs of a community through the creation of a visionary end story, and (3) creating an authentic pull strategy based on this vision. Let's consider each of these topics in more detail.

Differentiating what is called a pull strategy today from what is truly an authentic pull strategy. Marketing efforts have been migrating over the years precisely to an approach that is deemed to be a pull strategy. Evolving from such just-in-time manufacturing pioneers such as Toyota and Dell, a pull strategy manages inventory in stringent and cost-effective ways, such that a product is not manufactured and pushed onto a consuming public but is produced in response to a customer's order. But this pull strategy is nothing more than the older push strategy—engendering want through marketing—managed through operational efficiency. The product is still marketed heavily, the consumer is "educated" on the merits of the product and how it can be customized to individual preference. The end result, a *New York Times Magazine* article summarized, is mass customization, an assembly line of production in which the consumer becomes part of the manufacturing team by selecting the specific product that gets made.[7] My daughter's fondness for making a Build-A-Bear customized to her particular preferences is a typical example of customer as manufacturer. She thinks she is creating her own custom-made bear, a product she pulls toward her. In fact, she is the target of a marketing stratagem that has tapped into her desire to personalize a product. She is no more having her deep-seated need for creativity met than I am when I go online to order my own customized car.[8]

Depending on one's point of view, this marketing strategy is either a brilliant tactic of empowering the consumer or a cynical co-opting of buyer vulnerabilities. It's a sophisticated strategy that is becoming more widespread. But it is *not* a true pull strategy, nor is it likely to lead us in the direction of restrained consumerism or less manufactured need.[9] A sustainable business should hold itself accountable to a more ethical or virtuous orientation.

So what would a more ethical business orientation look like? An authentic pull strategy involves a business functioning as a result of responding to—being pulled by—the needs of a community.[10] With this in mind, we can revise the Brundtland Commission definition to come up with our own provisional description of a sustainable business: "a business that meets the needs of *a present community* without compromising the ability of *future generations of a community* to meet its needs."[11]

Granted this notion of a business responding to community needs is fraught with problems. First, most businesses function by identifying individual users or segments of users for their products and services, not by selling to larger corpuses such as communities. Second, a likely objection to our revised Brundtland definition has to do with an issue economist Milton Friedman raised decades ago. The purpose of a business, according to Friedman, is to maximize profits for its shareholders, not engage in issues better left to ethicists.[12] In such a view it is simply not the charge of business to self-legislate what is a necessary good or service and what is not.

A third objection emanates from the field of economic game theory. Let's imagine that tomorrow all businesses in a particular industry decided collectively to adopt an ethical orientation addressing the authentic needs of a community. In this scenario, game theory posits, there would always be a minority of companies, lured by extraordinary profit from being the only ones continuing to do business as usual, who would choose not to cooperate. As such, and anticipating this a priori, no other company would be willing to adopt a new business model for fear that it would end up going down this new road alone.

Finally, a fourth objection centers on the argument that the ethical orientation being promoted rests with the consumer, not the business. If reducing wasteful consumption is a key part of reducing our overall global impact, then the responsibility of that reduction rests on the shoulders of the consumer, not on business.[13]

The list of reasons as to why a business would not be willing to pursue a more ethical orientation focused on authentic needs is long. That's hardly a surprise. We need only recall my resistance to my sister Tovah's leadership from the middle (chapter two) to remind ourselves that we tend to dislike what we refuse to understand and that fear, by and large, is the mother of resistance: fear of change, fear of failure associated with that change, fear of being thought of as an impractical dreamer. A reframing of the issue is needed if we are to overcome fear and resistance.

Shaping a visionary end story. Instead of asking, "Why in the world would my business adopt a more ethical orientation centered on communal needs?" the approach needs to be, "How can my business respond to true communal needs?" The exercise of shaping an end story and then backfilling it is helpful in this regard. If, for instance, ten years from now, the *Wall Street Journal* were to feature an article on our company and how we had been pioneers in our industry for addressing true communal needs, what would that article say? What steps can we take today to make this hypothetical article a reality? What would our business need to look like to respond to the authentic needs of our community?[14]

Posing these types of questions has proved helpful in our own business, particularly in our brokerage division. Our brokers for the longest time felt powerless to move clients in a more sustainable direction since brokers function as "middlemen," facilitating transactions between buyers and sellers of land, between landlords and potential tenants. By shaping an end story and backfilling it, our brokerage division has reframed what it perceived as a position of weakness into a position of strong leadership. Our brokers want to be able to say twenty years from now that particular developers and development practices they actively sought years before influenced the careful, deliberate growth of our community. From this end story, our brokers have realized that their traditional role as "weak facilitator" enables them to lead from the middle. They have begun to educate themselves about sustainable practices. They think deliberatively about partnering with clients who are particularly focused on being good stewards of our coastal marshes and our heterogeneous, historic community. They are using the expertise of other colleagues at our company to educate and advise their clients on how adopting sustainable practices can improve financial performance.

Addressing authentic needs. Every business is a bit different, and the needs of its particular constituents vary from place to place. So perhaps the very first thing a business does to respond to its community's authentic needs is to take stock of what that community is all about. What does my community need—a stronger education for its citizens, baseline health care, affordable housing and better nutrition, effective transportation? And then comes the follow-up: What might my own business do to address just *one* of those needs? What expertise does my business have that could effectively be put to use to satisfy a basic community need, not as pro-bono work with a nifty marketing ribbon tied around it, but as part of my company's business model? It is helpful to leverage the perspectives of staff members by asking them what they think. Polling one's community is another obvious if neglected approach. As author

Bill McKibben notes, radio stations were originally required to assess the needs of their communities and provide a business plan of how they intended to fulfill those needs in order to stay in business. Otherwise a station's license would be revoked.[15] A sustainable business should consider tapping into local forums such as town meetings whenever possible and seek out opportunities to invite broad and diverse input.

A business must now, more than at any time in our history, hold true to Peter Drucker's famous dictum of staying close to the customer, not simply to the individual customer but to a collective set of customers. Learning to be pulled means being attuned to the real demands of a community. For the health-care industry this means rethinking its business proposition so that it is more about fostering health and less about denying or delaying treatment or providing care because of lack of proactive programs. For the legal industry this means reinventing itself so that it's more about forestalling and/or resolving conflict than litigating. For manufacturing this means migrating to life-cycle services rather than dead-end products. For agriculture it means finding ways to provide healthy, nutritious, inexpensive, locally produced food for the vast majority of citizens who suffer from malnourishment and obesity. For educators this means shaping a learning environment around curiosity, interdisciplinary thinking, lifelong literacy, and decorous public discourse rather than a curriculum built around standards and a checklist.

Learning to be pulled requires the lesson of letting go discussed in chapter three and applies that lesson to the market: letting go of one's own presumptions of what the consumer ostensibly wants and instead providing what consumers passionately care to have. What matter most—our health and well-being, the community we are a part of, and the natural world around us—are in short supply and high demand. It's not, as some would argue, about packaging experience.[16] In most cases, the "experience product" (Rain Forest Café, Chuck E. Cheese, Disney World, etc.) is more a simulacrum for a deeper need, one that remains unmet even as the experience is consumed. Learning to be pulled has more to do with touching that need, in large measure through deep listening to one's social and natural environment. Learning to be pulled entails asking permission in order to be provided a license to conduct business.

Obtaining permission to conduct business is traditionally thought of in narrow contexts like ordinances and regulations. The notion of permission, however, should be much broader and entail three major components: permission from society, permission from nature, and permission from ourselves. Not surprisingly, the three realms of nature, society, and self are intertwined in complex ways, making it challenging to tease them apart and view their workings independently. In many ways, as I hope to show by the end of this chapter, it is critical that we view them not independently but rather as overlapping circles in a Venn diagram, with the sustainable business operating at the intersection of all three. For the moment, though, let's consider each of these permissions in turn, beginning with permission from society or the social order.

Seeking Permission from the Social Order

Permission from society for a business to conduct its affairs sounds strange, calling for us to unlearn embedded assumptions about the hegemonic "rights" of our capitalist system. We need to understand the basic drivers of business, primarily the shareholder theory of governance. We then need to understand the history and ideology underlying this shareholder theory in order to realize how business has evolved to its current state, which is, in many ways, at odds with the social order. Only at that point are we well equipped to reframe things and suggest a different approach to the way business should be accountable to society. Let's follow this sequence of analysis in greater detail.

Business governance in the United States has long been shaped by a shareholder theory of ownership, in which a business's decisions are based narrowly on maximizing profits for its investors. In contrast, business governance in Europe has long been shaped by a stakeholder theory of ownership, a broader view that considers the interests of the company's workforce, the vendors that provide complementary goods and services, the town in which a business resides, even the nation from which a business gets its charter. Stakeholder theory carries with it standards of performance that extend beyond the profit motive, whereas shareholder theory is all about the financial bottom line. Stakeholder theory holds to a trustee theory of leadership. A business is not so much owned but held in trust for a broad spectrum of interests. Shareholder theory holds to an agency theory of leadership. Business leaders are the agents making decisions on behalf of the business's owners, its shareholders. Although in recent years there has been a tendency among European businesses to migrate toward an American shareholder model, and a converse tendency among American businesses to migrate toward a European stakeholder model, the two approaches to business and business accountability are still rather distinct.[17]

How did these two business models evolve? More specifically, how is it that the American business model seems so individualistic? Was it always that way?[18] Should it be? These are some of the issues underlying the concept of permission from society that are well beyond the scope of this book. Addressing this topic fully calls for a consideration of American concepts of individualism;[19] the relationship of individualism to land and notions of private property; the legal fiction of viewing an American corporation as an individual; and the odd fragmentation of political, economic, and social elements of our culture. Let's at least consider these issues briefly, so as to understand better what's involved in moving a sustainable business in the direction of a stakeholder model of governance.

A thumbnail sketch of the European conquest of North America would look something like this: The early colonists viewed America as a new beginning, far beyond the centralized and authoritarian structures and mores of Europe, a place where the basic rights of the individual to life, liberty, and pursuit of happiness could take root. And the land that they first saw? Pristine, apparently endless in abundance, a blank slate, an empty canvas. Early settlers proceeded to ignore the operational example of indigenous peoples, instead importing many practices familiar from the Old World.

How did we as a nation get to the point where, from such apparent blank-slate beginnings, the interests of the individual hold sway in significant ways over those of the general polis? These questions have been addressed in works by a number of historians,[20] all of whom seem to agree on these causes:

1. A fundamental myth of America as "Eden restored," with nature viewed as so abundant as to enable individualistic greed.
2. The development of ethical systems that divorced nature from culture and an agrarian economy that layered this divorce with a strong individualistic ethos centered on the yeoman farmer.
3. The belief, a departure from European sensibilities, that land ownership was a private and local matter. American business practices, entailing a narrower individualistic ethos and a shareholder theory of governance, evolved in a similar vein to that of the nation's culture as a whole.

Interestingly, these historians contend that our lack of a sense of history leaves us with the false impression that the way things are today is the way things have always been. An effort of historical recovery is called for. As these various scholars point out, we are largely unaware of a time in American history when a more collective, public spirit held sway, with a sense of the common as something shared by all and owned by none —a notion of place that has its roots in a public trust doctrine created almost 1,500 years old.

The public trust doctrine dates back to 529 C.E., when the Roman Emperor Justinian appointed a commission of ten legal experts to codify all of the unpublished edicts handed down by his predecessors. To this code the sovereign added the following: "By the law of nature these things are common to all mankind, the air, running water, the sea and consequently the shores of the sea."

This policy has had a complex history over the past 1,500 years, expanding and contracting based on political climates and attitudes toward the commons. French law in the eleventh century expanded the doctrine to include pastures, forests, and meadows. This expansion found its way into England in the Magna Carta in the thirteenth century, from there to the British colonies in America through the Colonial Ordinance of 1647, and from there into various state constitutions.[21]

It's a long, involved history. The basic issue pits a more public notion of land against the notion put forth in the eighteenth century by John Locke that private property was a natural right of individuals. At the end of the nineteenth century, for example, the United States Supreme Court still upheld the notion that a landowner should cause no harm either to immediate neighbors or the surrounding region. Over the past hundred years, however, this doctrine seems to have taken a backseat to the American belief in the right to life, liberty, and property. Our legislators, our courts, our regulatory agencies, our states, and our municipalities have become cowed into limiting their dominion because of what they view as the private rights of land owners.[22]

We can see the powerful sway of this individualistic credo in my own backyard of south Georgia, where developers are notorious for trying to shape the regulatory landscape in self-serving ways. Developers, for example, packed a so-called stakeholders' group to rewrite the rules for coastal development, which will effectively eviscerate the intent and spirit of the original, visionary, and nationally touted 1970 Coastal Marshlands Protections Act. It's a long story, one of politics as usual, with certain influential developers using their political clout to change the rule book to fit their particular style of play. This regulatory environment is less one of permission to build than entitlement to do largely what one pleases.[23]

There's an ironic—albeit deserved—consequence to such practices of entitlement. When a company such as ours appears before a local planning commission to request a variance from a particular ordinance—for instance, requesting from the City of Savannah permission to install a gray water system to use captured rain water for irrigation—the instant presumption is that the developer is trying to manipulate the system to its own advantage. When we enter a new market we inevitably face an uphill battle trying to convince local officials that we have the interests of the community at heart. While this seems unfair, we are simply reaping the fruits of contentious seeds planted long ago by businesses that have set the stage by looking to their own narrower interests at the expense of communal needs. Trust often slighted is difficult to earn anew.

The pendulum needs to swing back in the other direction, away from private dominion over property and back toward a public trust orientation. Environmental law scholar Eric Freyfolge expresses this sentiment quite forcefully, noting:

> A fairer approach would be to eliminate nearly all development rights. Landowners would then have no protected right to develop. Instead, they could develop only with permission from community leaders who would act, ideally, in accordance with a well-considered development plan. Those receiving permission to develop would be understood as receiving a benefit from the public. In exchange for that benefit, they would be expected to compensate the community in some manner commensurate with the economic value of their gain.[24]

While Freyfogle's argument may seem extreme to some, we need to consider moving from a narrow, overly restricted notion of what it takes to receive a permit to build to a wider and more encompassing concept of what works for the community.

Does the social component we have been addressing have broad applicability beyond the notion of land and building and property rights? I think so. Embedded in the public trust doctrine is a fundamental issue relating to the rights of the individual vis-à-vis the interests of the polis. At one time the rights of a corporation to conduct business were prescribed through government charter. While this is still formally embodied through the act of state registration, a corporation today is viewed as a fictional person, securing to itself certain protections from liability while preserving freedoms claimed by the individual. Alongside the movement toward greater claims for the rights of the individual has occurred greater protection for the ostensible rights of the corporation. Only during moments of particular corporate excess—the Enron debacle is one example—does the idea of protecting social interests through legislative action gain favor (e.g., the federal Sarbanes-Oxley Act, which created detailed rules for corporate accounting and is intended to forestall the type of fraud perpetrated by Enron).

By merging the ideas contained in several recent seminal writings on social and environmental justice issues, we can begin to see this dynamic more clearly. According to Jeffrey Sachs, there are five key steps to shaping an economy: stabilization, liberalization, privatization, social safety net, and institutional harmonization. A country first stabilizes its culture through a system of workable laws. Political stabilization fosters greater individual freedom and a growing sense of private property and ownership. This liberal economy then fosters the creation of governmental programs to support those individuals who function less successfully in the reformed economy, and the entire order results in a more stabilized culture in which judicial, legislative, executive, and economic systems function well together. A developing country lacking in these five steps, Sachs notes, tends to be caught up in a trap of poverty in which basic nutrition, health care, and mortality rates are low; birth rates and population growth are high, political governance tends to be corrupt; wealth is concentrated in a very few powerful hands; and a hand-to-mouth existence for the vast majority of the population leads to intense environmental degradation (desertification of lands, acidification of water sources, degradation of soils, deforestation, etc.).[25]

But even as developing countries fight their way out of this cycle of social and environmental injustices, other reinforcing issues present themselves. The problem comes when political stabilization facilitates a type of freewheeling capitalism, where the individual or corporation is largely viewed as having dominion over natural capital (air, water, land). As Paul Hawken has pointed out in his discussion of the British economist Arthur Pigou, the costs associated with the degradation of natural capital, though having an impact on the population at large, are externalized. A housing development, for instance, that, in the process of construction, disrupts the landscape and pollutes an adjacent stream, is not held accountable for the actual cost to society of such damage. Instead, this cost is said to be an "externality." The onus of paying for these externalities (cleaning up the river downstream) is passed on to the larger community. Such externalities, if not attended to, place added strains on the natural order. Greenhouse gas emissions, diminution of our air quality, degradation of our ground- and surface water, and the widespread use of untested and health-diminishing chemicals are all results of externalities, by-products of our economic system, the costs of which are absorbed by the social and natural order as a whole and not the offending party.[26]

The feedback loop Sachs and Hawken describe between them, where growing economic stabilization leads to free-market practices that externalize much of the true costs of a business, dovetail, with a well-regarded though little-discussed hypothesis by the Nobel-winning economist Simon Kuznets. Kuznets argued that economic development is initially a foe and then later a friend of environmental quality. In rising or developing economies, the focus is so single-mindedly on improving the financial situation of a citizenry that business practices run roughshod over the environment. As an economy matures, however, as the basic needs of a citizenry are met and a country becomes wealthier, more time, energy, and resources are spent setting stricter expectations for the environmental consequences of a business's activities.[27]

This leads to a forking path in terms of general business practices: Path 1, which we might call "fight," and Path 2, which we can refer to as "flight." Neither has particularly positive consequences for the environment. Neither places business in a particularly positive light. Both fight and flight are employed as basic tools by companies focused on doing business as usual.

Path 1, the "fight" path, looks like this: As a society matures and general concern for the environment increases, so too does public advocacy and oversight. The result is oftentimes changes in legislation (local, state, federal) as well as greater government oversight. What then ensues is corporate resistance, fighting back against legislation in the first place and hindering governmental oversight and enforcement of legislation on the back end. At times, business proves itself savvy enough to forestall legislatively imposed guidelines relating to a business' social responsibilities, typically by lobbying efforts that maintain cozy relationships with key legislators. And once environmental legislation is written? Businesses have proven themselves adept at keeping close tabs on regulatory activity by ensuring (1) that regulatory departments and programs are under-funded, or (2) that application of legislation is delayed for years as a result of "needed" additional study, or (3) that regulations are interpreted in ways that are "business-friendly," or (4) that regulations being promoted by one federal agency are hamstrung through the counter interests of another agency, or (5) that application of environmental regulation is tied up for years through litigation. Either business posture—forestalling environmental legislation from ever getting passed into law in the first place or managing the regulatory implementation of environmental legislation on the back end—implies a notion of business at odds with communal interests.[28] Sheldon Wolin and Robert Reich, two well-regarded scholars in the field of political theory, have noted that our political system has devolved to the point where government, rather than serving the population, has essentially become an instrument of big business.[29]

Path 2, the "flight" scenario, looks like this: In light of growing environmental (and labor) regulations in developed countries, businesses simply relocate much of their activity to developing parts of the world where regulations are more lax and where the five political steps outlined by Sachs have yet to evolve.

The entire sequence of this feedback system can be seen Figure 4-3 (on page 170), the Feedback Loop System.

We need a third path, a way out of these interlocking positive feedback loops. We need ways of inserting ourselves into critical aspects of these complex systems and changing our thinking and approaches to old practices. At the global, political level, solutions call for a multi-country infusion of investment that links the breaking of the cycle of poverty to governance reforms and environmental stewardship.[30] At the level of economic systems within countries, we need a "carrots and sticks" approach that equitably charges for the numerous environmental degradations that are currently externalized onto society and rewards actions that advance a green agenda. And at the legislative/regulatory level, we need a system that decouples the perverse sway business has upon government.

There are a number of differing viewpoints on how best to extricate ourselves from this feedback loop. In the following chapter I'll be addressing whether the impetus should come from government or multi-government collaboration, from big business, or from grassroots organizations and nonprofits. It is important to note that as long as each of

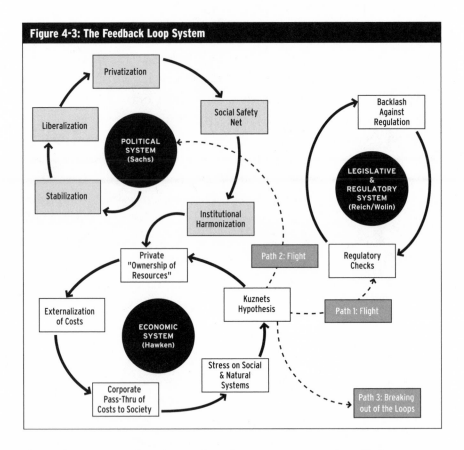

Figure 4-3: The Feedback Loop System

the major sectors of society points fingers at one another, little progress toward a restorative order is likely to be made. It will take congruent knowledge and action among all social sectors to break us out of this feedback loop.

What strides can business take today on its own initiative to help counter this loop? How might a business conduct itself if it assumed that the social system within which it operates actually matters? Economist Jeffrey Sachs offers up a tentative solution, one that evokes a notion of business more attuned to true societal needs:

> Each company needs to be part of the solution and needs to stretch its activities beyond normal market activities. This does not mean to turn the company upside down or into a charitable institution, but rather to identify the unique contribution the

company may make as part of a broader effort to solve a major social challenge.[31]

The third path calls for a renewed covenant between business and society. It calls for business to, in Sachs's words, make a broader effort to address a major societal/environmental issue. If businesses today were licensed by a social charter that established strict guidelines for conduct and accountability in order to remain in business, what would that social charter mandate?

I think such a charter would require a business to respond to social need as part of its license to do business. It would demand practices that facilitate safe, livable, inspiring, enduring, equitable places.[32] This charter would call for products and services that would engender a special feeling of attachment to place, foster a rich social web of connected people, provide linkages between business and the larger community that would give us a sense of belonging and facilitate connections to our ancestry and to collective memory.[33] Such a charter would echo an ethic of sustainable place, as defined by Timothy Beatley and Kristy Manning in their coauthored work *The Ecology of Place*:

> An ethic of sustainable place, then, is composed of a number of value dimensions, including: an ethic of interdependence; respect for the interests of future inhabitants and future generations; greater respect for the needs of the broader public, and personal responsibility to that community; humility and caution in using and manipulating nature and the natural environment; and a sense of kinship with the many other life-forms that inhabit the planet and respect for the needs of the broader natural environment.[34]

A business that seeks permission from society first seeks to recover and then understand the historical context in which it has traditionally functioned. Such a business questions the values it has always assumed were an immanent part of its workings, such as the individualistic ethos of American corporate life. It considers restraining its own self-centric orientation and its own limited accountability to shareholders. It begins to think about its overarching purpose and the links between that purpose and the broad, diverse stakeholder groups residing just beyond its siloed doors. A business that seeks permission from society thinks more deeply about those stakeholder groups—who they are, what their needs are—and considers the ways in which its own capacity to sustain business operations over the long term are tied to the interests and values of these stakeholders. It considers the prospect of creating a business model around lasting covenants. After all, if the single most critical strategy for a business is the retention of its client base, what more longstanding practice of customer retention exists than covenants with a community over the long term?

Seeking Permission from the Natural Order

What does it mean to get permission from nature? It's an odd, counterintuitive notion. Nature never gives you permission. As one legal scholar has noted:

> Westerners believed that they stood apart from and above all other species, divided from the rest by their superior reason, knowledge, and tools. Among all life-forms, they alone possessed moral value, or so they believed. This was an arrogance rooted less in scientific knowledge than in emotion and myth.[35]

While nature does not give us permission to encroach upon it, nature does give us strong hints when the rights we arrogate for ourselves entail overreaching. Sometime in the mid-1950s, in the early years of the baby boom, we overreached Earth's carrying capacity. We now emit twenty-five billion tons of carbon dioxide annually but are only able to absorb or sequester 40 percent of that amount through our land and water masses. The result has been a one-degree temperature rise over the past century, resulting in altered weather patterns, rising sea levels, and changes in typical behavioral patterns in nature. Worldwide fisheries, coral reefs, mangrove swamps, wetlands, forests, and arable soil are all in a state of collapse. With significant growth among the top seven emerging economies—the so-called E7 of China, India, Brazil, Russia, Mexico, Indonesia, and Turkey—our collective strain on nature's sources and sinks is going to call for multiple planet Earths in the next twenty-five years. We simply cannot continue with a mind-set of unabated, unlimited growth. Whether we want to point to global warming trends, or increasing desertification, or our inability to buffer ourselves from natural tsunamis, nature is clearly withholding permission for our civilization to grow beyond certain bounds.

We are long overdue to heed this message. It's a challenging task, since, in essence, we need, as biologist Edward Wilson suggests, to address both the cultural and genetic markers that have made up our evolutionary history over the past millennia:

> Few will doubt that humankind has created a planet-sized problem for itself. No one wished it so, but we are the first species to become a geophysical force, altering Earth's climate, a role previously reserved for tectonics, sun flares, and glacial cycles. We are also the greatest destroyer of life since the ten-kilometer wide meteorite that landed near Yucatan and ended the Age of Reptiles 65 million years ago. Through overpopulation we have put ourselves in danger of running out of food and water. So a very Faustian choice is upon us: whether to accept our corrosive and risky behavior as the unavoidable price of population and economic growth, or to take stock of ourselves and search for a new environmental ethic.[36]

There are a number of thinkers and writers today who believe we won't be able to shape such a new environmental ethic. Maybe they are right. But we need to start somewhere.

At our own company, we've begun to apply the principle of restraint to discussions around limits to our own growth. Part of that rethinking means putting a stake in the ground and saying we are going to build within established urban core areas where an infrastructure (roads, sewerage, etc.) already exists. We place particular emphasis on revitalizing existing sites where contamination exists (brownfield) or where there has been previous construction (grayfield), utilize embodied energy by targeting renovation of existing buildings, and try to restrict new construction to filling in urban pockets. As we move away from the urban core toward the urban fringe and suburbs, our willingness to develop projects diminishes. Figure 4-4 depicts our own rough guide to determining where and how we will develop, where we won't develop, and where we have major concerns and are hesitant about contributing to growth.

But this setting of limits addresses only a small part of the larger issue. We know there are both upstream and downstream effects of our actions. Any building we construct generates activity: additional residents and shoppers, additional traffic and pollution, additional waste. At some point, the very logic of my own argument for considering "permission from nature" begins to fall apart, begging the question, Why grow at all, since even limited growth results in natural degradation, just at a slower rate?

Perhaps this is the point at which hope and self-deception collide. The self-deception stems from the sense, expressed by historian Ted Steinberg, that "no culture is in complete control of its ecological destiny."[37] To assume otherwise would be naive at best, arrogant at worst, and most likely willfully blind. What, then—wave a white flag of capitulation? I think this is where hope enters the fray. As David Orr notes, "hope, real hope, comes from doing the things before us that need to be done in the spirit of thankfulness and celebration, without worrying about whether we will win or lose."[38] I would place special emphasis on the phrase *things before us that* need *to be done,* which touches on the management practice of addressing need. Fundamentally that is what is implicit in the notion of permission from nature: a covenant focused on addressing true need, couched as a hope that such a focus will be restorative.

Seeking permission from nature is by no means limited to real estate practices. Equivalent limits to growth maps can be developed for virtually all types of business. Interface, Inc., for instance, a manufacturer of carpets and flooring systems, has an ambitious plan, based on intensive work the company has conducted in taking stock of the environmental consequences of every aspect of its production, to have a zero

Table 4-4: Limits To Growth Chart							
	Brownfield	Greyfield	Renovate	In-fill	Acquire, Hold	New Construction	Greenfield
Urban Core							
Urban Fringe							
Suburban							
Country							
Wildlands							

net footprint on this Earth by 2020. The Business Alliance for Local Economies (BALLE) is a global forum of networks providing a wealth of information on and strategies for reducing our impact on the natural world. Numerous other multinational companies have signed on to the global reporting initiative (GRI), which provides a protocol for auditing a company's environmental footprint.

In fact, conducting an environmental audit is one critical step any company should take in its journey toward becoming a sustainable business. An environmental audit entails taking a detailed look at the daily life of a company, from how staff members travel to and from work and their travel elsewhere for business and conferences, the consumption of energy and water, and the production of waste. Evoking the principles of recovery (taking stock of one's daily activities) and restraint (reducing consumption), an environmental audit helps establish a baseline around which a company's collective sense of meaning and purpose is put into action.[39] A promising tool is the One Planet Business accounting method being developed by the World Wide Fund for Nature (WWF) and its partners, an effort to establish an international standard to assess a business's environmental footprint.[40]

There are additional steps a company should consider in the context of seeking permission from the natural order, among them:

1. Addressing whether a company's growth plans are built around the needs of the company and its shareholders or instead around larger stakeholder needs, with nature itself on the list of stakeholders

2. Considering designs that mimic strategies developed by nature
3. Focusing on cradle-to-cradle zero-waste designs and practices
4. Practicing a business model of optimization rather than maximization[41]
5. Local procuring of resources and materials and abatement of waste
6. Adopting use of the precautionary principle and avoiding making big bets where technology is viewed as the great cure-all and nature is likely to be the big loser[42]
7. Respecting biodiversity as a key business tenet, perhaps with the aim of adopting the Standstill Principle, which calls for no further deterioration of the environment.
8. Adopting The Natural Step's four-system conditions (reduce extractions from Earth, reduce substances produced by society, avoid taking more than can be replenished, fair and efficient use of resources)

Each of these steps forges greater connectedness between a business and the natural order, shaping a covenantal relationship that runs with the land.

Seeking Permission from Self

Permission from self is probably the most vague and abstract of the three permissions, but it may be the most fundamental. The use of *self* here, while rooted in the individual, is the company as an entity. Sometimes we pose this question in our company discussions: "What do we want to be when we grow up?" It seems an odd question coming from a business that is almost seventy years old. But that's the sensibility behind permission from self, a restless self-questioning about where we are headed, what we are evolving into, and if our direction is consonant with our collective values and purpose.

This company self-reflection takes many forms. For me this meditation takes its cues from narratives that comprise part of our collective conscience, exemplified by some of the stories recounted in this book. Since the notion of image seems so central to reflections on self, let's consider two images that help us think more deeply about a company's identity and the master narratives shaping who we are. Those master narratives concern the nature of beauty and the nature of truth.

The first image, Figure 4-5, is a painting of a familiar story, that of Narcissus and Echo. In the Greek myth, Echo, as punishment by Zeus's wife, Hera, for being the object of Zeus's affection, has lost the power of original speech—she is only able to repeat the words of others. Echo has fallen in love with a Greek youth named Narcissus, who has eyes for only himself. Echo finds Narcissus gazing into a stream or lake, looking lovingly at his own reflection. Narcissus, thinking the reflection in the water is another person, says to the image, "I love you." And Echo, watching the scene, repeats, "I love you." Narcissus believes the response comes from the image in the water and sits in self-rapture until he dies, when his mortal remains are transformed into the flower that today bears his name. Echo pines away at the loss of her love, her presence immortalized in the refrain of others' words.

The second master narrative is also captured in a painting, Figure 4-6, by Pieter Brueghel the Elder, depicting the building of the Tower of Babel. The story is from Genesis, immediately following the story of

Figure 4-5: *Echo & Narcissus*, 1903

John William Waterhouse, Walker Art Gallery, Liverpool, England

Figure 4-6: *Tower of Babel*

Pieter Brueghel the Elder, Kunsthistorisches Museum Wien, Vienna, Austria

Noah and the deluge, and essentially launches God's second go-round with the human experiment on Earth. Humankind, speaking with one voice, in one language, decides in unison to build a city and a tower with its top in heaven to avoid being scattered across the face of the earth. This overreaching concerns God to the point that he confounds their common language, scatters them abroad, and succeeds in halting the building of the city indefinitely.

These two narratives, so rich in nuances and resonances, help frame a conversation about permission from self. One captures our fascination with beauty and cautions against self-admiration. The other captures our fascination not only with building monuments of overweening self-importance but also with aspiring to divine truth, quite literally through our own construction. Together they capture two perils that are especially pertinent in the context of real estate development but also more generally in the business world and beyond: the drive for creating icons that reflect our own beauty and the drive for creating icons to reflect our own sense of knowledge and truth. Both are self-referential; both are egocentric.

I would like to believe that this drive to create icons of beauty and truth is something I left behind me, as a younger executive running a then-younger company. But that's wishful thinking. The Sustainable Fellwood project, with which I began this chapter, serves as an example.

Our neighborhood charettes for Sustainable Fellwood—largely a series of love-fests—were not without tense moments. A few participants in our brainstorming workshops took issue with the height of our senior housing complex. Others were not convinced about the large linear open-space park, feeling it cut off residents from one another. Some were concerned that the old neighborhood look and feel would be lost. Some neighborhood residents felt that all the businesses along the commercial edge of the development should be owned by African-Americans. Open staircases that we had designed to enhance public safety were critiqued as looking too much like fire escapes. Water features that we planned to enhance the overall aesthetics were thought by some to be hazards for young children. The plan for nondesignated parking spaces drew the concern that inconsiderate neighbors would park in each others' spaces.

As these comments were voiced to our team over the ensuing months, I felt my jaw tighten. *Breathe*, I told myself. I knew others on our team, who had spent upwards of a year trying to get all the pieces of this complex project to fit together, felt a similar anxiety. We knew what this project called for, right? We knew how it needed to look aesthetically and knew how it should flow from a day-to-day user perspective. We just knew how our plans and designs would enhance community. *Knew, knew, knew*. The hubris of beauty and truth, right before my eyes.

Alice Walker, many years ago, wrote a collection of short stories titled *In Love and Trouble*, and in that volume is a favorite of mine. "Everyday Use" is the story of a woman, quite poor and getting on in years, who has two daughters. One of the daughters lives at home with her mother, while the other left home and became a successful professional in New York. Both daughters are home as the story unfolds around a handmade quilt that the mother wants to give as a bequest to one of her two children. The daughter from New York desperately wants the quilt to hang on her apartment wall. She values the quilt not only for its exquisite handwork but also because it is rare and quite valuable. Meanwhile the stay-at-home daughter states her intention to use the quilt on her bed on cold winter nights. The mother gifts the quilt to the daughter who intends it for everyday use.

I try to keep the message of this story in mind. Yes, our intent with all of our projects, including Sustainable Fellwood, is to create something beautiful and inspiring, something with the intelligence of wise and restrained use of resources. Still, we have to remember that, no matter how special our current project, it is ultimately about everyday use, not about putting up a trophy project for all to admire. We do want our work to have a beloved quality to it, but that quality comes from how it feels to the user.

The epigram from Paul Coelho that begins this chapter captures this sensibility in all its complexity: that perhaps the hidden essence of the story of Narcissus emanates from the perspective of the lake, not from the perspective of humankind. Coelho's revision and inversion of a long-standing myth, to see the story not from the perspective of human vanity but from another vantage point entirely, is nothing short of revolutionary.

Permission from self, then, is no more (and no less) than letting go of the self-oriented perspective that so dominates our thoughts and actions. It means letting go at the company level, to share the process of creation with the larger community. It means also letting go of specialized knowledge that tends to make priests of us professionals who guard the gates of what we believe to be valuable and beautiful and true. Permission from self means recognizing that the beauty and wisdom of our work inheres in a larger, collaborative enterprise.

In this process of letting go we not only tap into what true community needs are all about but also take to a higher level the notion of what managing a sustainable business entails. From sustainable practices occurring within a business culture, we migrate to sustainable practices occurring in the larger community around us. From a value system that draws its strength from the sociability and solidarity of individuals in a company, we migrate to a value system that evolves around the shared restoration of a community.

Synthesizing Permissions: Three Performance Organizers

Thinking about the broader communal context leads us to consider the triple bottom line (TBL), the set of metrics that assess the economic, social, and environmental performance of a company. The term, which has become mainstream, is one my colleagues and I use to talk about how we evaluate projects both before and after implementation.

Our board reports regularly include a page on our TBL performance, despite the fact that we constantly adjust both criteria and depth of analysis. Part of this constant tweaking is because a TBL approach is relatively new, having its impetus in John Elkington's 1998 work *Cannibals with Forks*. There has yet to evolve a standardized TBL report. It's too recent a phenomenon. But part of our constant tinkering has to do with a problem embedded in the very wording of the metrics itself: *bottom line*. We have no problem analyzing our financial bottom line. But analyzing or even referring to the bottom line of our social and environmental criteria is problematic.

The financial aspect of a triple-bottom-line approach is a snapshot in time, typically defined by a company's fiscal-year performance. For us that financial performance includes our returns on equity and assets, our total return on the portfolio (income plus growth appreciation), our cost of capital, and so forth. Without a strong financial bottom line, our business (or any business) will not endure for long.

How we benchmark our financial performance against the market entails a more extended conversation. It is the consensus among my colleagues that, despite being a privately held company, we need to show returns in keeping with the returns of other real estate companies. Otherwise our arguments for attending to the other two parts of the triple bottom line won't carry as much weight in the community at large.

I don't believe it is likely for a deeply committed sustainable business to match the bottom-line financial return of some of the highest-performing, larger, publicly traded real estate development companies—often referred to as real estate investment trusts (REITs). Despite the fact that it now costs the same to build a LEED-certified building as it does to build conventionally, the REIT model is different. The REIT focus is on building quickly (and usually inexpensively), tenanting fast, and getting out by flipping to others within about four years, before the ongoing cost of capital maintenance begins to reduce returns on the initial investment. It's a financial model built for speed, not place and people, and the returns are hard to beat. Having said that, our three-year moving average on total return is still within the lower part of the REIT performance range. In fact, we have demonstrated in an extended financial analysis of our performance over a ten-year time span that our investment in sustainable initiatives has realized roughly a 29 percent return on investment.[43]

Despite this strong financial performance, part of our rationale for developing a triple-bottom-line approach to performance is motivated by a desire to change the way a business is evaluated, to say, "Hold on, there are other measures that accrue to the overall performance and success of the company that we need to account for." These elements, such as a company's purpose and the meaning it ingests into work, translate into greater ease of hiring and retention and result in reduced personnel costs. And there are reduced costs of operation associated with systems and practices that, by being more attuned to the environment, reduce waste. These two elements enhance a company's financial bottom line. We have seen the effects firsthand with some of our retail tenants, whose financial performance has received an eye-popping boost through lower utility costs. And yes, we do see reduced risk through how and where we choose to build. In the years following Hurricane Katrina, when insurance premiums throughout the coastal southeast have skyrocketed, ours have remained unchanged. Social and environmental aspects of what we do positively affect our financial performance.

Moreover, shaping a business strategy along three performance objectives has the distinct advantage of sheltering a company from the boomerang effect of market exuberances. In the credit crisis of 2008, for example, a project such as Sustainable Fellwood moved along nicely; it was addressing a pent-up social need for affordable housing, not betting on the vagaries of the second-home, speculative-investment market. Construction costs were kept low ($85 per square foot), utility costs were a fraction of conventional housing projects, and demand for such affordable rental units has been high. Granted, even a project like Sustainable Fellwood is not entirely isolated from market conditions, since the financial engine driving this development is based on the pricing of low-income tax credits, the demand (and pricing) for which has dropped in this recessionary environment. Nevertheless, Sustainable Fellwood has proven to be a viable financial deal in an economic climate when virtually all other types of development have suffered.

But we short-change the power and effect of sustainable business practices when we evaluate the contributions of our social and environmental orientation solely within the context of a bottom line. There is the thorny problem of trying to define concretely what those social and environmental criteria should be—and also how to measure them.[44] But even more problematic is that social and environmental criteria are measured on a different scale. A financial bottom line is quantitative and can be captured as a moment in time. Contrast that with social and environmental metrics, which are partially qualitative in nature and are best measured over a time continuum.

Measuring a company's financial bottom line is much like looking at the gauges monitoring a scuba dive, gauges that tell how long you've been diving, how deep you are, and how much air you have left. The social aspect of the dive, however, has to do with the experience of exploration in a group setting. The environmental aspect of the dive includes the overall health of the coral reef and the land-based society that "services" the area both before and after the dive. In other words, the time scales of measurement for these three criteria, as well as the qualitative components of the measurements being taken, are very different. By translating the social and environmental effects of business decisions into a bottom line, we confirm environmental historian Donald Worster's critique of sustainability as dressing up a business wolf in sheep's clothing:

> It may inescapably lead us back to using a narrow economic language, to relying on production as the standard of judgment, and to following the progressive materialist world-view in approaching and utilizing the earth, all of which was precisely what environmentalism once sought to overthrow.[45]

Instead of speaking about a bottom line, I would suggest an alternative nomenclature, one about three performance organizers (3-PO): financial performance, environmental impact, and social consequences. To many people, differentiating between a triple bottom line and three performance organizers may seem like semantic hairsplitting. I believe the differences, however, are important.

Our three performance organizers, of course, include the financial bottom line. In addition we need to consider the overall environmental impact of our business practices. This would take into account our overall environmental footprint as well as the Limits to Growth Chart (Figure 4-4), which considers where we develop. Also factored in would be both the downstream and upstream effects of our activities, the opportunity to use cutting-edge approaches to reducing a building's footprint, conserving energy, and reducing our carbon emissions. The social consequences are the most elusive of all to calculate. They include aspects such as the catalytic nature of our project (and whether that catalyst is good or not), our affinity for a location's people and place, and the extent to which we address community needs. A 3-PO matrix is provided in Figure 4-7. While the criteria here are tailored for real estate, this 3-PO tool is easily adaptable to other businesses.

Coda: Running with the Land

We began this chapter by looking at the story of Jack and the checkers players. The story illuminates aspects of a covenant implicitly negotiated in the taking of a photograph. Transparency, trust and intention, processes of engagement, mutuality of needs: These are some of the elements of covenantal action embedded in this story. We then built upon that story by considering covenantal action in the context of a specific development project. Sustainable Fellwood involves expanding the circle of our own company to a larger brain trust of equally committed stakeholders. In the process of broadening this circle, we saw how it's possible to take values and practices inherent within a business and extend those values and practices into the larger community. Sustainable

Figure 4-7: Three Performance Organizers	
3-PO Headings	**3-PO Criteria**
Financial Performance	Total return: What is the total return on real estate assets and equity?
	Fee income: Is there opportunity for fee-related income (development, brokerage, etc.)?
	Financing: What are our sources for debt and equity for this project?
	Incentives: Are there financing/tax incentives (historic, new markets, etc.)?
	Time: What is likely to be our total time in the deal?
	Risk: What is our risk associated with the hold period?
Environmental Impact	Carbon emissions: Does the project enable us to meet our commitment to the 2030 Challenge?
	Nature of the site: brownfield, urban-infill, urban fringe, greenfield?
	Infrastructure: Does the project cause carry-over impacts demanding additional infrastructure (e.g., sprawl)?
	Potential for reuse: Does the project entail new construction or restoration?
	New techologies: Does the project provide an opportunity to utilize consumption-reducing technologies?
	Natural features: Does the project enhance or detract from key natural features (marsh, river, etc.)?
	Waste: What are the upstream and downstream consequences of this project?
	Consumption of natural capital: What are the upstream and downstream effects of the project?
Social Consequences	Alignment: Are our partners, local decision-makers, etc. aligned with our values?
	Extending the circle: To what extent does the project engage a broader stake-holder base?
	Ripple effect: Does the project faciliate catalytic development that would revital-ize an area?
	Addressing needs: To what extent is this a "pull" (as opposed to a "push") project?
	Equity and equality: To what extent does this project redress social imbalances?
	Diversity: Does the project lend itself to a mix of uses and users, promote tolerance?
	Educational outreach: To what extent does the project serve as a teaching tool about sustainable practices?
	Aesthetics: To what extent might the project facilitate the creation of lasting beauty?
	Context: To what extent does the project enhance the unique historical and social aspects of a place?

Fellwood also epitomizes a response to community needs, entailing a process of learning to be pulled rather than imposing our presuppositions about what the community should have.

This process of being pulled leads to a deeper consideration of a business as a set of activities calling for a charter in order to engage in commerce. A business that's striving to be sustainable is less a right than a responsibility, accountable to the social and natural environment as well as accountable to itself in basic ethical ways. This accountability of business to nature and society evokes a sense of covenants running with the land.

The phrase itself—*covenants running with the land*—is resonant. It suggests commitments of a timeless nature that carry over from generation to generation. Brian Hall, the cocreator of the Hall-Tonna Values Inventory, notes that companies with visionary leadership require a time frame of about fifty years, involving the active engagement of several generations.[46] The sociologist Elise Boulding proposes that we view the present as a two-hundred-year span of time— a continuum comprised of the past one hundred years and the upcoming century.[47] The People of the Six Nations, known more familiarly by the French term Iroquois, embrace a sense of timelessness that extends even further into the future: "We cannot simply think of our survival; each new generation is responsible to ensure the survival of the seventh generation."[48] Stewart Brand, in his discussion of the planning and building of a long-term mechanical clock in the Snake Mountain range of eastern Nevada, suggests a span of time reaching ten thousand years into the future. Covenants that run with the land are imbued with a similar sense of timelessness.[49]

Such covenants also connote a link between community and land ethic. Our society's need for overall health and well-being mirrors a similar need for our land. These two needs run together, sharing the same path, complementary goals, equivalent pacing. This connotation courses through our company as we have evolved over time. Taking stock of people and place, recovering a deep sense of context, imply a covenantal relationship to where we reside and to those with whom we live. Our hiring practices focus on creating long-term covenants with

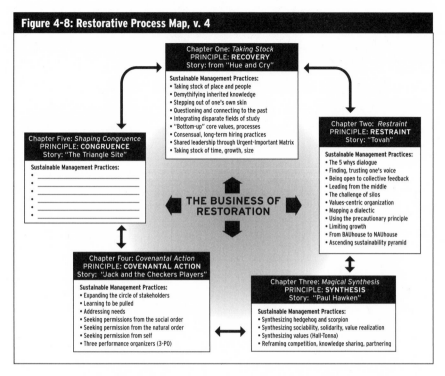

Figure 4-8: Restorative Process Map, v. 4

Chapter One: *Taking Stock*
PRINCIPLE: **RECOVERY**
Story: from "Hue and Cry"

Sustainable Management Practices:
• Taking stock of place and people
• Demystifying inherited knowledge
• Stepping out of one's own skin
• Questioning and connecting to the past
• Integrating disparate fields of study
• "Bottom-up" core values, processes
• Consensual, long-term hiring practices
• Shared leadership through Urgent-Important Matrix
• Taking stock of time, growth, size

Chapter Five: *Shaping Congruence*
PRINCIPLE: **CONGRUENCE**
Story: "The Triangle Site"

Sustainable Management Practices:
• _____
• _____
• _____
• _____
• _____
• _____

Chapter Two: *Restraint*
PRINCIPLE: **RESTRAINT**
Story: "Tovah"

Sustainable Management Practices:
• The 5 whys dialogue
• Finding, trusting one's voice
• Being open to collective feedback
• Leading from the middle
• The challenge of silos
• Values-centric organization
• Mapping a dialectic
• Using the precautionary principle
• Limiting growth
• From BAUhouse to NAUhouse
• Ascending sustainability pyramid

THE BUSINESS OF RESTORATION

Chapter Four: *Covenantal Action*
PRINCIPLE: **COVENANTAL ACTION**
Story: "Jack and the Checkers Players"

Sustainable Management Practices:
• Expanding the circle of stakeholders
• Learning to be pulled
• Addressing needs
• Seeking permissions from the social order
• Seeking permission from the natural order
• Seeking permission from self
• Three performance organizers (3-PO)

Chapter Three: *Magical Synthesis*
PRINCIPLE: **SYNTHESIS**
Story: "Paul Hawken"

Sustainable Management Practices:
• Synthesizing hedgehog and scorpion
• Synthesizing sociability, solidarity, value realization
• Synthesizing values (Hall-Tonna)
• Reframing competition, knowledge sharing, partnering

people who desire meaning and purpose in work. Our practice of the principle of restraint implies a covenant having to do with limiting our growth. The magical synthesis of values—both within a company and beyond—integrates disparate values into a covenant of shaping a new order. With this overall flow of our discussion in mind, we return to our Restorative Process Map (Figure 4-8).

The shaping of covenants still leaves us with questions pending: How can a business foster change not just on one project but in a town or region as a whole? Is the pace of change suggested in this chapter too incremental to redress the degradation of land and community occurring at a macro level? How does a sustainable business leverage its culture and relationships to restore who we are on a larger plane?

These questions will be addressed in the following chapter. For now, it's worth bearing in mind an admonition voiced by the writer and pathologist Lewis Thomas, who expressed wariness of our capacity, as a species, to pool our collective abilities and knowledge: "Although we are by all odds the most social of all social animals—more interdependent, more attached to each other, more inseparable in our behavior than bees—we do not often feel our conjoined intelligence."[50]

For Thomas, conjoined intelligence conveys the degree to which humans share their knowledge with one another. But the concept also has broader implications, having to do with shared sensibilities and practices. At stake in a sustainable business is precisely this question of pulling it all together, of conjoining not only what we know but what we feel—and beyond that, conjoining what we both know and feel with what we do and with whom we collectively join forces to make this restorative enterprise a reality. With those challenges in mind we turn to the following chapter.

CHAPTER FIVE

SHAPING CONGRUENCE

The environmental awakening is clearly the result of realization by larger and larger numbers of people that society must begin to study, analyze, and act in terms of larger and larger units—that is, whole cities, states, regions, nations, and regional groups of nations. Ultimately and logically this reasoning means working rapidly towards international coordination of management strategies and rules of conduct, as the well-being of the whole biosphere soon will be the overriding concern of all mankind.

—Eugene Odum, *Ecological Vignettes*[1]

Throughout this book we have been discussing the management of a sustainable business in terms of an ever-expanding circle of engagement with both land and community. A sustainable business grows and matures through such an outward-radiating pattern.[2]

But there is still much work to be done. A sustainable business must face the challenge of expanding its sphere of values and influence beyond that of a broad set of stakeholders to encompass an entire social order. Another outward-rippling movement is called for, one that absorbs the best thinking, knowledge, and wisdom from all four major sectors of society—business, government, academia, and the nonprofit world (or civil society organizations[3])—and brings all four sectors into congruence to shape a sustainable world.

Congruence, as I use the term in this chapter, is defined as "agreement," often connoting a sense of harmony. Shaping congruence entails engendering harmony and agreement among all sectors of society with the intention of creating a sustainable order.[4] Without congruence the fostering of a land-community ethic is largely impossible. And without the active collaboration of all sectors of society, congruence does not exist.[5]

There are challenges to shaping congruence, challenges illuminated with these two brief exercises.

Exercise 1. Imagine you are at a town hall meeting, attended by the key people from your community: local government officials, prominent business executives, highly regarded scholars and administrators from the local college, and some active community organizers representing several influential volunteer groups. They are here because you are proposing a specific reform that could have profound effects on the entire community for generations to come.

You get up to speak. Say out loud the following three sentences: "I believe with all of my heart that this reform must be passed in order for our community to survive over the long term. Not only that, but I believe, also with all of my heart, that without the active support of all of you this reform will never come to fruition. And finally I believe that all of you here in this room have come to pledge your support for this reform, and I know that you will do everything in your power to see that this reform is not only passed but implemented."

Now ask yourself if you have an internal reaction to your speech and whether there is a skeptical little voice in the back of your head saying, *Who am I kidding? I don't really believe that. Maybe I am saying that for rhetorical flourish, but I really don't need the support of everyone here tonight to get this reform passed. And if I did need everyone . . . yeah, right—everyone in this room is pledging support? I've got four major sectors of the city in this room. When was there ever a time when government, business, academia, and the nonprofit world agreed on anything?*[6]

Exercise 2. Fold your arms across your chest, as if you were looking disapprovingly at someone else. Look down at your arms and notice which arm overlaps the other. Now relax your arms by your sides.

Repeat the sequence, folding your arms across your chest, taking notice of which arm overlaps the other, and relaxing.

Did you find that the same arm "dominated" the other each time? If you are like the vast majority of people, the answer is yes. Now repeat the exercise one more time, only this time, make a point of placing your nondominant arm on top. Awkward?

I can't take credit for inventing these two exercises. The first is borrowed (with some poetic license) from business author Peter Senge and will be cited later in this chapter in another context. The second is borrowed from business management scholar and author Dennis Meadows, who several years ago kicked off a speech with the arm-crossing experiment. Both exercises have a lot to do with shaping congruence.

Exercise 1 is intended to tease out the underlying doubts and biases most of us harbor regarding collaborative effort. These biases need to be acknowledged, confronted, and overcome to see clearly the four keys to fostering a sustainable order, namely:

1. To recognize that congruence is indeed necessary
2. To believe that shaping congruence is actually possible
3. To comprehend that shaping congruence can occur in multiple ways
4. To understand that it will take not just one silver-bullet strategy but rather multiple strategies of shaping congruence operating in parallel to achieve a land-community ethic

Exercise 1 is about transcending one's biases in order to see the need for and possibility of shaping congruence. It works primarily on a cognitive plane.

Exercise 2 is a little more involved. Most people are genetically wired to prefer the dominance of one hand over the other. Moreover this is a genetic preference that becomes culturally hardened over years of repeating the same pose. It's what scientist Edward Wilson refers to as an epigenetic rule, a trait or tendency to do something a certain way because genes and culture, nature and nurture, have co-evolved to determine that specific behavior. No wonder, then, that the charge to swap dominant and nondominant arms seems so awkward to most people. It doesn't feel "natural." We've been genetically wired and culturally hardened to fold dominant over nondominant.

Exercise 2 has a lot to do with the *challenge* of shaping congruence. Each sector in our society, evolving over millennia, has become hardwired genetically and culturally to distrust the others. Persuading each sector to work collaboratively with the others is a lot like asking people to fold their arms counter to what is familiar and comfortable. It doesn't feel natural. And yet this very "unnatural" action needs to occur if a land-community ethic is to be effected.

This chapter focuses on some of the challenges in shaping congruence—as elucidated by our two exercises. This chapter also considers one strategy for shaping congruence, through the actions of a sustainable business widening its circle of engagement to encompass all sectors of a social order.

We begin by looking at the story of a business deal that fell apart because it lacked congruence.

THE STORY

This is a story about one of our failures. It started when a local architectural firm approached us about developing a site owned by Armstrong Atlantic State University in Savannah, which is part of the University System of Georgia. The site was a twenty-seven-acre parcel, triangular in shape, located along one of the city's main north-south thoroughfares (Abercorn Street) and across the road from the university president's office and the rest of the Armstrong campus. The university wasn't sure what it wanted to do with the property. Theywere interested in talking to us because of our recently completed work elsewhere on a sustainable retail development.

Frankly I was skeptical about even talking to Armstrong. I didn't think Armstrong specifically or the university system in general would be interested in our sustainable ideology. My colleagues and I didn't want to waste their time—or ours—on pitching an idea that seemed foreign to the way the state Board of Regents was rumored to operate. Still, our company spends considerable time doing outreach, education, and advocacy, so I thought, *What the hell. We'll send a team over to Armstrong and at least talk about it.*

We met with a handful of senior administrators and listened to their needs:

- They wanted to hold on to the land, not sell it.
- They needed something that would be at least partially cash generating, to realize the value of the land they wished to retain.
- They viewed this site, situated across Abercorn Street from the president's office, as an opportunity to create a "gateway" branding opportunity for the school.
- There had to be flexibility of use to accommodate the university's growth.
- They were trying to address the region's acute shortage of health professionals and so needed immediate additional classroom space for their School of Public Health. Other classroom, office, retail, and even hotel needs also could be addressed.

Surprise, surprise, they were not put off by our sustainable focus. Our team left that meeting feeling energized. We immediately regrouped with our architects and over the course of a day created a preliminary sketch, based on Armstrong's key program requirements. We introduced a lot of pervious paving to minimize storm water runoff. We envisioned using green roofs to reduce heat gain and energy use. We had down-lighting at night to minimize light pollution and rain-collection systems integrated into the roofs to irrigate the native landscaping. We were off and running.

Here is where things got interesting. One of our team members happened to say, "You know, I think we need to walk the site to see what we've got."

"Oh, it's nothing but a bunch of scrub pine," someone replied. "It's a scruffy site."

In fact, that's how the site had always looked like to me driving up and down Abercorn. Still, the idea had merit. I was already feeling chagrined. I spend a lot of time talking about the need to take stock of both people and place before doing anything. And here I was planning a site without even seeing it. *I really am an idiot*, I kept muttering to myself.

We called some folks from the nonprofit Savannah Tree Foundation to join us for a walk through the Triangle Site—as we were now calling it. The Tree Foundation had been our partner on several prior projects. We have an ongoing tree-planting program that helps their organization with its mission of beautifying neighborhoods and helps us reduce our environmental footprint through carbon sequestration. The Tree Foundation had also provided artful suggestions on native plantings and landscaping for some of our other developments. And so that next morning a group of four, two from Melaver, Inc., and two from the Savannah Tree Foundation, hiked through the Triangle Site.

The site (shown in Figure 5-1) is sandwiched between the Armstrong campus on one side (A) and multifamily housing on the other (B), with an FBI crime lab (C) and a Boy Scout Headquarters (D) located along the periphery. The edges of the property are a dumping ground from the neighboring multifamily developments and are indeed fringed largely with short, stubby slash pine. My first impression of the site was that it looked, from the curb, just as it did at sixty miles an hour flying down Abercorn—scruffy.

But as we walked the property we found a little gem of what biologists used to call a climax forest, one riddled with longleaf pine among other old growth. Moreover, even though the largest commuter artery in Savannah—six lanes of the single major

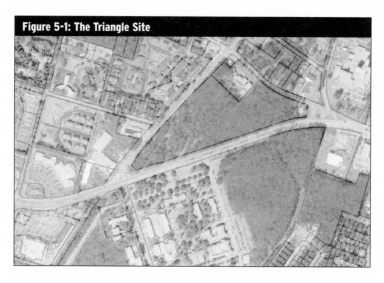

Figure 5-1: The Triangle Site

source of urban sprawl in our community—was only one
hundred yards away, you couldn't hear the traffic. Right in the
heart of junk-food, shopping-center heaven was . . . a different
world. As we enjoyed the quiet of our walk, Dale Thorpe from
the Tree Foundation said softly, "You know, our foundation
has nothing really to say in this, but it would be a shame to cut
all this down."

We agreed.

So we returned from our walk, reconvened our team, ripped
up the old plan, and created a new development proposal. The
new plan called for retail and classroom space along two corners
of the triangle where the site was already almost completely
degraded. We left intact the core of the site, except for some
walking trails that connected the two development ends. To add
to the effect we decided to locate the university's new Health
Services Department on one end of the site, which seemed to fit
naturally into the sustainable spirit of the project.

This, we thought, *is the right way to approach this site.* In
fact, this is the only way we would agree to move forward
with the project. We were also sure that Armstrong would
never go along with such a concept, since we would be leaving
untouched a major portion of the twenty-seven acres.

We returned to Armstrong, confessed that we had originally tried to sketch out a plan without even walking the site, and told them what we had found on our morning hike, using a huge longleaf pine cone as a visual aid. We showed them the new plan and then stated emphatically that we wouldn't build it any other way. Period.

They loved it. I made a mental note: *Martin, be careful about making cynical assumptions about the close-mindedness of others to paradigm change. People and institutions can be more on board with new ways of thinking than you presume.* We had quick follow-up meetings on the financials. There were a few challenges, arcane regulations relating to the amount of rental versus classroom/administrative square footage a university can build. But we thought we could manage those issues with some creative ground leasing. We met with a few folks high up in the Board of Regents, since they would be funding it. They too were on board.

But this is a story of failure, not success.

What happened next should not have surprised, but it did. The State Department of Transportation (DOT) arrived on the scene. The DOT had been quietly eyeing the increased congestion along Abercorn for several years. Because of their earlier construction of the Truman Parkway, which connected the suburbs of Savannah to the downtown core, the DOT now needed to widen Abercorn to accommodate the traffic build-up caused by use of the Truman. The DOT's intention was to take a swath along Abercorn for that purpose, including the Triangle Site.

Deal dead. Game over. Armstrong briefly considered contesting the DOT's plans to take the Triangle Site by eminent domain before deciding there were better uses of its time and political capital.

Identifying the Challenge of Congruence

I've reflected a lot about what that deal teaches us. Many of the lessons are indeed positive, having to do with sustainable management practices we've discussed in previous chapters.

Lesson 1: Start with authenticity and intention. Your reputation precedes you. Armstrong contacted us because they had seen some of our work nearby and trusted that we would bring the same sensibilities to their property. We set aside our original skepticism relating to Armstrong and the Board of Regents, assuming good intent by all parties unless facts proved otherwise.

Lesson 2: Align for the long term. In this situation three different groups—a business, a nonprofit, and an academic institution—had been in the community for a long time. Our all being long-time, local stakeholders meant there was a greater likelihood that our interests would be aligned in terms of the long-term interests of both the particular site and the community.

Lesson 3: Keep an eye toward expanding community. We contacted the Savannah Tree Foundation, with whom we had partnered on other projects. Over time the Savannah Tree Foundation realized that we weren't just bringing them in to get a cosmetic seal of approval. I think they trusted us enough to feel we would listen respectfully and deeply.

Lesson 4: Be transparent. We were open with Armstrong about what we would and would not do. We confessed to our stupidity of not walking the site initially. We kept the Savannah Tree Foundation updated as the process unfolded. Armstrong was up front with us when it came to discussing the lengthy and frustrating process of navigating the bureaucracy of the Board of Regents and worked with us to create an expedited timetable. We worked with an open financial plan so that it was clear from the get-go what the costs would be, how the financing would work, what our fees would be, and what leasing rates needed to be achieved.

Lesson 5: Establish consensus. In our discussions with Armstrong, we expressed concern that one day a future administration would plow down the trees we worked hard to preserve. We tried to persuade Armstrong to create a permanent conservation easement on the property. That's especially challenging since the university doesn't pay property taxes. They were not willing to go that far, and we understood. So we said, "Fine, but we're going to develop and brand it in such a way that any future president would face a firestorm of criticism if he or she decided later to build on it." Armstrong could live with that. While not a legal permanent easement, our agreed-upon plan created a sizeable undisturbed green space that would likely run with the land.

What we did not do, however, was shape congruence among all sectors of the community. We had ignored completely the role that government (in the form of the DOT) could play in the Triangle Site. Use of the Five Whys mirror dialogue helps to illuminate our blind spot:

Q1: Why did you ignore a key stakeholder on this project?

A: Probably because we defined the project too narrowly in site-specific ways. We didn't connect the dots between the site, the traffic along this site, and the future plans to extend the Truman Parkway. DOT didn't seem to have a stake in this project.

Q2: Why do you think your scope on this project was too narrow?

A: Because our thinking was too static. While we typically do traffic studies before developing a project, those studies focus on the short term, not the long term—static thinking having to do with time. We also did not connect the micropicture—what was happening in this particular area along Abercorn—to macro traffic problems. Static thinking having to do with limited geographical perspective.

Q3: Why was your thinking too static temporally and geographically?

A: As real estate developers focused on specific projects, we didn't consider the master plan for the entire south side of Savannah, developed over twenty years ago. Nor did we give much thought to a similar transportation plan for the region developed around that same time by a separate government entity.

Q4: Why didn't you give much time or thought to this overarching master planning?

A: Because it didn't seem to have much relevance to us back then. In fact, back then, we were still running a grocery business, which we thought didn't have much to do with master planning.

Q5: Why didn't you see the connection between running your grocery business and the efforts of governmental entities to do what they do?

A: Because they are part of a separate sector of society that by and large keeps to itself. We didn't have a sense of relevance or entitlement: that what government does holds interest for us or that it was our responsibility to weigh in with our own thoughts and opinions.

This Five Whys dialogue teases out the challenges of congruence: tunnel vision, a sense of disenfranchisement from the other sectors, a self-limiting role in or even complete retreat from active engagement in the body politic. Shaping congruence runs headlong into a critical obstacle to managing a sustainable business: siloed thinking and siloed action. As a nation, we collectively wall ourselves in to our respective compartments, consigning what we perceive to be the work of others to, well, others.

It is arguable that our team gave up too readily and should have fought DOT over its intended taking of the Triangle Site. There's merit to this argument, though a company of our small size is always concerned about the lack of resources (people, time, and money) to fight a protracted battle. Armstrong briefly considered this option before deciding it wasn't worth it. And we demurred. But this issue of a lack of resources is a smokescreen for several deeper issues.

First, though we wish we had been at the table decades ago, when municipal land planning and transportation issues were being hammered out, I don't think our company, back then anyway, had evolved to the point where we would have objected to what was being planned. No, this regret has more to do with a longing for a land-community mind-set to have been part of the planning process decades ago. But isn't that a lot to ask, something akin to Monday-morning quarterbacking of a game that took place decades before? Maybe, but I think beneath the wistfulness is a cautionary tale applicable to the present.

The fate of the Triangle Site was set in motion decades ago with a commitment to a single mode of transportation (the car) tied to a single concept of growth (suburban sprawl). The Triangle Site is simply the remnant of what was once a magnificent forest, hacked away bit by bit over time as sprawl ensued. The decision to build the Truman Parkway was an effort to solve the problem of moving suburban residents to their jobs downtown more efficiently. The more recent issue—widening Abercorn—is a result of the additional traffic caused by the Truman Parkway. We are all familiar with this type of sequential logic, reminiscent of the ring in the bathtub (from *The Cat in the Hat Comes Back*) spiraling out of control. The feedback loop of car manufacturing to the creation of a national highway system to easy access to cheap land outside urban centers to suburban sprawl has played out in virtually every town in America over the past hundred years.

Lessons Derived, Lessons Applied

The deck was stacked against our efforts to save the Triangle Site once our community as a whole yielded without much engagement with or visionary thinking about suburban expansion that began in Savannah in the 1960s. The lack of visionary, collaborative, local/regional planning back then—more specifically, the lack of coordination between land planning and transportation—led us to this day. We do indeed reap what we sow.[7]

This is a lesson our company has begun to absorb, recognizing that our work is tied in intricate ways to our involvement (or lack of involvement) in the planning efforts of the larger community. If recognition of our inextricable links to the other sectors of society begins today, then, as architect William McDonough and chemist Michael Braungart note, "negligence begins tomorrow":

> Once you understand the destruction taking place, unless you do something to change it, even if you never intended to cause such destruction, you become involved in a strategy of tragedy. You can continue to be engaged in that strategy of tragedy, or you can design and implement a strategy of change.[8]

This strategy of tragedy is wrapped up in a mind-set of siloed thinking and behavior. The strategy of change has everything to do with shaping congruence. We may have missed a critical period many years ago by not becoming engaged with the master planning going on in our community. But similar long-term planning is going on now, is always going on across virtually every region in the country. How do we take some of the lessons learned from the story of the Triangle Site and apply them to issues currently facing us? The question, while directed toward what our company needs to do going forward, is also addressed to all aspiring sustainable businesses. It is a question that should engage us all.

Our company's to-do list for our region is rather long. Among the issues high on my own personal radar is addressing the unprecedented growth occurring along the Georgia coast and the pressures this growth is creating on critical natural systems.

A collaboration of a non-profit group (the Georgia Conservancy), two governmental entities (the Department of Natural Resources and the Association of County Commissioners of Georgia), and a private foundation (Woodruff Foundation), is heading up a visionary project to conserve large portions of the rich, fragile one-hundred-mile stretch of wetlands, salt marsh, barrier islands. and back-barrier islands running the full length of Georgia's coastline. It's a complex ecosystem with five major riverways, each a unique habitat, winding their way toward the coast. Piping plovers, swallow-tail kites, rare species of pearly mussels, gopher tortoises, eastern indigo snakes, and West Indian manatees comprise just a fraction of the area's numerous endangered species. Its hammocks have been designated one of America's "last-chance land-scapes." John Teal, eminent marine biologist who started his profes-sional career studying the salt marshes of Sapelo Island, Georgia, has noted that despite being a robust ecosystem, our salt marshes are never-theless receding, for reasons still uncertain. Changes in sedimentation rate, sea-level rise, dredging, and increased human pressures, including development, are all contributing factors. "To save marshlands," Teal notes, "we need to do things at all political levels."[9] Spending time walking along parts of maritime forests or simply gazing out along the soft green and taupe pastel stretches of spartina marsh grass reminds me of an observation by Aldo Leopold: "If, then, we can live without goose music, we may as well do away with stars, or sunsets, or Iliads. But the point is that we would be fools to do away with any of them."[10]

We would also be fools to live without this coastal treasure just outside our back door. The consortium of groups (The Georgia Conservancy, the state Department of Natural Resources, the Association of County Commissioners of Georgia, and the Woodruff Foundation) is working to map the region with an eye toward designating (1) areas that are off-limits to development, (2) small corridors that create linkages between no-growth areas and that are themselves restricted in the amount of development activity that can occur, and (3) areas that are designated for high-density human activity. The concept is not new, taking cues from similar strategies undertaken in the Adirondacks[11] as well as from a more recent and local campaign to create a conservation corridor linking Okefenokee Swamp to Osceola National Forest.[12] It is a long-term, visionary conservation plan, one that may take decades or longer to enact.

I'd say we have time, all the time in the world. But because policy decisions being made today—much like the master planning that occurred more than twenty years ago on Savannah's south side—are not so easily (if ever) reversible, I personally feel a sense of urgency and impatience setting in. A sea change needs to occur in our thinking about the coast. John Muir, just starting out on his journey as a naturalist, walked along this same coast about 150 years ago, making his way at the age of twenty-nine from his home in Indianapolis and walking to the Gulf Coast before eventually sailing to California and living the remainder of his life out west. His thoughts from this maiden journey echo quietly yet cogently today:

> You bathe in these spirit-beams, turning round and round, as if warming at a camp-fire. Presently you lose consciousness of your own separate existence: you blend with the landscape, and become part and parcel of nature.[13]

A critical part of shaping congruence, perhaps *the* critical part of shaping congruence, is this merger of self into colleagues into community into a social order into nature. This sense of wholeness is also at the heart of a restorative business.

Having identified the challenge of congruence, how do then we address it? In the context of Georgia's coast, it will take more than just the work of the Georgia Conservancy and other environmental groups to conserve critical parts of this ecosystem. How does congruence get shaped to make that vision a reality? What should our own role be in helping shape congruence? In the larger context beyond our region, a similar set of questions needs to be posed. With the bubbling up of environmental consciousness everywhere, something now loosely referred to as a sustainable movement, how can we connect the dots of all this activity?[14] How do we transcend silos that separate sectors of our society and the thought and knowledge each possesses?

Little Boxes, Little Boxes, Little Boxes Made of Epigenetic Codes

A few years ago I came across an exercise conducted by a cognitive psychologist (Figure 5-2 on page 204).

Using this diagram, the psychologist asked which letter in the four frames seemed the most different. Answers to the question varied, as some respondents focused on the relative size of the letters, others on their relative curvilinear nature, and still others on differences among the fonts.

The researcher showed this same diagram to a young girl, most likely his daughter. And here's what she said: "The letter *t*." It took me a moment to see what she was referring to—the lines demarcating the four frames. That is what congruence is about: being able to see the connective tissue when we've been conditioned to compartmentalize.[15]

What if we replace the letters in the four frames with the names of four major sectors of our society—government, academic institutions, nonprofit organizations,[16] and business—and ask ourselves how they might come together? (See Figure 5-3 on page 205.) In the context of managing a sustainable business, the question is, How does a business

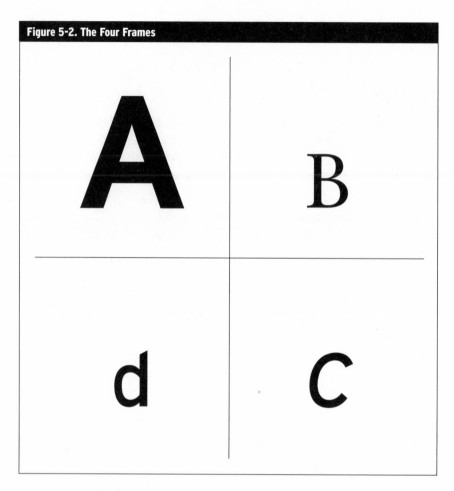

Figure 5-2. The Four Frames

integrate its thinking and its activities into that of a larger whole? In the more specific context of our own company, the question looks like this: How do we weave our own business activities into the policies being shaped by local government (land planning, affordable housing, transportation, waste management), knowledge shaping by academic institutions (curriculum development that includes ecological design or environmental education, research into alternative energy), and social issues being addressed in the nonprofit world (homelessness, poverty, illiteracy, etc.)? In other words, if the *t* in our diagram represents the vision of a land-community ethic, what does a business need to do differently to foster common ground at the intersection of these four sectors?

The issue of congruence doesn't just occur broadly across *what* we

Figure 5-3. Four Societal Sectors	
Governmental & Judicial Institutions	Business
Non-Profit & Social Justice Organizations	Academic Institutions

do professionally in our respective sectors. We also face the issue of congruence in the way we think, ask questions, process information, and formulate knowledge. It's what biologist Edward Wilson calls the issue of consilience (a term he uses for the ways in which different fields of inquiry coalesce), which he captures in a familiar matrix (see Figure 5-4 on page 506).

Wilson's consilience matrix is probably self-explanatory for those familiar with academic institutions; it's a system in which teachers and scholars become expert in one field or specialty with little regard to or substantive understanding of the links to other disciplines. But the consilience matrix has relevance beyond the world of academia. Businesses usually organize themselves by function or department.

Figure 5-4. Wilson's Consilience (Unity of Thought) Matrix	
Environmental Policy	Ethics
Social Science	Biology

Finance, operations, and sales and marketing are typical divisions within a company, and with those divisions come discrete ways of thinking. In the context of this consilience matrix, managing a sustainable business entails asking how one integrates the disparate boxes of thought into a collective whole.

If we refer back to our discussion of taking stock of place (chapter one), we can see that the integration of knowledge can be overwhelming and intimidating. Knowledge of one's locale calls for a sense of history, economy, anthropology, sociology, biology, geology, hydrology, botany, and so on. Layered upon this baseline of thought across disciplines are areas of knowledge specific to a particular business. For instance, as real estate developers, we need to have a certain level of expertise regarding design (urban, architectural, landscape, interior, general land planning), engineering (structural, mechanical, electrical), high-performance green systems, organizational design, financing, marketing, public relations, construction management, and brokerage.

Impossible, one might argue, for any one business to have that broad a spectrum of knowledge in-house, much less the capacity to integrate these disciplines. Precisely. Such an integration of thought and knowledge across multiple disciplines insists upon a type of collaborative brain trust—a village of thinkers and doers with different expertise, all coalescing around certain central ideals.[17] In other words, congruence. Considering the Four Societal Sectors matrix (Figure 5-3) and Wilson's Consilience Matrix (Figure 5-4) together, I would suggest that congruence is about the ways in which unity of action (how the sectors in our culture engage with one another) and unity of thought (how we think about things) come together (see Figure 5-5 on page 208).

Here's how this Congruence Matrix reads. In the post–World War II years—the 1950s and a good part of the 1960s—scientific knowledge of the way our environment worked was fragmented (low degree of unity of thought), and the degree to which our sectors worked together was also fairly low. The huge controversy over pesticide use, most notably DDT, sparked by Rachel Carson's book *Silent Spring* (1962), can be viewed as a good indicator of lack of congruence in the population as a whole.

Then came what, in many ways, was a golden age, the 1970s, in which synthesis of thought and action was at its peak (note the high point in the graph). The Environmental Protection Agency was created in 1970, the Clean Water Act was passed in 1972, the Endangered Species Act in 1973, the Safe Drinking Water Act in 1974, and the National Forest Management Act and the Resource Conservation and Recovery Act in 1976. Here we begin to find much greater unity of action among the four major sectors and more consolidated research. It is at this time that Eugene Odum, preaching a gospel of holism captured in the chapter's opening epigram, was in his heyday.

And now we are in the early twenty-first century, where we have never had greater integration among our various branches of knowl-

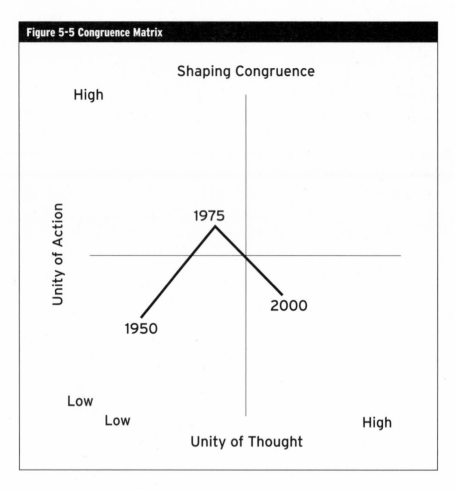

Figure 5-5 Congruence Matrix

edge. Why? Despite the complexities of the natural world, we are collectively beginning to fill in major pieces of the puzzle, owing in part to the proliferation of research from the past twenty years.[18] But unity of action is low, with a strongly siloed approach to action among the four sectors. *Why* is this happening?[19] And *what* can we do about it?

We can begin to understand the *why* when we consider what Edward Wilson calls epigenesis, a concept introduced in the context of Exercise 2 at the beginning of this chapter. Epigenesis involves the ways in which our genes co-evolve with how we shape culture:

> Genes prescribe . . . rules . . . that [shape] the acquisition of culture.

> Culture helps to determine which of the prescribing genes
> survive and multiply from one generation to the next. Successful
> new genes alter the . . . rules of populations. Altered rules change
> the direction . . . of cultural acquisition.[20]

Essentially, Wilson is talking about adaptive management on a grand scale. How we have developed over thousands of years is a result of a trial-and-error dance between genes and culture, with certain genes winning out, shaping culture, and causing further genetic adaptation. Kin selection, parental investment, mating strategies, social status, territorial expansion and defense, contractual agreements: All, Wilson argues, are shaped by the interplay of genes and culture.

It's this last piece, *contractual agreements,* that I want to focus on because contractual agreements are closely related to the principle of covenantal action. If our notion of contractual agreements or covenantal action has been shaped by a trial-and-error dance between genes and culture, it behooves us to know as much about this dance as possible. As Wilson argues, "contract formation is a human trait as characteristic of our species as language":[21]

> Because personal familiarity and common interest are vital in
> social transactions, moral sentiments evolved to be selective.
> And so it has ever been and so it will ever be. People give trust
> to strangers with effort, and true compassion is a commodity
> in chronically short supply. Tribes cooperate only through care-
> fully defined treaties and other conventions. They are quick to
> imagine themselves victims of conspiracies by competing groups,
> and they are prone to dehumanize and murder their rivals during
> periods of severe conflict. They cement their own group loyalties
> by means of sacred symbols and ceremonies. Their mythologies
> are filled with epic victories over menacing enemies.[22]

The issue of tribalism in contemporary American culture is a complex landscape of shifting identities and allegiances. As Alexis de Tocqueville famously observed in his two-volume *Democracy in America* (1835,

1840), our culture is characterized as a nation of associations—loose-knit, close-knit, small and large—running the gamut from shared hobbies to organized sports to cause-related activities. If de Tocqueville were alive today to revise *Democracy in America*, he might update this original observation by noting the competitive and contentious nature of our associations. It's a sense of competition that not only pits one business against another; or one academic institution against another; or local, state, and federal parts of our government in internecine conflict; but it also has each of these sectors squaring off against one another.

Despite the obvious complexity of this contentiousness American culture today can be viewed as having evolved into four large and distinct tribes, the four societal sectors: a government tribe that legislates and manages our political relations, a business tribe that pursues economic interests, an academic tribe that conducts research and disseminates knowledge, and a nonprofit or civil society tribe that is essentially the mechanism for addressing spiritual or ethical concerns as well as a channel for the members of society inadequately represented by the other three sectors. Moreover, there is a natural defense mechanism genetically and culturally built into our system that limits the degree of trust and compassion each sector has for the others.

We have seen examples of tribal defense mechanisms throughout this book. The keynote address delivered by Florida governor W. S. Jennings at the 1902 Turpentine Operators' Association annual convention (chapter one) not only suggests the excesses of the turpentine industry in wiping out the region's longleaf pine but also hints at government's desire to combat both the turpentine industry and its practices. The appearance of Nader's Raiders in Savannah in the summer of 1970 (chapter one) set the stage for a confrontation between local businesses and a nonprofit research and advocacy group. The story of a group of Georgia real estate developers trying to eviscerate the state's 1970 Coastal Marshlands Protection Act (chapter four) pits business and government and environmentalists against one another.[23]

If adversarial tribalism shapes the way our major social sectors engage with one another, we really are in a pickle. It's the dilemma underlying Exercise 2 in the opening of this chapter. How do we learn to comfortably cross our arms differently? How do we rewire the epigenetic codes we have developed over centuries? What do we do about this lack of trust and true compassion across sector (tribal) lines? We are faced, as geographer Jared Diamond has noted, with collapse on a global order. A critical antidote to this potential collapse is creating congruence among our various tribes, our societal sectors.[24] So how do we achieve that, given the epigenetic inclination among tribes or social sectors to keep to themselves?

Multiple Strategies of Shaping Congruence

There are a numerous ways to bring all sectors together in the interest of shaping a sustainable order (see Figure 5-6).

Each approach comes with its own notion of who is leading the charge (business or government, for instance), as well as what processes (top-down, bottom-up) are being employed. Each approach has its strengths and weaknesses. Ultimately, it will take all of these strategies, each working within its own capacities, to effect critical change.

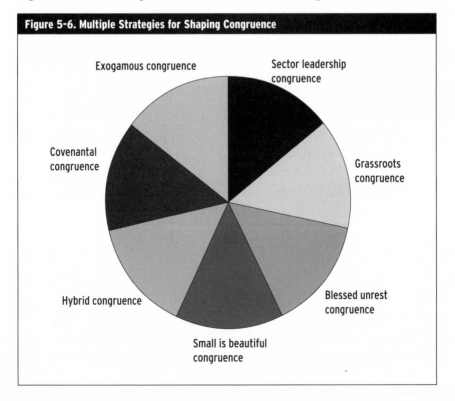

Figure 5-6. Multiple Strategies for Shaping Congruence

Exogamous congruence

Sector leadership congruence

Covenantal congruence

Grassroots congruence

Hybrid congruence

Blessed unrest congruence

Small is beautiful congruence

One approach, if you can call it that, places faith in severe external shocks to the system as a means to move us in a sustainable direction (exogamous congruence). Another approach is to look for top-down leadership from one of the four social sectors, thus galvanizing the other sectors to get on board (sector leadership congruence). A third approach is to place hope in aggressive grassroots activity, largely at the local level (grassroots congruence). A fourth perspective is that these small grassroots activities amount to a quiet, sustainable revolution on a global scale (blessed unrest congruence). A fifth approach shares the same bottom-up approach as grassroots congruence but locates the leadership less in community organizing and more around small businesses and others that fill the vacuum of leadership in a community or region (small is beautiful congruence). A sixth approach is neither top-down nor bottom-up and is based on partnering around shared areas of interest, usually between two sectors of society, often business and nonprofit (hybrid congruence).

Finally, I would like to suggest something I'll refer to as covenantal congruence, which is neither top-down nor bottom-up but has more in common with leadership from the middle. Covenantal congruence is the focus of the remainder of this chapter. Before delving in to the details of covenantal congruence, let's consider the other approaches to shaping congruence.

Exogamous congruence. We could, I suppose, pin our hopes on what economists call exogamous events, a fancy word for shocks that occur from outside the social system and that can have profound influence upon it. For instance, growing awareness of global warming through greenhouse gas emissions would be one such shock to the system. Disappearance of most of Lake Chad and a large portion of the Aral Sea accelerates awareness of increased desertification on a global scale. Additional category four and five hurricanes would alert us to the dangers of rising sea levels and the urgency behind reducing carbon emissions.

There are at least three big problems with external shocks to the system. First, you can't control when they occur (they are external). Second, while the aftermath of an exogamous shock might galvanize a whole society into action, that's hardly much solace for those who have suffered the devastating consequences of the shock itself. Third, it's not clear if or how these shocks will change our general mode of operation as a society. Hurricane Katrina is a cogent example. Writing about changes to the Louisiana bayou *several years before Katrina hit*, Mike Tidwell noted that the Gulf Coast is losing twenty-five square miles every year and that New Orleans, which a century ago was fifty miles from the coast, is now only twenty miles inland. One key antidote, Tidwell notes, would be the investment of some $14 billion to facilitate the Mississippi's older flow patterns, which would help retain a high portion of the silt that is washing out into the gulf. Years after Katrina there's still little movement on that front.[25]

Meanwhile development activity in my own backyard along the Georgia coast has increased since Katrina, a sure indication that lessons intended to be learned about basic services provided by our wetlands have gone unheeded. So much for exogamous influences. They come in with a bang, creating an immediate firestorm of concern, but can dissipate in strength as quickly as they arrive. A final comment on exogamous events: The term itself is a bit of a misnomer, since properly construed, many so-called natural disasters that humankind faces are of our own making.[26]

Sector leadership congruence. A number of eminent thinkers writing today look to leadership from one of the four major societal sectors for a solution. It's an argument of first among equals, with one sector playing the leadership role and pulling the other three along in its wake. Typically, though not always, the two big guns at the table are business and government. Ryuzaburo Kaku, former head of Canon, contends that, while individuals and governments can do their part, it is really to business that we need to look for substantive change, since corporations have a degree of wealth and influence that the other sectors lack.[27] The economist Jeffrey Sachs and public-policy thought leader Robert Reich take a different tack, placing faith in government to resolve some of our most fundamental social and environmental dilemmas.[28]

While Kaku, Sachs, and Reich (among others) differ on the locus of leadership, all share a sense that leadership from one particular social sector will be the driver of transforming our thoughts and actions and creating a sustainable order and that the process for shaping congruence will be a top-down process. There are numerous examples that seem to support such arguments, with recent sustainability moves by Wal-Mart and GE in the business sector and leadership roles provided by countries such as Sweden in the government sector indicating that top-down leadership from a single sector is a powerful, paradigm-changing force.

Congruence led by a major social sector and shaped by a top-down process begs some questions. Just how collaborative is the nature of the congruence? Just how much agreement or harmony (to use two dictionary definitions of the term for a moment) is cobbled together here?

The move to look for leadership per se is an interesting one. In essence this move is a response to a question framed in a competitive way: Who (among you) is *most* capable of taking the lead? The solution offered—whatever it is—reaffirms tribal boundaries. The move to be first among equals reaffirms the epigenetic rules Wilson discusses. I don't think that this is necessarily bad, but I do think it inhibits real agreement and harmony among the social sectors. When it comes to addressing acute environmental issues quickly and resolutely—such as carbon emissions and global warming—such a top-down approach has significant merit. When it comes to addressing longer-term problems related to biodiversity and overall consumption practices such a top-down approach, because of its lack of broad engagement from all sectors, may be problematic. Sector leadership congruence, in short, seems suited to addressing single, big-ticket issues quickly.

Grassroots congruence. The classic grassroots perspective is one that most people are probably familiar with. It is well articulated by journalist Mike Tidwell in the closing chapter of *The Ravaging Tide*, which is tellingly titled "The Bottom-up Solution: A Grassroots Rebellion":

> We need nothing short of a social and economic revolution in this country. . . . And history shows that change of this revolutionary sort almost never begins with the people at the top, with the people in political power who see the problem clearly and then act as catalysts, infecting the rest of us with the need to act. No, this is not how it happens. The average person has to demand action fast. . . . No one should think for a second

that our government will take care of this crisis without our full, insistent participation at every step. Nor will mainstream environmental groups, headquartered inside the Beltway, lead us out of this mess.[29]

Several parts of this approach are worth mentioning. It stakes its authority both on historical grounds and on the grounds that traditional loci of leadership have abnegated their responsibilities. Where precisely is the congruence shaping in this scenario? Tidwell devotes considerable time in *The Ravaging Tide* to discussing the process of founding an organic corn co-op in his hometown of Takoma Park, Maryland, for the purpose of fostering grassroots support for corn-fueled home energy. The process he describes doesn't sound too much like congruence-shaping as much as wearing down his adversaries. But his is just one example among many others. The town of Schoenau, Germany, for instance, through a door-to-door grassroots campaign, managed to supplant a corporate utility company with one owned and run by the citizens of the town.[30] Here again, though, there's an adversarial quality to the grassroots effort that belies the more collaborative nature of congruence.

The strength of a grassroots approach lies in the localized nature of change. It is well suited to specific challenges to sustainability at the local level. When it comes to specific fights over water or air quality or waste-disposal practices or green space conservation, for instance, grassroots efforts seem particularly effective. When it comes to more systemic issues such as climate change or desertification, a grassroots approach seems to be lacking in its capacity to shape broad stakeholder congruence with effective results.

Blessed unrest congruence. This concept, taken from the title of a book by Paul Hawken, basically follows Hawken's argument that there is a movement afoot, without overarching leadership, without an overarching ideology, without even being aware that it comprises a movement. This movement, consisting of somewhere between one million and two million nonprofit groups worldwide working on intertwined issues of social and environmental justice, has no grand coordinated plan. Nevertheless, the cumulative effect of this activity will be one that moves us in the direction of shaping a land-community ethic worldwide. Do the organizations trip over each other at times? Do they sometimes conflict with one another? Would the movement toward a land-community ethic move less cumbersomely, more efficiently, were there more formal ties and programs linking them all? Perhaps yes.

But the beauty of this approach, Hawken argues, comes from its supremely flexible capacity to shape and implement a vision without that vision being narrowly prescribed or controlled by any entity. It is an approach that has a strong sense of place and people (being localized and decentralized), practices restraint in the sense that no one entity imposes its sole vision on the social order, and facilitates a dialectical play of disparate voices.

Does this approach move us toward harmonious agreement (congruence) around a land-community ethic? Perhaps. Its very diffuse nature suggests a certain paradox at its core: On the one hand, it covers the full gamut of social and environmental justice issues humankind is concerned with; on the other hand, because of its very expansiveness the capacity of this approach to bring order out of chaos is in question. It is not clear in this case whether a whole will eventually evolve from its parts. Perhaps the fairest evaluation of blessed unrest congruence is this: It is built for (eventual) congruence but might be lacking in sufficient agency to actually shape congruence. It is, by any account, a fascinating phenomenon. Its strength is in its potential to shape systemic change over the long term. It has almost infinite entry points, enabling all of us to join in and support causes and initiatives that speak to us individually. It is built, to use Stewart Brand's term, for "the long now." Its weakness is its lack of capacity to shape broad coalescence around critical issues over the near term.

Small is beautiful congruence. This type of congruence shares with Tidwell a sense that changes in thought and action need to come from a bottom-up approach. But rather than deriving from individual action, this perspective places hopes on small businesses and nonprofit organizations that assert themselves when governments are not responsive to environmental concerns.[31] For example, David Suzuki and his foundation work on behalf of the Great Bear Rainforest in British Columbia, an area comprising about 15.5 million acres and one of the only temperate rainforests left on this planet. Here's how Suzuki describes it:

> [It] is a narrow strip of forest pinched between the Pacific Ocean and the coastal mountain ranges, fed by high rainfall blown off the ocean. It supports the highest biomass . . . of any ecosystem on the entire planet. It's home to a quarter of the world's remaining temperate forest, a truly magical place where Sitka spruce, hemlock, western red cedar, and Douglas fir tower as much as a hundred meters into the sky. This ecosystem is also home to many of the world's last healthy salmon runs, as well as geoduck clams, pods of killer whales, murrelets, spotted owls, grizzlies, wolves, otters, sea anemones . . . and much more.[32]

For many years, environmentalists, indigenous First Nation groups, logging companies, and government officials fought tooth and nail over the legal and administrative rights to this land. Eventually, these stakeholders worked to develop trust for one another, shaped a shared vision that met the needs of the community without compromising the future needs of the community, and eventually led to a revolutionary type of management plan that sustains the needs of all.

This is an interesting type of congruence, one a sustainable business shares strong affinity for and can learn much from. This approach involves a nonprofit organization (Suzuki Foundation) being invited into or inserting itself into an extensive series of discussions with citizens, businesspeople, and government officials to address each one's immediate concerns but also to step away from those concerns to take the long view of each group's respective vision for the area.

This process has many positives. It starts with recovering a sense of place and people. The process also restrains any one sector from imposing its vision on the larger group, instead serving to be open to the play of dialectical voices, all of whom are heard and validated. It focuses on the overarching meaning and purpose not just of each group but of the entire land area and community. It does not force or impose synthesis but enables synthesis to magically bubble up through the play of voices, and this synthesis radiates out to others beyond the region as a model for how to create congruence elsewhere.

Small is beautiful congruence has a larger reach in terms of both space (geography) and time than grassroots congruence. It is built for more complex issues for the longer haul. It takes the time necessary to build coalitions and shape covenantal processes. Its weakness is that it is not built to tackle systemic problems on a global level in the here and now.

Hybrid congruence. This is an interesting strategy, rather recent as far as sustainable approaches go. It is neither top-down nor bottom-up but instead involves partnering efforts usually between a business and a nonprofit on a single issue of interest to both. A few recent examples[33] include the following pairings:

Coca-Cola | World Wildlife Fund
Chiquita Bananas | Rainforest Action Network
Royal/Dutch Shell | Greenpeace
Goldman Sachs/TXU | Natural Resources Defense Council
eBay | World of Good
Unilever | Oxfam
Trigen | City of Chicago

Another version of hybrid congruence is suggested by the biologist Edward Wilson, who relies upon academia for the knowledge-based portion of problem-solving, while placing his hope largely on the nonprofit sector (with assistance from government) for taking that knowledge and shaping it into action-oriented steps through the conservation of large, critical hot spots around the globe.[34]

The strength behind such partnerships comes from the mutual leveraging of powerful and influential entities or brands to reduce a company's environmental footprint (or conserve regional resources) in some meaningful way. Also promising are the foundations of trust being built across sector lines. The weakness of such relationships is that they tend to focus on a single issue of importance to both parties, do not often involve other sectors in their work, and because of the topical nature of the work of are uncertain duration. Moreover, as Peter Senge notes, such partnerships are still in their infancy and have a long row to hoe before substantive collaboration will occur:

> It is enormously difficult to actually build the capacity for successful collaboration. Mutual distrust runs rampant between NGOs and corporations. Most governments have little history of building such collaborative efforts with the other sectors, and most, sadly, still see little need. Typically, organizations from these three sectors have different technical know-how, speak different languages, and focus on different stakeholders. There is little to bring all of them together—other than the urgent need to do so.[35]

Let's recap the positive and problematic characteristics of the various strategies for shaping congruence. Exogamous congruence has the power to galvanize on a global level, but it is a reactive strategy. Sector leadership congruence brings with it significant power and influence but lacks a consensual or collaborative feel. Grassroots congruence may work through consensus and collaboration but probably lacks the power and significance to have broad reach and impact. Blessed unrest congruence works collaboratively and augurs tremendous reach and impact but leaves questions unanswered as to whether its broad theoretical reach will cohere. Small is beautiful congruence epitomizes quasi-leadership from the middle, amalgamating the strengths of top-down and bottom-up approaches, but may not be a replicable model. Hybrid congruence brings with it the powerful coalition of major brands but is limited in its outreach to all sectors and seems best poised to tackle single issues over a limited time frame. An overview of these comparative strengths and weaknesses is shown in Figure 5-7 on page 220.

Each strategy for shaping congruence carries a notion of leadership. Each features processes endemic to its structure (top-down, bottom-up, leading from the middle). Fortunately, there is no need to choose among them. They are all in motion at the present time. In fact, it's the very presence of multiple approaches to shaping congruence that may give us the greatest hope for fostering a land-community ethic.

Table 5-7: The Comparative Shapes of Congruence							
	Type of Leadership	Degree of Collaboration	Power and Influence		Time Frame for Paradigm Changing Results	Issue Focus	Proponents
			Globally	Locally			
Exogamous congruence	N/A	N/A	Uncertain	High	Short-term	Single	
Sector leadership congruence	Top down	Low	High	High	Short-term	Single	BUSINESS: Ryzaburo Kaku, Ray Anderson; GOVERNMENT: Jeffrey Sachs, Robert Reich, Joseph Romm
Grassroots congruence	Bottom up	High	Low	High	Medium/Long-term	Single/Multiple	Mike Tidwell, Mark Dowie,
Blessed unrest congruence	Bottom up	High	High Potential	High	Long-term	Multiple	David Korten, Paul Hawken
Small is beautiful congruence	Middle/Shared	Medium/High	Low/Medium	High	Medium-term	Single/Multiple	David Suzuki, Bill McKibben, E. F. Schumacher, William Greider
Hybrid congruence	Top/Shared	Medium	High	Low/Medium	Short-/Medium-term	Single	Peter Senge, Fred Krupp,
Covenantal congruence	Middle/Shared	High	Medium	High	Long/Medium-term	Systemic	Living Above the Store

In the April 13, 2006, issue of *Science* magazine, scientists Stephen Pacala and Robert Socolow published an article in which they identify fifteen distinct strategies that individually are insufficient but collectively will reduce our carbon emissions to sustainable standards. They argue that it will take a combination of these strategies to reduce our global emissions to manageable levels. So too with the issue of shaping congruence: It will take a plethora of congruence strategies, some built for the long term and some for the short, some around single issues and others around multiple concerns, some that are global in reach while others are very local in nature. The good news is that we don't need a single silver-bullet strategy: We need them all. The challenge for an organization is finding the congruence strategy that best fits its capacities.

Covenantal Congruence and Systems Feeling

Covenantal congruence takes all of the principles of covenantal action discussed in chapter four and applies them to an entire social system. Unlike sector leadership and grassroots activities, this type of congruence is based upon shared leadership among all sectors of a community, arising through a middle stratum and cutting across all tribal boundaries. Unlike blessed unrest congruence, this structure is rooted in a specific locale, with a more definite shape and structure to it. While small is beautiful congruence is typically shaped by stepping into a leadership void that has been abnegated by government, covenantal congruence is typified by business being an equal participant at the table with all social sectors. Unlike hybrid partnering, covenantal congruence is inclusive in its partnering and is systemic in its approach to social and environmental problems. Maybe the easiest way to capture this particular type of congruence is to provide a simple example of covenantal congruence in action.

A while back, our head of sustainable initiatives, Tommy Linstroth, simply announced to us that because of a unique set of circumstances the community had a golden opportunity to institute a recycling program, and we had to do something about it. We were used to Tommy by then. He came to us through a nationwide search and assumed one of the first such positions created for a real estate company. He had a background in environmental science and had planned to pursue environmental policy issues while working for a nonprofit, but he was intrigued by the idea of working with a for-profit business. He also sported a gold earring in each ear, played a wicked game of soccer, and was as laconic as any stereotypical Midwesterner. I'm still trying to figure out his communication style.

Over the next two-plus years Tommy, our CFO, Denis Blackburne, and a handful of others in the community took on the recycling-program project, carefully building a strong, broad stakeholder base of businesses, nonprofits, academic institutions, neighborhood associations, and civic organizations. Before we knew it Tommy was the "Green Guy" around town. He was inspiring. The recycling movement was contagious, even if the political process was damn near frustrating at times. As a result of this group's efforts Savannah now has a nascent recycling program, including the hiring of a city staff member dedicated to education and outreach in the community.

Our company involvement with this recycling program, albeit a small project of limited scope, epitomizes the nature of covenantal congruence. It also captures the essence of a sustainable business coming into its own, in large part through use of the principles and management practices we have discussed throughout this book. Our engagement with this program began by addressing a need that we were pulled toward, not because of something we as a company felt we needed to push onto the community (chapter four). That awareness of a need itself came about through taking stock of place and people (chapter one). While initially some of my colleagues and I thought we knew what the city's strategy for waste management should be, we restrained imposing our own views in the interest of cultivating creative brainstorming among our many stakeholders (chapter two). Eventually a shared vision for managing the city's waste and a set of flexible strategies and tactics emerged through this group process (chapter three). The group of core stakeholders then fanned out across the city seeking greater compact with the community (chapter four).

In this example of congruence shaped through covenantal action, the leadership is shared and diffuse. It is neither top-down nor bottom-up but akin to leadership from the middle. Moreover, no single social sector plays the dominant role in shaping the congruent vision. The vision and action plan comprise a magical synthesis welling up from each and all. It has rippling-out potential. The same broad group of stakeholders who came together to implement a recycling program has leveraged its joint experience to implement a number of other innovative initiatives in the community: the use of LEED guidelines for institutional construction projects, adoption of the International Council for Local Environmental Initiatives (ICLEI) program by the city to reduce carbon emissions, and the passing of a county resolution to be the greenest county in Georgia. Finally, and this is a key point in terms of a sustainable business realizing its highest potential, covenantal congruence occurs when the issue at hand (recycling in this case) is the concern of all social sectors but not the primary business of any one. Covenantal congruence takes place on a playing field on which all participate but that no one owns.

We can think about this last concept in the context of a management practice that has been with us throughout this book: letting go. We first encountered this in chapter two, where a leader of a company learns to restrain personal drives in the interest of fostering a broader play of dialectical voices. The practice is extended in chapter four, where a company learns to let go of its tendency to push goods and services onto the community, in lieu of allowing itself to be pulled by community needs. Here we extend the practice of letting go yet again, with the sustainable business being pulled in the direction of a land-community ethos, in which all social sectors come to the table in a spirit of participatory stewardship.

How does this happen? What enables a sustainable business to step out of its own skin, as it were, to let go of epigenetic rules it has been conditioned to, in order to shape congruence? Peter Senge, the organizational guru and popularizer of the notion of the "learning company," contends that "the discipline of building shared vision lacks a critical underpinning if practiced without systems thinking."[36] He may indeed be right. But Senge is framing the issue of a vision for a business in terms of the company itself, not in terms of a larger land-community ethic.

Once we reframe the question of building a shared vision for a social order, the critical discipline involved is as much about systems feeling as it is about systems thinking. Marc Gunther, a senior editor at *Fortune* magazine and someone who has written persuasively on the need for businesses to operate out of a sense of personal belief systems, nevertheless wonders if a system can manifest feelings.[37] It's a good question. Perhaps the difficulty here is a semantic one, linking an inanimate object with sentient capabilities. My own experience, one shared by organizational writers and thinkers such as Arie de Geus, Peter Senge, Stewart Brand, and Paul Hawken, is that a business is very much an organic entity, one in which we far overemphasize rational and analytical faculties to the detriment of feelings and sensibilities. As renowned political scientist Murray Edelman has noted:

Emotion and reason are commonly assumed to be separate categories. It is often assumed that they displace each other. But neither of these can appear without the other, and they qualify and modify each other.[38]

It is high time that a prescriptive account of business practices for the twenty-first century address the extent to which thinking and feeling are intertwined.

In our own company, I've identified six qualities to systems feeling that are basic management tools for shaping covenantal congruence: mastering powerlessness and unworthiness, spiritual intelligence, recognition of complexity, recognition of interconnectedness, boundary spanning, and subsidiarity. Let's consider each in a bit more detail.

Mastering powerlessness and unworthiness. Peter Senge has a passage in *The Fifth Discipline* that I wish to draw on in the context of the recycling group's efforts. This passage should sound familiar, since it was the basis for Exercise 1 at the beginning of the chapter:

> Many people, even highly successful people, harbor deep beliefs contrary to their personal mastery. Very often, these beliefs are below the level of conscious awareness. To see what I mean, try the following experiment. Say out loud the following sentence: "I can create my life exactly the way I want it, in all dimensions—work, family, relationships, community and larger world." Notice your internal reaction to this assertion, the "little voice" in the back of your head. "Who's he kidding?" "He doesn't really believe that." "Personally and in work, sure, but not community and the larger community." Most of us hold one of two contradictory beliefs that limit our ability to create what we really want. The more common is belief in our powerlessness—our inability to bring into being all the things we really care about. The other belief centers on unworthiness—that we do not deserve to have what we truly desire.[39]

If we recall the Five Whys dialogue earlier in this chapter regarding the Triangle Site, we can see elements of this sense of powerlessness and unworthiness in how our company once viewed its role as a business in civic affairs. By contrast, Tommy and his group of community stakeholders serve as an alternative, healthier model, epitomizing the transformative power that comes when people don't feel or practice powerlessness and unworthiness. Tommy never questioned whether we as a company were entitled to enter the political arena, never doubted the power that one company has to be an agent of change.

Spiritual intelligence. Rather than working within the boundaries of a given situation, Tommy and his group of stakeholders' first move was toward what philosopher Danah Zohar terms spiritual intelligence, to sense the need for a different situation.[40] This sense extends well beyond identifying a need for a different approach to waste management. The spiritual intelligence embedded in Tommy's actions extends deeper, relating to actions and thoughts that transcend typical tribal boundaries. The "different situation" implicit in his group's actions is one in which the social sectors feel both worthy and empowered to engage one another without thinking twice about—without even seeing—the walls between them.

With that shift comes a reshaping of land and mind.[41] Our business is no longer bounded simply by the projects we are specifically engaged in but encompasses everything around it. Government is no longer this monolithic other but becomes part of the process of change. Our perception of the boxes that served to pigeonhole each of the tribal sectors begins to fade from view, and the *t*, which seemed invisible to us at first, becomes a positive sign of convergence and integration.

Recognition of complexity. While our two-year involvement with the recycling program was frustrating at times, it also fostered both a recognition of and deeper appreciation for the complexity of systems. In ecologist and philosopher Aldo Leopold's words:

> The outstanding scientific discovery of the twentieth century is not television, or radio, but rather the complexity of the land organism. Only those who know the most about it can appreciate how little is known about it. The last word in ignorance is the man who says of an animal or plant: "What good is it?"

> If the land mechanism as a whole is good, then every part is good, whether we understand it or not. If the biota in the course of aeons, has built something we like but do not understand, then who but a fool would discard seemingly useless parts? To keep every cog and wheel is the first precaution of intelligent tinkering.[42]

While Leopold refers specifically to the complexity of the natural world, his idea applies equally well to our societal sectors and how they interact. They are complex, they are not always comprehensible, we may wish to discard useless parts, but they are all part of our own evolution. And so while we tinker, we need to hold on to every cog and wheel.

Recognition of interconnectedness. Alongside this recognition of complexity comes a recognition of interconnectedness. You can feel this most easily in smaller cities such as ours. We didn't understand, still don't understand, and perhaps never will understand all the inner workings of this social interconnectedness. But it is there nevertheless, creating further unexpected and positive linkages.

Sean and Chris, who work for the City of Savannah and who discussed and argued and brainstormed with us about recycling, took off their city-servant hats at times to sit with us on other nonprofit boards. Chris, for instance, was a primary behind-the-scenes influencer in getting the city to adopt a gray-water ordinance our company was advocating. Sean is working quietly with a municipality-wide group of environmentalists and businesspeople to assess and evaluate our city's carbon emissions through the ICLEI program, which Tommy Linstroth not only has been promoting for several years but has written a book about.[43] Patty, also a member of our recycling group, is spearheading a multisector, multiyear task force to make good on a county resolution to turn Chatham County into the greenest county in Georgia. Howard, a prominent long-standing businessman in Georgia and also part of our recycling group, has been instrumental in fostering a knowledge-based business economy focused on sustainable practices. Harold, one of the city's most influential attorneys, has quietly leveraged his political capital to lobby on behalf of numerous sustainable initiatives in the community.

We often joke about the fact that there is no such thing as a secret in our city. But there is an elemental truth underlying the joke, a feeling that we are far more involved with one another than any of us is consciously aware. It sometimes feels as if our business is involved in virtually every environmental issue relevant to our region. That sense is probably not far off base. We are, in organizational design lingo, boundary spanners.

Boundary spanning. Boundary spanners are those in an organization whose social network extends well beyond the boundaries of a company. Boundary spanners are those with a rich social capital because of the wide-ranging and diverse people with whom they maintain contact.

What is striking to me is the degree to which most everyone in our company is a boundary spanner, functioning with a high degree of civic involvement in much the same way that Tommy does. When considering how a company can maximize its influence on the larger community, the degree to which this company is comprised of boundary spanners is particularly important. So too is the capacity of each boundary spanner to see and foster synthesis among the many seemingly unconnected dots out there.

In more typical companies, boundary spanners are utilized to help with business development. They reach across to other companies and beyond to other tribal sectors, facilitating business development and strategy. Boundary spanners in the conventional sense work in a centripetal way, bringing others into a business's fold. But boundary spanners in a sustainable business work centrifugally, moving the business outward in the direction of a higher calling.

There is another intriguing difference between boundary spanners in a conventional business and those in a sustainable business. In a conventional setting boundary spanners zealously guard their social contacts, since these are the value an individual provides to an organization. Sharing those contacts with colleagues makes it possible to more easily replace the individual. In a sustainable business, however, where knowledge is shared across the company, so too are the social contacts of boundary spanners. The result is an overall enriching of the company's broad stakeholder base, with odd and serendipitous connections added to the complex array of relationships all the time. These connections are so rich and multifaceted that even in a small company such as ours it is often challenging to connect the dots among them. In trying to get a handle on this proliferation of networks, we have had to develop an internal website. Even so, it's hard to keep up with. In a conventional business boundary, spanners create silos of networked relationships. In a sustainable business, the network expands geometrically.

I don't believe it's possible to go out and hire a whole bunch of boundary spanners. They more or less come with the territory. Boundary spanners find you. If you create a company focused around a sense of shared purpose, and you develop a culture of dialectic engagement and enable a synthesis of purpose to magically bubble to the surface, and you broaden that sense of company mission to include a larger group of like-minded stakeholders, you will have fostered an environment where people are not mandated to but rather become of their own accord passionately engaged in the needs of the larger community. A management practice of self-restraint and letting go, enabling staff members to realize their higher potential, results in a complex web of thoughts and activities encompassing all aspects of community life. In other words, the boundary-spanning nature of most of my colleagues is woven into the culture of the company. Without intending to, our company was constructed to transgress tribal boundaries and leverage relationships. When we as a company are doing our job properly, the boundary-spanning capacities inherent in our staff members naturally emerge.

Subsidiarity. Complementing the strong presence of boundary spanning within our company is a notion of subsidiarity. Subsidiarity, which has its roots in Catholic teachings, is based on the notion that "it is an injustice, a grave evil and a disturbance of right order for a larger and higher organization to arrogate to itself functions which can be performed efficiently by smaller and lower bodies."[44] In other words, social issues are to be handled by the lowest authority competent and willing to address the problem. Subsidiarity seems to fit our company and our social mission, for it meshes a three-generation-long business history with a local context that we know intimately. The concept enables us to take huge and seemingly intractable problems and tackle them effectively at the community level.

Subsidiarity is important because it enables a company such as ours to translate global challenges into local, prescriptive action. It facilitates the mastery of powerlessness and unworthiness.

When I read the far-reaching writings of a Paul Hawken or a Jeffrey Sachs or a David Suzuki or an E. O. Wilson, the experience is both exhilarating and dismaying; exhilarating because of the breadth and depth of thoughtful analysis and dismaying because there seems to be no earthly way to get one's hands around such global issues. No wonder, then, as Al Gore points out in *An Inconvenient Truth*, we seem to move so quickly from a position of denial (that environmental problems exist) to one of despair (a feeling of being incapable of doing anything about it). Senge's comments regarding powerlessness and unworthiness forcefully reassert themselves. But relocated and recontextualized in a smaller setting, the problems facing us not only seem manageable but easily command our attention. As they should, given the fact that "natural systems, such as habitats, watersheds, and species composition, change every few miles or so on this planet."[45] And as with natural systems, so too is it with social systems—changing every few miles or so and calling for our involvement.

Taken together these six qualities—mastering powerlessness and unworthiness, spiritual intelligence, recognition of complexity, recognition of interconnectedness, boundary spanning, and subsidiarity—create a system of feeling within a company that restoration of community is doable. In fact, it would be well nigh impossible for a company with this system of feeling not to be mission driven. Systems feeling hearkens back to a concept we discussed in chapter one: creating a space for meaning. We want everyone at our company to find something they feel passionate about in the community and engage deeply with it. We don't mandate it by any means, but more often than not following one's passions just happens. More than that, my colleagues bring the company to that issue and to that passion, so that, lo and behold, we find ourselves as a company intertwined into virtually every critical issue that our community faces. You can't design this a priori. What you can do is provide space for colleagues to link the sense of meaning they find within a business organization to the sense of meaning they each find in the community at large. Covenantal congruence evolves from this permeable exchange of meaning that occurs between a company and the larger social order beyond.

The question arises as to whether any business can afford to devote much staff time and energy on boundary-spanning and congruence-building activities. It's a valid concern. Companies have always engaged in a version of congruence-building activities for the purpose of value creation, although often without a completely integrated ideology behind this practice. But given the degree to which economics and the environment are intertwined, the question should be inverted to ask, Can a company afford not to engage in congruence-building activities?

Shaping congruence is basically a new twist on a very conventional practice. Those of us who have been involved in business for several decades or longer are probably very familiar with the standard practice of many businesses to "seed" their presence in the community through participation on committees and boards such as the United Way or Red Cross or a local chamber of commerce. This has been a time-honored tactic businesses employ to kill two birds with one stone: give the nod to community involvement and give-back while both enhancing brand equity and enriching the network for business development.

Congruence shaping takes this practice to a whole different level in a few basic ways. First, there is the issue of integrative thinking: a fundamental awareness on the part of a restorative business that the various social and environmental justice issues facing a community are all interrelated rather than one-off charitable gigs. Second, there is the practice of centrifugal engagement: Rather than a business strategically placing its staff members in various high-profile nonprofits for its own purposes, a restorative business provides the space for staff members to engage themselves through their own particular passions. Third, there is the issue of the virtuous circle: No reductive accounting is done to assess whether the efforts to shape congruence enhance a company's financial bottom line; the effort is simply made as part of what makes a values-centric company tick. And yet, as we ultimately discovered in the course of analyzing ten years' worth of effort advocating for sustainable issues, there is a strong financial benefit to doing so.[46] Moreover, as we discussed at length in chapter one, the company that intends to stay competitive in the hiring and retention of skilled employees needs to be mindful of a labor market that more and more seeks to integrate work with meaning. Creating a company culture that focuses on shaping congruence as part of its overall business strategy fulfills a workforce's possibly ultimate desire of integrating the various aspects of one's life into a purposeful whole. Which is why the term *systems feeling*, while seemingly a contradiction in terms, is particularly apt—providing for a suffusion of mind and heart.

From Shareholder to Stakeholder to Placeholder

In chapter four we addressed notions of business governance, contrasting the historical European tendency to view business from a broad, stakeholder perspective versus the American tendency to view business from a more limited shareholder perspective. A sustainable business needs to be accountable to a broader stakeholder group.

As a sustainable business widens its circle of engagement, from covenants with stakeholders in the community to a broader sphere of engagement involving the shaping of congruence around a land-community ethic, it's time to jettison the notion of stakeholder for something I'd like to call a placeholder. This change in terminology may seem to be a simple semantic shift. But I think the change is significant.

Objectively speaking, *stakeholder* simply refers to someone (or some entity) who has an interest or stake in a specific issue. But the term also carries a connotation of position, of having a fixed perspective on things, as in a stake fixed into the ground. Too often these days, like the discussions centered around the rules applying to marshland protection on the Georgia coast, most stakeholders come to the table with fixed positions representing their own agendas. In issues broadly affecting our land and our community, like the master planning of the south side of Savannah decades ago or discussions of marshland protection, who within that region would *not* have a stake in the debates? In short, as we begin to move from a discussion of covenants involving a group of local stakeholders to a wider group encompassing a community, I think it is incumbent upon us to speak of placeholders, not stakeholders.

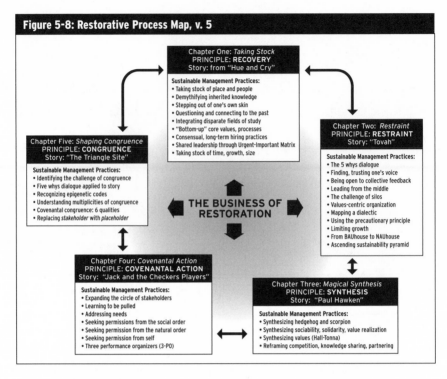

Figure 5-8: Restorative Process Map, v. 5

Chapter One: *Taking Stock*
PRINCIPLE: **RECOVERY**
Story: from "Hue and Cry"

Sustainable Management Practices:
• Taking stock of place and people
• Demythifying inherited knowledge
• Stepping out of one's own skin
• Questioning and connecting to the past
• Integrating disparate fields of study
• "Bottom-up" core values, processes
• Consensual, long-term hiring practices
• Shared leadership through Urgent-Important Matrix
• Taking stock of time, growth, size

Chapter Five: *Shaping Congruence*
PRINCIPLE: **CONGRUENCE**
Story: "The Triangle Site"

Sustainable Management Practices:
• Identifying the challenge of congruence
• Five whys dialogue applied to story
• Recognizing epigenetic codes
• Understanding multiplicities of congruence
• Covenantal congruence: 6 qualities
• Replacing *stakeholder* with *placeholder*

Chapter Two: *Restraint*
PRINCIPLE: **RESTRAINT**
Story: "Tovah"

Sustainable Management Practices:
• The 5 whys dialogue
• Finding, trusting one's voice
• Being open to collective feedback
• Leading from the middle
• The challenge of silos
• Values-centric organization
• Mapping a dialectic
• Using the precautionary principle
• Limiting growth
• From BAUhouse to NAUhouse
• Ascending sustainability pyramid

THE BUSINESS OF RESTORATION

Chapter Four: *Covenantal Action*
PRINCIPLE: **COVENANTAL ACTION**
Story: "Jack and the Checkers Players"

Sustainable Management Practices:
• Expanding the circle of stakeholders
• Learning to be pulled
• Addressing needs
• Seeking permissions from the social order
• Seeking permission from the natural order
• Seeking permission from self
• Three performance organizers (3-PO)

Chapter Three: *Magical Synthesis*
PRINCIPLE: **SYNTHESIS**
Story: "Paul Hawken"

Sustainable Management Practices:
• Synthesizing hedgehog and scorpion
• Synthesizing sociability, solidarity, value realization
• Synthesizing values (Hall-Tonna)
• Reframing competition, knowledge sharing, partnering

Placeholders come to the table in the interests of the place they are a part of, not in the interests of a position held by a particular profession, person, or sector in the community. Placeholders come to the table with open minds and a more altruistic mind-set. They also come prepared for the table itself to be moved—prepared, in fact, to help with some of the heavy lifting.

Completing the Picture

Since the early chapters of this book, we began mapping out a process of working collaboratively through an ever-expanding set of circles of contexts and relationships. That process began by taking stock of people and place, then using those contextual touchstones to become more reflective of self and other in a dialectic of statement and challenge, agreement and disagreement. That dynamic tension helps foster greater synthesis within a business community and then ripples outward to create covenants that run with the land, working with key stakeholders in the larger community.

We have focused our attention in this chapter on broadening that synthesis and covenantal action to encompass the larger community of a municipality and region, trying to foster wholeness among the key sectors in a society. This movement toward shaping congruence orients a business more deliberately in a restorative direction, by linking the journey of the business to the journey of the larger community. In other words, the collective *we* that comprises all of us at our company cannot restore itself if that process is separated from the restorative work of the *we* of the larger culture. With this in mind, we can now fill in the remaining block in our Restorative Process Map (Figure 5-8).

Coda: Moving the Table

This notion of a business and its social culture being joined at the hip recalls an issue raised by Jared Diamond toward the end of his monumental study *Collapse*. Diamond identifies four categories of failure that may dog our efforts to stave off environmental collapse: (1) failing to anticipate a problem because of the perception of creeping normalcy; (2) failing to perceive the problem once it arrives; (3) failing to solve the problem because of competing interests, perverse subsidies, and the like; and (4) attempting to solve the problem and failing. Although Diamond doesn't explicitly say so, it would seem from his work and the work of scientists and others studying environmental issues that we are currently experiencing a combination of failures 2 and 3. Of interest to us, particularly in the context of this chapter on shaping congruence, is the third point, failing to solve the problem because of the epigenetic code of tribal factionalism. Diamond also finds this problem of competing interests to be absolutely critical. Toward the end of his book, he leaves the reader with a question that I find to be perhaps the most penetrating and challenging of any confronting us today:

> It is painfully difficult to decide whether to abandon some of
> one's core values when they seem to be becoming incompatible
> with survival. At what point do we as individuals prefer to die

than to compromise and live? . . . Nations and societies sometimes have to make similar decisions collectively. All such decisions involve gambles, because one often can't be certain that
clinging to core values will be fatal, or (conversely) that abandoning them will ensure survival. . . .

Perhaps a crux of success or failure as a society is to know
which core values to hold on to, and which ones to discard and
replace with new values, when times change. . . . Societies and
individuals that succeed may be those that have the courage to
take those difficult decisions, and that have the luck to win their
gambles.[47]

Changing one's core beliefs and practices—beliefs and practices that
brought us to the table in the first place—in the interest of survival
works on so many levels. Diamond here is mostly referring to a culture
or society changing its course of action so as to avoid the demise experienced by the inhabitants of Easter Island, the Mayans on the Yucatán
Peninsula, and the Vikings in Greenland. Using this lens, the charge for
managing a sustainable business is clear: We bring other sectors of the
culture to the table, and then we move the table.[48] To come to the table,
we may need to abandon some of the core beliefs and practices that
have kept us feeling secure in our own tribal or social sector worlds. To
move the table, we may need new core beliefs and practices centered on
a collective restoration of land and community.

The question of changing core beliefs and practices in the interest of
survival also needs to be addressed at the company level. Our company
is, after all, a real estate business, one that focuses a lot of its energy on
development. And there is very little, if anything, truly sustainable about
development. Everything we do has consequences for the environment.[49]
Perhaps we should consider closing up shop, or at least try another line
of work?

It's not a trivial consideration, nor do I think it should be posed as a
straw argument, only to be parried away as part of an academic exercise.
I don't have a totally satisfactory answer. Maybe the charge for us as a
business is to bring ourselves and others to the table and then move that

table in ways and in directions we may not have envisioned at this stage in our evolution. That dialectical play of voices without a prescribed goal is a process that occurs within our company daily. Perhaps a similar openness to dialectical questioning, with a much broader group of placeholders throughout the social order, is called for. I think some of that dialectical questioning at the broader level is happening now with our company. I'll get back to you on how it plays out.

I'm concerned that when I discuss the process of building community from within a business outward to the larger society that I am conveying a message of linearity—that I or we have certain goals in mind that we are engineering through a step-by-step, deliberate, orchestrated process. That's not the case. Instead what has evolved over the years is a process of finding meaning and purpose in the society of others and allowing that social sense of purpose to pull us in directions we only vaguely grasp at that time. That collective movement has to feel right. It's oftentimes an intuitive sense, experienced well before rationality kicks in, that embracing a certain direction and a certain decision and a certain set of stakeholders just makes sense. Malcolm Gladwell devotes an entire book, *Blink*, to the intuitive aspects of decision making. He notes, in one salient passage:

> Our world requires that decisions be sourced and footnoted, and if we say *how* we feel, we must also be prepared to elaborate on *why* we feel that way. . . . I think that approach is a mistake, and if we are to learn to improve the quality of the decisions we make, we need to accept the mysterious nature of our snap judgments. We need to respect the fact that it is possible to know without knowing why we know and accept that—sometimes— we're better off that way.[50]

It is quite possible that, at some stage in our evolution as a company, we will decide that we cannot be developers and still speak passionately about a land-community ethic. For the moment, anyway, we see our profession, properly construed, as making a positive contribution to the overall health of our land and community. Might our own arrogance be showing? It is possible that we fall prey to these humanistic myths that all problems are solvable; that all problems are solvable by people; that problems are solvable either by technology or by solutions inherent in the political, social, or economic world; and that when the chips are down, all we need to do is apply ourselves and work together to find a solution before it's too late.[51]

In this context, it seems helpful to draw upon Alice Walker's notion of everyday use as a touchstone and inspiration. Does our overall purpose make sense? Do we get up in the morning and feel energized by the sense of making a difference in our community? Do we feel that we are working in covenantal terms with others outside the four walls of our office? Does each person's individual sense of trying to realize his or her greatest potential dovetail with a similar sense of aspiration for the community as a whole? Does it all seem to come together, almost of its own volition? Do we love what we do and with whom we work and what we accomplish? Can we answer these questions in the affirmative without a little voice in the back of our head saying, "Whom am I kidding?" I think the answer is yes.

A sustainable business has a sense, even if it can't be fully articulated, that its processes, relationships, connections, and activities somehow, despite their complexity, comprise a whole. Restoring that overarching sensibility of wholeness is what a sustainable business is all about.

CHAPTER SIX

LIVING ABOVE THE STORE

*Away from home we were ashamed of the junkyard.
Our daddy was a junk dealer, but when we filled out his
occupation on forms from school we wrote "salesman."
We weren't allowed to socialize outside of school, so
classmates didn't come home with us, and we didn't go
to other kids' houses. We knew nobody else lived like
we did, but we didn't know how they lived. We knew
they were wasteful and threw perfectly good things in
the garbage, which ended up at our house. We thought
that meant they were better than we were.*

—Janisse Ray, *Ecology of a Cracker Childhood*[1]

*I grew up along the coast of Georgia and South Carolina.
. . . After having found photography to be my path in
life, I left the South and traveled throughout the world,
making images that I hoped would give my life direction. Occasionally I would return home to the South, to
my family. And I would photograph, only to leave again
for points north, east, and west. There was something
distinctly different about the images I made while I was
home—something that ultimately was missing from the
images I had made during my travels. That something is
what compelled me to come home for good.*

—Jack Leigh, *The Land I'm Bound To*[2]

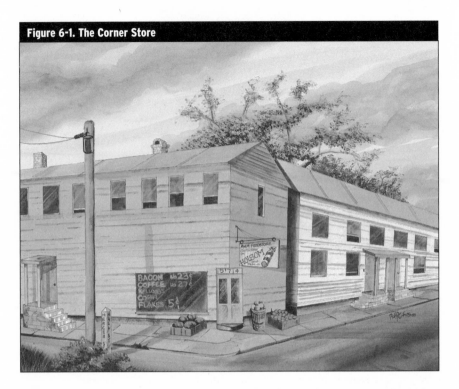

Figure 6-1. The Corner Store

Figure 6-1 is an image of the building that housed our original M&M Food Store in Savannah. I never knew that store, which opened in 1940 and closed eight years later when my grandmother Annie and my father, Norton, opened a larger store a few blocks away. I drive past this old building, though, from time to time and once in a blue moon I take a walk in the neighborhood. Every so often I think about purchasing this place and relocating our office there, thinking it will connect me more strongly to family roots. And then I think, *Nah, I don't really need to do that*. The stories my dad and my aunt tell about those days provide enough connective tissue.

Millie, my aunt, remembers most the terrible smell of slaughtered chickens coming from the area out back from the store proper. She was ten at the time. My father, four years older, recalls helping out with the slaughtering occasionally, though he tells such stories in an offhand manner that conveys this was just part of running a family store. More memorable for him were the full-service counters and how, when they moved to the new store in 1948, this old-fashioned approach was replaced by self-service. Both reminisce about their mother, my grandmother Annie, a blend of tough mother and savvy businesswoman.

Miss Annie (as people always called her) and her two kids never lived above this store, though the rich interlacing of business and home life meant they were never far away. I know the feeling, as do my two younger sisters, Tovah and Ellen. The business permeated everything we did. It was another family member at the table at mealtimes and a source of endless stories about colorful characters who worked with us. It was my job on weekends and during summer vacations and the source of moral understanding and wisdom, even if we didn't realize it at the time.

Once, years later, when we were about to open our third store, the business was picketed because our parents had signed an open letter in the local newspaper, urging everyone to support desegregation of our public schools. I remember crossing the picket line the day that store opened, and I recall some of the hateful things people were saying and had written on their placards. But mostly I remember being confident that our parents had done the right thing and that these other folks had gotten it wrong. I didn't know until years later that the entire business was mortgaged to the hilt and that such a boycott, had it been successful, would have ruined the company. Knowing that now makes our underlying sense of doing the right thing all the more powerful.

I recall meetings at our house late at night after we were put to bed, for organizations our parents were involved in back then. Those too made an impression about the nature of a local business being connected to the community. And I remember, after I was sixteen and able to work full time, driving home with my dad in the evening and hearing him talk about whatever had happened that day. Maybe it was that a key store manager had been lured away by a larger paycheck from a competitor. "That's OK," my father would say, perhaps more to himself than to me. "No one, not even me, is irreplaceable."

Other lessons back then were less warm and fuzzy. My father's and my aunt's management styles seemed to be based on intimidation and on motivating workers to avoid mercurial tempers that could flare up unexpectedly. The thought took hold—I don't know when—that if I ever had responsibility for others, my approach would be different. Sometimes, these days, when I suddenly snap and lash out at someone, I cringe and wonder just how far the apple has fallen from the tree. There was also the lesson of the time clock, punching in, punching out. As a kid I used to love the accumulation of punched-out entries on my card, indicating the gradual accruing of dollars I would see by the end of the week. As I got older, though, it felt demeaning, and I wondered if a system of trust could work just as effectively, perhaps even better.

I could probably fill a whole chapter with such vignettes, but I think the general sense I want to convey is clear. These fragments of memory from the store below carry up to where we live. John Muir spoke of his experience in nature much more eloquently when he wrote, "There is not a fragment in all nature, for every relative fragment of one thing is a full harmonious unit in itself. All together form the one grand palimpsest of the world."[3]

Palimpsest. It's one of my favorite words, referring to a parchment that is used several times over, the earlier scribblings rubbed over to make room for later expressions, though always there underneath. A layering of thoughts and ideas one upon the other, over time, a canvas reused. *Living Above the Store* has a lot to do with recovering those prior layers and integrating them into what we do currently. This restorative act is a basic activity of our company today. It evokes the rhythm of our work, the resonances we try to give voice to in the larger community.

THE STORY

There is one palimpsest I would like to devote a bit of time to here, another story from our grocery-store past. When I was no more than six and my sister Tovah was four, our father took us to the store one Sunday morning toward the end of the year (grocery stores were closed on Sunday in those days) to help with year-end inventory. We counted cans of soup and tins of tuna fish and packets of gum, and even at our young ages there was little illusion that this was fun. It was pure tedium, right up there with sorting coupons at home, another of our least-favorite jobs. We kept at the inventorying for close to half a day, when dad said it was OK to call it quits. What a relief. I grabbed a grocery cart and began whizzing down the empty aisles, hopping on the end of the cart after I'd gained enough speed, riding it like kids do on skateboards or scooters. I was having a blast. There was no one around, and the night crew had just finished waxing the floors so I was able to zip around quickly. And then I rounded the last aisle of the store, the dairy aisle.

In those days we didn't put the cartons of fresh eggs in a refrigerated display case. Instead they were stacked high in midaisle, a tall tower that shoppers found hard to resist. I was so intent, so thrilled at how fast I was moving on that wonderfully waxed floor, so relieved to be free of the tedium of taking inventory, that I never saw it coming. The grocery cart, with me aboard, slammed smack into the display of eggs.

When my own kids were younger they were amazed—hell, I was amazed—at just how wide a swath a spilled cup of milk will cut. No mess they've ever made compares to the scene that day in the dairy aisle. There were eggs everywhere. Whites and yolks strewn down the entire back half of the aisle, cartons that ended up . . . I didn't know cartons could fly that far.

I wish I could remember what my dad said to me immediately afterward. I'd like to think he rushed to see if I was all right. I'd like to think he tried to assure me that it was OK, that the financial loss of those eggs wasn't a big deal, that the time it would take to clean up that mess was something a business dealt with all the time. I can't remember. But I do remember the shame of that moment, the sense that as the boss's son, I was showing a careless and wasteful regard for things.

Lessons from Broken Eggs

While this story has been in my memory most of my life it is only recently that I've linked the two halves, connecting the act of taking inventory with the consequences of breaking eggs. I'd previously thought of them as two distinct stories: one providing the background, the other the foreground. In the course of writing this book, however, I've come to see these apparently distinct moments as two halves of one story.

The value of stock-taking. Much of what I have tried to describe and analyze in the preceding chapters has been about inventorying or taking stock—of people and place, of oneself, looking at our strengths and weaknesses as a company, considering what needs we address in the larger community. Taking stock can be a restorative activity. But in taking stock of everything around us our assumptions about things we have, how we got them, and what our inventory is likely to look like next year are tested, challenged, and in many ways broken asunder. What, then, is restorative about the broken eggshells of prior assumptions?

William Bridges, a professor of English literature who changed professions in midlife to become a business consultant, writes about managing transitions in our lives. At the core of his work is the notion of a neutral zone, where one takes time to come to terms with the past—a profession left behind, a prior relationship, the death of a close friend or family member—before moving ahead to plan what comes next. It is a time of reflection, Bridges argues that Americans, with our feet set firmly forward, particularly neglect. Bridges's thesis has far-reaching implications for our moment in history, when we should be taking time to better understand the course of our evolution as a species before plunging ahead. Humankind indeed seems to be occupying an uneasy space at the present time, between the stories and mythologies we once took stock in and the new narratives in which we will place our hopes.

But how do we write this story of our next chapter in history when we have done such a poor job of exploring and understanding and utilizing that which has come before us? As historian Daniel Boorstin notes:

> The nine cities of Troy, each built on the ruins of its predecessor, were accumulated over millennia, from the Stone Age till Roman times. . . . The Old World . . . more often than not . . . was built on the rubble of their ancestors' disappointed hopes. In America the archaeology of fast-moving men on a nearly empty continent was spread plain and thin on the surface. Its peculiar product was the abandoned place (the "ghost town") rather than the buried place. Its characteristic relics were things left by choice before they were used up.[4]

It's a familiar comment on the American sense of land and space: a history of restless expansion toward the new after partially consuming the old, a lighting out for the new territories on the frontier. This practice of discarding rather than reusing the old is one we have seen at work in the settling of the colony of Georgia, where a typical parcel of land was worked for a short, intense span of time and then abandoned for another parcel to be similarly exhausted in short order.

Our notion of self has been similarly portable: We can leave our feudal and European past behind and reshape our identity in the New World. This aspect of our culture has given rise to creativity and entrepreneurship and a general can-do spirit that is still attractive to many around the globe. But there is a downside to this dynamic sense of movement. Both Boorstin and Bridges touch upon it: a moral impatience and restlessness that does not take the time to rework the fabric of what has come before, to reuse those past ruins to build more solid foundations. There is something compelling about restoring what we've damaged, rather than moving on down the road to wreak havoc elsewhere. To a neutral zone of time, as articulated by Bridges, we need to add a neutral zone of space, to reflect on what next needs to be built (or not built) on prior ruins. Things broken, whether something as trivial as eggs or something much more profound like a dysfunctional economic order, call for pause and reflection.

Recognizing gaps in our knowledge. I wish I had remembered that egg cartons were stacked up freestanding in the dairy aisle. Or that the momentum of a grocery cart, moving along a well-waxed floor, takes a long time to stop. Some knowledge comes to us almost instantaneously. Other insights have to wait for, say, a physics course in college. Most of what we think we know is replete with gaps and requires time until gaps are filled in and information evolves into wisdom.

The marsh geomorphologist Denise Reed speaks to this issue of being cognizant of our ignorance when she made this observation about life on the coast: "Coastal restoration is much more complex than is generally understood. No one likes to admit it, but there are real gaps in our knowledge of how the coast works."[5] It's not just on the coast where our knowledge is spotty; it's throughout all of nature. We can act impulsively, as did those who trapped beavers in North America for the European craze for fur hats in the seventeenth century and thereby decimated a keystone population critical to nature's strategy for recharging our groundwater.[6] Those trappers did not intend to wreck the hydrology of North America. They were just trying to make a living. Nevertheless, their lack of knowledge of the systemic linkages in nature ultimately resulted in the transformation of our landscape.

We can act with what we believe to be forethought and rationality, such as the creation of a national grid system pushed through by Thomas Jefferson in the Land Ordinance Act of 1785 or later by the Homestead Act of 1862, which fostered the movement west through the promise of 160 acres of land per family.[7] But such ostensible forethought and rationality also sets in motion undesirable events (farming and ranching practices in arid ecosystems that eroded the land), events that again emphasize how little we know about the workings of nature. And we now seem to be moving into a new phase of environmental consciousness, placing our faith in science and technology to help us manage our ecosystems.[8]

Lost in this funhouse of human agency is a lack of humility about what we don't know and the willingness to place big bets on actions whose consequences are uncertain.[9] From time to time in business trade publications we find stories about entrepreneurs who bet the survival of a company on a big idea. We're fascinated by these cowboy creatives, a modern variant on the free spirit of America. But they're not laying down big bets with their own capital. As such, the personal consequences of their being wrong and losing are low. A responsible business thoroughly investigates the downside of a decision, ensuring that the gaps in knowledge are minimal to nonexistent. It has no intention of taking a business gamble of such magnitude that if the decision proves to be a bad one the entire company goes under. So why are we making big bets with our land and community, given the even more dire consequences if we bet wrong?

Our own family grocery business grew slowly and deliberately, opening our second store twenty-two years after the first in 1962, and our third location in 1971. With each new store opening, my father carefully researched the growth patterns in the city, the changes in consumer demand to better understand better what goods and services to offer, the changing thoughts about business practices that would help him manage several locations. Even then he sweated every new opening—not just initially but in the ensuing years as well. Dad knew better than anyone the gaps in his own understanding of the market and that successful grand openings did not necessarily translate into long-term positive results. His approach to decision making was grounded in deep study and forethought mixed with a sense that it took a long time before he would truly know the consequences of what he decided. He was reluctant to compound an initial, venturesome decision with other entrepreneurial moves until he knew he was on solid ground. His approach reminds me of the precautionary principle discussed in more detail in chapter two. Recognizing gaps in our knowledge, understanding that the road ahead has obstacles we are only dimly aware of, being deliberate and proactively cautious as we chart our growth forward as a business: These are helpful lessons to derive from living above the store.

Embracing the dialectic of creative rule making and rule breaking. I suppose it's virtually inevitable that a story about broken eggs ends up with a moral about not being able to make an omelet without cracking a few. But my interest is not so much about pain leading to gain. I'm more interested in the complex dynamics of breaking out of one's context.

The writer and philosopher Danah Zohar, in *SQ: Connecting with Our Spiritual Intelligence*, makes the point that the humanist tradition has been dominated by rational thinking, our intelligence quotient (IQ). In recent years, more attention has been paid to what we know emotionally or intuitively, our emotional intelligence or quotient (EQ). Zohar's work focuses on wrapping both IQ and EQ ways of understanding our world in the larger mantle of spiritual intelligence or spiritual quotient (SQ). If IQ is about what we know and EQ is about coping emotionally with a given reality, the SQ facilitates our questioning of that reality. Zohar notes:

> It is in its transformative power that SQ differs mainly from EQ. [M]y emotional intelligence allows me to judge what situation I am in and then to behave appropriately within it. This is working within the boundaries of the situation, allowing the situation to guide me. But my spiritual intelligence allows me to ask if I want to be in this particular situation in the first place. Would I rather change the situation, creating a better one?
>
> . . . Our culture is not stable. There is too much rapid change, ambiguity and uncertainty for us to be able to rely on wiring diagrams established in our first 18 years to get us through the rest of life. We have to use that third kind of thinking which involves creative rule-making and rule-breaking, so that we constantly rewire our brains as we go along.[10]

The need for creative rule making and rule breaking could not be more critical than at the present time. I think one would be hard-pressed to take stock of the state of the world today and not harbor a suspicion that things are not working out that well. Moreover, the kind of thinking that has shaped the current state of affairs—which assumes that we can continue to consume ever greater quantities of fossil fuel, dump eight billion tons of carbon into our atmosphere, and increase the overall temperature of the planet without facing the consequences of global warming—is not likely to get us out of this mess. Unfortunately, as the economist John Kenneth Galbraith has noted, we are hardwired to cling to conventional wisdoms:

> We associate truth with what most deeply accords with self-interest and personal well-being or promises best to avoid awkward

effort or unwelcome dislocation of life. We also find highly acceptable what contributes most to self-esteem. [Economic and social behavior] are complex, and to comprehend their character is mentally tiring. Therefore we adhere, as though to a raft, to those ideas which represent our understanding.[11]

What is needed is a viewpoint that illustrates that this old raft is leaky, an iconoclastic challenging of conventions that are no longer tenable. It's interesting in this respect to consider the term *iconoclast*, which has its roots in the notion of breaking icons or false idols and was originally a positive term connected with demythologizing and revealing the true nature of things. Today the term has a somewhat more ambivalent valence, connoting someone who may be a free thinker but may also be something of a troublemaker, stirring up the pot unnecessarily.

Egg breaking has a similar set of connotations. On the one hand, it's not that wise to launch ourselves impetuously down some new technological aisle without carefully considering what might be ahead. On the other hand, creative rule making and rule breaking can be positive, leading us to question the situation in which we find ourselves. In other words if the overall health of a system is to be nurtured, we need to be wise about which elements of that system need changing and which elements should be conserved.

I think back to our days in the grocery business, which was very conservative in its approach to growth, but iconoclastic in other respects—such as when my father began to hire minorities for leadership roles within the company. Or his inclusion on the shelves of so-called generics, cheaper-priced but equal-quality products that lacked the marketing pizzazz of national brands. Or the decision to move away from loss-leader pricing—a standard advertising practice of selling certain staple goods at a loss, to be made up from the overall volume purchasing—in favor of everyday low pricing. I can recall some of my father's senior management staff balking at his innovations. But he was insistent, and in the long run he was right. It was one factor among many that enabled us to hold on to a significant market share in town.

I keep these lessons in mind in the context of our real estate company, which aspires to this same iconoclastic tradition. It should. Sustainable business practices, after all, entail recovering older customs and values while also rewriting the rules. Living above the store provides a space within which to manage this play of continuity and change.

The significance of healing words. I don't recall what my father said to me immediately after I turned the green-and-white checkerboard vinyl floor into a yellow mess. But I'm fairly certain they were not words of reassurance at a time when a soft touch would have gone a long way. Ethicists, child psychologists, and spiritual leaders perhaps understand this best. Rabbi Joseph Telushkin's book, *Words That Hurt, Words That Heal*, should be a mandatory part of any business curriculum. The basic premise can be culled from the title and is one that any grade-school kid knows intuitively: You can do more damage with a critical comment than any amount of goodwill can create over the long term. Conversely, an encouraging word, when the situation would seem to call for reprimand, goes far.

The words I most have in mind are *thank you*. In a weeklong business seminar that John Ward and Ivan Landsberg conduct for family businesses, Ward queries almost rhetorically: "Why is it that the thing which is the least costly part of compensation to provide management is, for family businesses particularly, the most reluctantly given—saying 'Thank you'?"[12]

This same rhetorical question applies to businesses in general, particularly those aspiring to be learning companies. Learning companies by their very nature engage in creative rule making and rule breaking. They challenge so-called conventional wisdom. They try things that are untested. Learning companies also break eggs unintentionally on occasion. That's OK. In fact, it's better than OK. Breakage and failure are critical aspects of learning.[13] Anything other than the words *thank you* under such circumstances shuts down creativity and instills a basic fear of failure in its place. It's hard to be creative when the fear associated with failing is in the air.

There have been numerous times over the course of our company history when we have ventured into uncertain territory: the commitment to do all of our developments using LEED as a baseline, converting existing buildings to LEED, transferring green technologies and strategies to affordable housing projects, signing on to the 2030 Challenge with the commitment to dramatically reduce carbon emissions in all of our projects. These are cross-the-Rubicon moments. And my colleagues and I are often torn at such times, knowing that each public raising of the bar carries with it both the positive value of being in the vanguard of necessary change but also the negative consequence of possibly setting ourselves up for failure. Knowing that "failure" in this regard will be applauded is a critical element in a restorative business' repertoire.

So why the words *thank you*? I think because they acknowledge the opportunity provided to us to learn from our mistakes as well as the commonality embedded in the learning process. They are words that validate, words that restore, words that exhort us to pick ourselves up, wipe the egg off our face, and try again.

Retreat

Poet-writer-farmer Wendell Berry writes almost rapturously about living a unified life where the place of work and the place of home are integrated into each other:

> Once, some farmers, particularly in Europe, lived in their barns—and so were both at work and at home. Work and rest, work and pleasure, were continuous with each other, often not distinct from each other at all. Once, shopkeepers lived in, above, or behind their shops. . . .
> The modern specialist and/or industrialist in his modern house can probably have no very clear sense of where he is.[14]

Berry is probably right: A greater integration of work and home provides us with a moral compass that is lacking in the modern world. But to have a sense of the value of this integration you need to have some perspective, create some distance, retreat. Warren Bennis, an authority on leadership issues, is someone who places considerable value on the need to step away from the familiar: "All executives should practice the new three *R*'s: retreat, renewal, and return."[15]

But how do you retreat when you've seemed to live above a store your whole life? It's not a rhetorical question. The store seems to be with you always, like Janisse Ray's sense of the junkyard, quoted in the epigram to this chapter. And, as Ray suggests, this constant presence of living above the store, quite honestly, isn't always that easy to deal with. Bennis's three *R*'s framework provides at least a roadmap toward stepping away from the family store. It's a roadmap we'll be exploring throughout the remainder of this chapter, though we will add a fourth *R*, that of restoration, in the concluding section.

I thought I managed to step away from the family store when I went off to college, certain I would not return to my hometown. During the summer prior to my senior year I lived in Americus, Georgia, with my maternal grandparents. During the day I worked on the Lutz sweet potato farm. Nights I usually went over to one of the workers' houses to drink malted beer and swap stories. Weekends I spent researching my senior thesis, a study of Koinonia, a utopian experiment founded in the early 1960s outside of my grandparents' home (*Koinonia* is the Greek word for "communion through intimate participation"). Much of the research involved taking down the stories of those who lived at Koinonia, as well as residents, both white and black, in the surrounding communities. Many aspects of this utopian community were appealing: its focus on the land and creating a self-sufficient economy based on simple labor and basic needs, its democratic ethos of shared leadership, its diverse social composition. Blacks and whites lived together at Koinonia, worked the fields together, broke bread together at their communal meals. Several social justice movements and programs spun out of Koinonia, including the well-known international organization Habitat for Humanity. It was for that time and place a radical experiment in community that pissed off the local white establishment. An economic boycott of Koinonia took effect for a while. The boycott culminated in a drive-by bombing that killed no one but was intended to intimidate and communicate a message to residents to pack up and go elsewhere. The bombers were never caught. Koinonia is still there.

For me, though, despite many compelling features Koinonia, like most utopian experiments, lacked a sense of greater communal connectedness. It was isolated, separate. Utopia, from the Greek meaning "no place," works well by drawing clear boundaries between the small community it constructs and its larger context. This sense of an inclusive, small, tight-knit *we* versus a larger *they* seemed artificial. Koinonia was all about community, shaping its own ideal sense of how a diverse group of people should live together. But it was not of community. It lacked a basic sense of living above the store, of being part of a larger social order.

From undergraduate work focused on community and utopian experiments, I headed to graduate school and what I thought would be a career teaching literature. For me, retreat and renewal comes from literature. It provides the chance, even if it's momentary, to slip out of the store and see life through different eyes, wear different experiences. I did not realize this for a long time. In fact, only toward the end of my graduate studies did I get an inkling of the restorative nature of stories and storytelling. During my oral exams the historian Andy Delbanco asked me a question I'll never forget: "Martin, what to you is the most frightening moment in American literature?"

The question stopped me and my theoretical knowledge of texts dead. He was asking a "feeling" question, an "experience" question. Literature wasn't about being scared or inspired or saddened or touched, was it? It was about structures and strategies and mis-readings on the part of authors and readers and about the text itself, no? A frightening moment in literature? Was he kidding? He wasn't.

Delbanco proceeded to tell me what he considered the most frightening moment in American literature: chapter 93 in Melville's *Moby Dick*, which is tellingly titled "The Castaway." Pip, the black cabin boy on the ship, takes the place of an injured sailor on one of the small whaleboats used to harpoon the prey. The whaling sequence for Pip and the other sailors should have been as follows: A whale would breach near a whaleboat, one of the sailors would harpoon the prey, the whale would take off, pulling the small whaleboat behind it (the so-called Nantucket sleigh ride), and eventually tire, at which point the crew would bring the whale alongside the main ship, where its parts were dissected and packed in the hull.

Pip, game to fill in for the injured sailor, is nevertheless scared of the small boat and the impending hunt. And so when a whale breaches nearby, Pip leaps out of the boat just as the whale is harpooned. The whaleboat takes off, pulled by the whale, and Pip is stranded in the water, watching his crewmates recede quickly out of sight.

In order to appreciate better the force of this story it helps to locate ourselves within the world Pip experienced. Imagine being out on a vast ocean, waves pushing you up and pulling you down as you tread water, trying to keep afloat, your wet clothes a hindrance. You see no one in any direction all the way out to the horizon, and though you know your mates are out there somewhere in a small boat, you have no hope that they will find you. The sun is high and strong and starting to bake your skin. You're thirsty and dry-mouthed, but there's no fresh water to drink. You hope the sun will start to wane, hope the afternoon will trail off into a cooler night air, and then think about the blackness of the ocean and sky at night. And all you can do is try to stay afloat as long as possible.

Here's Melville's description of that moment:

> It was a beautiful, bounteous day; the spangled sea calm and cool, and flatly stretching away, all round, to the horizon, like goldbeater's skin hammered out to the extremest. Bobbing up and down in that sea, Pip's ebon head showed like a head of cloves. No boat-knife was lifted when he fell so rapidly astern. Stubb's back was turned upon him; and the whale was winged. In three minutes, a whole mile of shoreless ocean was between Pip and Stubb. Out from the centre of the sea, poor Pip turned his crisp, curling, black head to the sun, another lonely castaway, though the loftiest and the brightest.
>
> . . . The sea had jeeringly kept his finite body up, but drowned the infinite of his soul. Not drowned entirely, though. Rather carried down alive to wondrous depths, where strange shapes of the unwarped primal world glided to and fro before his passive eyes. . . . He saw God's foot upon the treadle of the loom, and spoke it; and therefore his shipmates called him mad. So man's

insanity is heaven's sense; and wandering from all mortal reason, man comes at last to that celestial thought, which, to reason, is absurd and frantic; and weal or woe, feels then uncompromised, indifferent as his God.

Eventually, the whaleboat crew returns, finds Pip, and hauls him back into the boat. But from that day forward, Pip, who has lost his sense of reason, can only babble incomprehensibly and is to all intents and purposes a lost soul.

I come back to this passage every once in a while to understand more fully Melville's dense, eloquent writing. I'm not sure I'll ever get the full hang of what he's talking about. But Delbanco was right. That sense of being alone on the open sea, no one in sight, abandoned by one's shipmates, doubtful that any one will return, is frightening. That moment lost at sea captures the full magnitude of the notion of retreat.

There are other meanings in this passage that I have come to notice over time. There is, for sure, a sense of nature, wild and untamed, irrespective of human efforts to subdue it through economic ventures like whaling. There is also that sense of need for community in the face of such wildness. It is a need that goes unaddressed as Pip's shipmates abandon him to pursue economic opportunity—fortune and fame—in the guise of capturing a whale. And finally there is that sense of senselessness, of being set adrift alone, without boundaries and context and values, without colleagues that don't know enough to turn back, and leaders who keep forging blithely ahead, unaware of the damage left in their wake.

If I had to sum up concisely what a nonsustainable business is, I would point to this passage—illustrating the jettisoning of basic values in the wake of economic opportunism. If I had to look for a contrasting example to the experience of living above the store, it would be Melville's description of becoming a castaway.

Renewal

Bennis does not indicate when the process of retreat ends and the process of renewal begins. There probably isn't a neat demarcation between the two, as each person discovers for him- or herself when that transition happens. For me, it probably occurred when I joined an old college friend, Ben Sher, on an eighteen-month trek across Africa.

I was at a crossroads then—at the end of my time in graduate school, about to take on a professional career but not ready just yet to make that call. The grocery store business had been sold to Kroger not too long before, but my father was still running the operation on behalf of the new owner. We had yet to begin the rebirth of the company as a real estate business. Ben and I had been talking on and off since our undergraduate days about an extended journey together, and so here seemed the time to make good on that promise.

I bought and outfitted a jeep in Gibraltar and met Ben in Algiers, setting off on a route that would take us across the Sahara to Lagos, Nigeria; from there through the forests of the Congo to Mombasa, Kenya; and from there snaking our way south and west through Tanzania, Zimbabwe, and Namibia; and then on back to South Africa, where I eventually sold the jeep and returned home. For a little over a year and half, Ben (as well as his wife and their newborn son) and I lived "in the bush," except for moments of respite in cities like Nairobi and Bulawayo and Capetown.

It's an odd thing, travel, situated uneasily between the surface voyeurism of tourism and the depth of residing in a place. Ben and I were *with* place, but not *of* place, seeing our own culture as if for the first time through the lens of cultures that weren't familiar to us. The stories of our time in Africa could fill this entire chapter and more. I'll focus on a few moments that particularly fostered a sense of renewal, facilitating a readiness to return home.

There was, first of all, my home away from home, the jeep, clearly organized by the influences of growing up in a grocery business. Part of the back of the jeep contained our kitchen equipment; another, massive amounts of dried, nonperishable food items. Another section of the back of the jeep was devoted to fresh foods—eggs and the little bits of fruit and produce that we would pick up in village markets (often nothing more than a roadside stand with a few items arranged on corrugated cardboard). There was a small prep area in the back for cooking, a set of shelves containing reading materials, and even a small refrigerator hooked up to the car battery. Lining the inside panels of the jeep were twelve twenty-liter jerry cans, six for water and six for diesel fuel. We topped off both fuel and water whenever we could, since supplies of both in many parts of our travels were often hard to come by. I slept in a fold-up tent installed on the roof. It's funny when I think about it now: I was literally living above the store.

Initially I had no view out the back from the driver's seat because the jeep was so crammed with provisions. Over time I lightened the load. Even with less stuff it was not lost on either Ben or me the surfeit of materials we were carrying with us in comparison to everyone we met along the way. Facing us every day of our journey was the fact that roughly half the planet's inhabitants lived on less than two dollars a day. We learned to make what we did have go farther, especially water. One hundred twenty liters of water, my total carrying capacity, would, based on American consumption patterns, be gone in a day. With often weeks between clean sources of water (it took us about two months to cross the Sahara), we clearly needed a strategy of conservation for the long haul. All these lessons—making do with less, conserving what we had, experiencing the stark disparity between the haves and have-nots—became an integral part of what we would bring home.

Also memorable were the places to which we were invited along the way. There was the elementary school in rural Tanzania where Ben and I sat in on a sixth-grade marine biology class. Here these kids were, living more than three hundred miles from the Indian Ocean, a place they might never see, and yet learning detailed aspects of the coastal environment. I learned more about the Georgia coast in that simple, concrete-block classroom halfway around the world than I had ever been exposed to as a child living twenty miles from the Atlantic Ocean.

There was also a rural health clinic in Tanzania that we visited, which was heavily supported by the Norwegian government. It was an incredible facility, clean, well staffed by a local nursing contingent and a cadre of local and foreign doctors, and reasonably provisioned in terms of medical equipment and medicines. *Reasonably provisioned* is the operative phrase here, since this small clinic in the Western world might be expected to treat forty or fifty patients in the course of a day. This clinic was overrun, however, by hundreds of AIDS patients, critical-care and triage cases spilling down the halls and out into the sun-baked courtyard, a sea of need that would challenge most of us to rethink the Brundtland Commission definition of *sustainability*.

Lessons from these two site visits are many and only apparently discrete: Our visit to the Tanzanian schoolroom underscores our own lack of environmental education in the United States. The health clinic visit underscores our own incapacity to fathom (or unwillingness to see) the complex spiral of poverty in much of the world. But the two are intertwined, with degradation of the natural order—for example, depleting adjacent forests for basic fuel—often serving as a short-term means for the poorest parts of the world to survive.[16] That too became a lesson with which to return home.

There were occasional respites from our journey when we would arrive in a major city, always a bit of a jarring contrast. In Nairobi we agreed to house-sit for an expat on vacation, a common-enough practice within the Western tribal world. The expat had someone "familiar" (read: "white") to guard the house, while the Western traveler (in this case Ben and I) got palatial digs for free. The expat family, typically headed by a business executive or diplomat, lived in its own guarded compound located within a larger luxurious subdivision mostly inhabited by other foreign businesspeople and dignitaries. The house and its surroundings were worlds away from the vast majority of the city's residents, although the extreme wealth of the one and the extreme poverty of the other made the house a constant target of theft. Armed guards typically patrolled the house and neighborhood twenty-four hours a day. Meanwhile, inside the compound, a team of gardeners, cooks, house-keepers, and drivers provided the expat residents with whatever they wanted. Our instruction set as house sitters included the charge "not to spoil the house servants." I take away from that distasteful moment the sense that most businesses today in many ways function like these expat families: siloed from the general populace, concerned primarily about protecting the wealth ensconced behind high walls, and mistaking their lives in gilded cages as somehow liberating and desirable.

The most dangerous moment of our year-and-a-half journey occurred through our own foolish actions. Ben and I were crossing the Sahara and decided, midway, to take a one-hundred-mile shortcut between two points on our itinerary. The Sahara is a beautiful landscape, an engaging place of shifting views and tones of color as arresting as anything I have seen. The general route through the Sahara is well marked and traveled, with white piste markers planted along the way every few miles and well-beaten, rib-jarring corrugated expanses of track that are easy to navigate if difficult to drive. Ben and I decided we preferred an off-road, softer-sand, quieter route and so took a shortcut, triangulating between two points, off the beaten path. And nothing happened. But halfway through our three-day shortcut, when we were sitting out in the evening light admiring a gradual swirl of sunset pastels that looked like God was finger-painting in the sky, it occurred to us that if our jeep broke down, we would probably die. We were too far away from the main piste to walk for help, and even at that, the main road saw only a few passersby a day on a road that could easily be five miles wide. Even if a diesel lorry or water truck or local jitney happened to pass by, a remote possibility to begin with, it would be highly unlikely that they would pass anywhere near us. And forget the idea of anyone finding us along our self-selected shortcut. The lesson of community, the need for others even at the edges of self-reliance, hit us powerfully. Even Thoreau, ensconced at Walden Pond for more than two years, enjoyed the gifts of chocolate-chip cookies from nearby Concord. It was the lesson of Pip, literally brought home to us.

After about eighteen months in Africa I returned to Savannah, ready (if not exactly prepared) to begin my work with this old-new family business involving real estate.

Return

Samuel Johnson, the English writer and critic who compiled the first English-language dictionary, wrote one of the more compelling essays I have ever read on the complex dynamics of returning home. Appearing in *The Rambler* on October 15, 1751, the essay tells the fictional story of Serotinus, a young man who leaves his village to seek fame and fortune elsewhere.

Serotinus is successful in business and so retires at a young age to devote the remainder of his life to hedonistic pleasures. But he becomes obsessed, in his early retirement, with thoughts of returning to his hometown, fantasizing about how his return would cause some to admire him, others to approach him with hope that he would bless them with his philanthropy, and still others to regard him with awkward respect and terror of his power. Serotinus further spins out his fantasies, imagining the noblesse oblige with which he will meet and greet the acclamations of the locals. He scripts his return with methodical precision and sets out for home. Here is what Serotinus finds:

> I had been absent too long to obtain the triumph which had flattered my expectations. Of the friends whose compliments I expected, some had long ago moved to distant provinces, some had lost in the maladies of age all sense of another's prosperity, and some had forgotten our former intimacy amidst care and distresses. Of three whom I had resolved to punish for their former offences by a longer continuance of neglect, one was, by his own industry, raised above my scorn, and two were sheltered from it in the grave. All those whom I loved, feared, or hated, all whose envy or whose kindness I had hopes of contemplating with pleasure, were swept away, and their place was filled by a new generation with other views and other competitions; and among many proofs of the impotence of wealth, I found that it conferred upon me very few distinctions in my native place.[17]

The name *Serotinus* is a Latin word meaning "late blooming" or "late maturing." It's an appropriate name for someone whose drive to succeed in the outside world has inhibited internal growth. While Serotinus seems to have retreated, renewed himself, and returned home, he has not engaged in any substantive way in the type of growth trajectory Warren Bennis contemplates. His is not a trajectory of true discovery and self-restraint. As such, his return home brings him squarely back, emotionally and spiritually, to the disquieted youth he had always been. Serotinus, whose name could be parsed out as "Sir-Rot-in-Us,"[18] does indeed suggest a person whose external successes belie a certain rottenness on the inside. Facing that rot-in-us head-on facilitates our understanding of returning home, as well as the restorative processes of which returning home plays an important part.

Although I wasn't aware of it at the time I returned from Africa to begin working with Melaver, Inc., the message underlying Johnson's essay was apt. Eventually we have to "put our own inner house in order."[19] Such housekeeping, a largely internal ordering of one's thoughts, feelings, and experiences in the context of returning home, includes these five deliberate acts: recovering an instinct for place, restraining certain (prior) patterns of behavior, integrating or synthesizing one's memories with the collective memory of the community, using one's liminal status as a returnee to foster covenantal relationships, and immersing oneself into the body politic as a full and complete member of the social order. Let's consider each of these acts in a bit more detail.

Recovering certain instincts for place. Serotinus's homecoming reflects very little sense for place beyond its serving as a stage to showcase his arrival. Most of us, fortunately, are more in touch with our surroundings. Steve Olson, the Georgia State University professor who is the focus of our discussion of the Hall-Tonna Values Inventory in chapter three, kicked off one of our company retreats by asking our staff to close our eyes and imagine a place that provides a sense of calm. The vast majority imagined a scene from nature. I was no different, creating in my mind's eye a picture of the dunes and sea oats just beyond the porch of our house on Tybee Island. It was one of the first places I returned to upon landing in Savannah from Africa.

This tendency to find serenity in certain images from the natural world is referred to as the savanna instinct. It's not the wide-open expanse of the ocean (e.g., Melville), nor the enclosed world of a dense tropical forest (e.g., Africa), but is something in-between. A savanna landscape provides a pleasure of green vistas, a sense of protection and wonderment, and enables one to make of nature a personal, special place.[20]

Camille Kingsolver, a contributing author to her mother Barbara Kingsolver's work *Animal, Vegetable, Miracle,* notes her firsthand experience of such places:

> When I was a kid, summer was as long as a lifetime. A month could pass without me ever knowing what day of the week it was. Time seemed to stretch into one gigantic, lazy day of blackberry picking and crawdad hunting. My friends and I would pretty much spend our lives together, migrating back and forth between the town swimming pool and the woods, where we would pretend to be orphans left to our own devices in the wilderness. School was not on our minds. Our world was green grass, sunshine, and imagination.[21]

Recovery of this savanna instinct, then, is a constant renewal of an emotional bond between nature and ourselves. For me this entailed a reconnection with landscapes long familiar: houses along the Georgia coast—at least the older ones—sited well back from the ebb and flow of tides, the accretion and erosion of sand. There was also the landscape of the urban core of my hometown, which called for extensive green open spaces to help with air ventilation and rainwater conveyance and overall sociability.

The return home calls for a recovery of the savanna instinct.

Restraining certain (prior) patterns of behavior. It's an odd feeling to enter an American grocery store after spending extended time shopping in the street markets of Africa. The huge, long aisles, the seemingly endless assortments of cereals, and cookies, and sodas—who needs all this stuff? It's an interesting twist, coming from my grocery background.[22] I thought back to the wares spread out on old recycled fifty-five-gallon drums in numberless villages throughout Africa. OK, so that's a bit too lean and scarce, but do we need all of this junk? The question links back to Serotinus, the epitome of conspicuous consumption.

Putting our own house in order means getting our hands around our own consumption practices, understanding the extent to which such practices are tied to issues of self-esteem, and learning to be more comfortable with ourselves and less comfortable with our selves' wanting more. That's a mouthful, easier to say than do. I have a long way to go in that regard. But I feel that our best hope for reducing our impact on our home is less acquisition, less consumption, less waste. Serotinus's pleasure-seeking excessiveness is not pretty, particularly when multiplied on a national or global order. If our collective impact on the globe is calculated by our population times the amount we acquire times the efficiency of our technologies (often referred to as IPAT or $I = P \times A \times T$), the greatest potential for moderation is in our consumption practices.

A helpful tool in moving us toward restrained consumption comes from an unlikely source: the twelve-step program originally developed by Alcoholics Anonymous and now utilized by numerous organizations to address recovery from addictive, compulsive, and behavioral problems. The twelve-step program is characterized by these components:[23]

- Admitting that one has a serious, uncontrollable problem
- Recognizing that an outside power could help
- Conscious reliance upon that power
- Inventorying and admitting character defects
- Seeking deliverance from these defects
- Making amends to those one has harmed
- Helping others with the same problem[24]

If we attended a twelve-step program aimed at fostering a sustainable social order, it might sound like this: "Hello, my name is Martin, and I have a problem with overconsumption. It's a struggle. I feel as though I'm divided against myself, split between what I think and how I often act.[25] Each year at our company retreat we give the 'Bigfoot Award' to the person who has the largest negative impact on the environment. I 'win' it every year. My consumptive addictions go beyond travel to nice clothes, unusual watches. These purchases make me feel better, for at least a short time. And then the feeling tends to subside, until the next wave of consumptive purchases ensues. I need the society of you all to help me realize that my sense of purpose cannot come from a bottomless shopping bag."

"Hello, our name is Melaver, Inc., and we have a problem with over-consumption."

"Hello, our name is Georgia, and we have a problem with overconsumption."

"Hello, our name is America, and we have a problem with overconsumption."

In this case, the outside power that can help us is, paradoxically enough, ourselves. Just as there is no "away" in the sense of throwing things away, our outside power resides in each other. Leveraging that outside power, inventorying and admitting the compulsive behaviors in one another, recognizing our global fellowship, seeking deliverance from those defects by helping each other with our addiction: These are some of the critical first steps that will help us formulate a multiwedge strategy for restoration. The move toward home, to my mind, entails a more thoughtful acknowledgment of who we each are, a deeper understanding of the help people and place can provide us, and a profound determination to leverage those "outside powers" to enable us to make amends and help others with the same problem.

Integrating one's memories with the collective memory of the community. After having been away for so long, your memories can play tricks on you. Despite Serotinus's narcissism, people in his hometown were not living their lives wondering what he was doing.

But the challenge of memory, in one's absence from home, goes deeper than that explored in Johnson's essay. There was so much, for example, that I had forgotten in the time I was away. Simple things in some respects, like the actions of the dunes and sea oats in front of our Tybee house. I remember as a kid watching my mom gesturing and screaming at folks to stop uprooting the sea oats along the dunes. She looked like some frantic sailor at sea, gesticulating wildly in the air for help—which, in a sense, she was. She would explain to my sisters and me that the sea oats helped secure the dunes, which in turn impeded erosion. I understood but still cringed and ducked out of sight every time Mom expressed her thoughts loudly and clearly to the sea-oats pickers.

Years later Tybee has a series of wondrous secondary and tertiary dune structures along much of its eastern shore. Sand fences protect most of the dunes from intrusion and erosion, while bridges now carry beach-combers from parking areas to the water without touching the dunes. Still, every once in a while a visitor trespasses the dunes to pick a few sea oats. And there I am, screaming at the top of my lungs to tell him to stop. *My God*, I think, *I'm becoming more like my mom by the year.*

That's using collective memory on a small, personal scale. The lessons of collective memory on a larger scale are easily found, provided one is open to them. The group of German Protestants from Salzburg, who accompanied Oglethorpe and established the neighboring settlement of Ebenezer, were farmers and so brought with them agrarian knowledge and practices that were desperately needed by the tradesman and arti-sans who found Savannah.[26] More recent examples of needed collec-tive memory include understanding which methods of oystering ensure a stable crop each year, or knowledge of how marsh grass serves to filter impurities, or knowledge of how houses need to be sited to make use of prevailing winds and provide shelter from the summer heat—knowledge the inhabitants of our coastal area once knew but have lost over time. With our culture on the move relentlessly, changing jobs and residences every four years, we have lived through two generations of not having much experience of staying put in one locale, sharing collective experi-ences, living in human habitats of quality.

Putting our own house in order entails the pursuance and cultivation and transmittal of collective memory.

Leveraging one's liminal status to foster covenantal relationships. Serotinus blew a golden opportunity. When I look back at the eco-mafia group that comprised our recycling task force in Savannah (chapter five), it is striking that almost all were returnees to the community. They were able to view the community through bifocal lenses, melding the old-timer's sense of the way things are typically done in the community with the newbie's sense of innovation and potential. Returnees, in short, occupy a special position as boundary spanners in a community, with the capacity to connect history to possibility, continuity to change.

I can remember as a kid going out to dinner occasionally on Sunday evenings and the constant interruptions from other diners as they dropped by our table to say hello. I hated this sense of intrusion and embraced the anonymity that retreat to other locales offered. Now I have come to enjoy the rich, complex social network of my hometown, the sense of interconnectedness of it all.

Ours is a town of tight connections. This is in stark contrast to the loose-tie cities that attract the swoop and swarm of "cultural creatives" who move about from one culturally hip town to the next without putting down substantive roots.[27] But if this creative class truly is looking for deeper ties to community, as one sociology scholar contends, our communities need to learn to be equally adaptive and creative in finding ways to incorporate new people into the old. The new provide our communities with rich nutrients from other ecosystems, if we will let them. Our communities need to function socially like our marsh grasses do biologically: as an ecotone, a liminal space between different environments, absorbing the incoming so as to recharge the system on an ongoing basis.

Creating covenantal relations within a community involves a two-way adaptive capacity, integrating the new into the old with the resultant mix being neither entirely new nor entirely the status quo. As someone who stepped away from Savannah for an extended period of time, only to eventually return, I see my community with the lens of both an outsider and an insider—a sentiment Jack Leigh seems to express in the epigram that opens this chapter. It is this bifocal vision that facilitates the fostering of covenantal relationships within a community.

Immersing oneself into the body politic as a full and complete member of the social order. One of the things that struck me on my visit to that elementary school in Tanzania was the informed, polite, and yet challenging ways in which a sixth-grade class of students engaged Ben and me in a discussion of American politics, U.S. foreign policy in the Middle East, and the image of Africa in the minds of most Americans. Their passion and knowledge and engagement was inspiring. It's still very much with me to this day, as a touchstone not just for how I would like my own kids to be, but how I would like to engage in the public sphere. Putting our own house in order means becoming informed and engaged citizens, relearning the art of deep listening as well as honest and respectful disagreement. These arts, critical components of educated, communal discourse, have been on the decline for decades but seem to have virtually disappeared since the repeal of the Fairness Doctrine in 1987.[28]

Over time, my colleagues and I have gradually become more politically engaged: lobbying for a recycling program, advocating for a graywater ordinance (one of the first of its kind in the country), pushing for various institutional buildings (schools, libraries) to adopt green building practices, pushing for various carbon-reduction strategies throughout the community, and so on. Perhaps more significant than these initiatives, however, is the quiet evolution we have undergone in terms of our willingness and capacity to engage in the public arena. It's a subtle and quiet change, largely unremarkable to the casual observer, and, for those who live in pockets of political activism in the United States, probably not all that newsworthy. But it's a significant change at least at the local level in my hometown. I feel it personally. Those who return "from the wilderness," I think, not only have the capacity to recognize that old-style siloed politics will not be transformative. They are also well positioned to assist in what author Gus Speth refers to as shaping a new environmental politics that spans the full range of social and environmental justice issues.[29] Living above the store means engaging with what's transpiring on the streets below your windows.

Restoration

After a period of retreat and renewal I returned home, having never really left in the first place. My journey toward restoration is wrapped up in the journey of my colleagues at work. We are like the band of travelers from Chaucer's *Canterbury Tales*, a motley assortment bound together in a common journey, a moveable feast, picking up fellow travelers along the way, bringing in more people who become part of the community. Before we realize it, the collective *we* in the process of restoring ourselves grows beyond the confines of our small business to envelop a small social order.

My own journey toward self-restoration is also wrapped up in the palimpsest of stories played out before me, stories that come from the mind-set of living above the store. They are stories of place and stories of people. Some of those stories have to do with learning to say no to paths that lead us away from who we are, as in the case of our negotiations with Balch & Bingham in their Birmingham law offices. Some of those stories entail failure, as was the case with the Triangle Site, clarified as a larger role we needed to play in the community. Some of those stories read like cautionary morality tales: a sister who led me to reflect on overweening pride or a guide such as Paul Hawken who led us to a meditation on value. Some stories carry with them promise and hope, such as our engagement with the Fellwood neighborhood. There are stories about family and staff wrestling with the notion of identifying a higher purpose for a business and stories about colleagues at work who help exemplify what that purpose is. Each story functions much like Kermode's notion of a new classic that is placed on a bookshelf among the prior classics: shifting ever so slightly the way we were positioned before, enabling us to rethink what we have said and done in the past so as to renew our sense of what still needs to be done.

Many of the stories told throughout this book address a variety of fractures in our culture that leave us isolated from one another, disjointed relationships with the land around us, disconnections among the sectors of our society. Embedded in these stories of restoration are acts of repair, acts that involve travel back to the time and place of the initial rupture, travel that is as much emotional and spiritual as it is physical.

Stories of restoration, acts of repair. A psychologist might point to my story of the broken eggs as a master narrative in this regard: a journey back in time to revisit, repair, and ultimately restore damage done years before. Perhaps that is the case. It gives me pause to consider that a lifelong focus on sustainable practices and community perhaps originates in a moment of disruption experienced long ago. Living above the store engages us in a palimpsest of stories we have lived with intimately most of our lives, an engagement that asks of us, What do we want to make of these experiences that have come before us? How do they all fit together?

These stories, then, serve as a bridge, connecting a sense of being to a sense of becoming, connecting the company we have always been with the company we are evolving into. The stories told throughout this book, stories that involve both principles and practices of living above the store, are the basis for our becoming a sustainable business.

Coda

During our travels in Africa, Ben and I found ourselves waiting around in the town of Kisingani (in what is now the Democratic Republic of the Congo) for a ferry to take us down the Congo River to Bukavu, located on the border of Rwanda and Burundi. I think we waited about two weeks, but there didn't seem to be much of an alternative. The overland route to the border, a distance of some five hundred miles, was seldom traveled and said to be less of a road than a slow slog through extensive stretches of mudholes that, it was rumored, could mire us down for six months until the rainy season ended. Much preferable to put our jeep on the ferry and enjoy a nice float downriver. It was the familiar route everyone took.

And so we waited for two weeks, until the ferry finally arrived.

Our jeep was second in line to be loaded onto the ferry, just behind a Unimog, a huge German surplus military jeep with tires as tall as our vehicle. The crane lifted the Unimog, swung around to position it onto the ferry, and then, without warning, cables came loose, and the Unimog was dropped into the Congo River.

Pandemonium ensued for the rest of the day: yelling and screaming all around, frantic though vain attempts to save the Unimog, and equally frenetic energy focused on fixing the crane.

And so that next morning, Ben and I were faced with a dilemma: stay the course and have our jeep loaded onto the ferry, despite our sense that the crane and its attendant systems were broken beyond repair, or take a chance on driving the five hundred miles to the border along an unknown, unchartered route.

We took the path less traveled.

Of the many stories that are laid, one upon the next, to provide a rounded sense of the restorative business I have been a part of, this one is foundational. Strange that it is only recently that I have been able to recall it. Its moral, at least for me, is fairly clear regarding the path business must take in the years to come.

We know already—or at least we should—what the well-traveled road has wrought. It seems myopically foolish to queue up to go down that route. True, that route is so familiar. And with that familiarity comes a sense of security and safety. But at the end of the day it's a false sense of security. We cannot rely on that route to get us where we need to go. And the alternative? The route Ben and I chose was indeed less populated with travelers. And we did have our adventures. At one point, the only time during our extended time in Africa, our jeep skidded off the slick, wet clay path, and we ended up with our jeep listing precariously, its two front wheels about four feet off the ground. But practically a whole village from nearby came to our rescue, righted our jeep, and sent us on our way. I could not think of a more apt extended metaphor for the sustainable path facing us all than the way this particular journey played out: pursuing an unfamiliar but necessary course that entails the helping hands of an entire community to get us through the rough patches.

This story of forking paths recalls another story from Africa, though it's not mine. It's a moment from Joseph Conrad's *Heart of Darkness*, adapted into the film *Apocalypse Now* (and transplanted to the jungles of Vietnam/Cambodia).

In the film Captain Willard, played by Martin Sheen, is sent by the military to retrieve a rogue general, Kurtz, played by a demonic and overweight Marlon Brando, who has holed up in the deepest recesses of the jungle and created mayhem and destruction. When Willard finally confronts Kurtz face-to-face, the general tells the captain contemptuously, "You're nothing but an errand boy sent by a grocery clerk."

That line has always gotten under my skin. But as it turns out errand boys sent by grocery clerks have an important mission to play. Some errand boys, like Pulitzer Prize–winning author James Alan McPherson, grow up to write powerfully about social justice. And other errand boys get to be part of a real estate company that is trying to make a difference in the community, shaping a land-community ethic that is ecologically sound and ethically mature.[30]

All of us, whether we work in government, in the not-for-profit world, in academia, or in business, confront situations that are, in various ways, like Kurtz in *Apocalypse Now*, laying waste to our communities. All of us face a choice similar to the one confronting Ben and me many years ago, between an untenable status quo and a sustainable alternative whose path is but hazily comprehended. I would like to suggest we each take stock of where we are and where we are going. And recognize that in small but significant ways, we errand boys, you and I, sent by grocery clerks, have an important mission to play in communicating a vision of a land-community ethic, in demonstrating how a sustainable ethos is practiced, in shaping a broad covenant running with the land, and in showing that living above the store can be deeply restorative.

OPERATING INSTRUCTIONS

*In some sense, we've run out of our story, which was the
story of taking power over nature. It's not that we've
finished that, but we've gotten ahead of ourselves, and
we don't know what the next story is after that.*
　　　　—W. Daniel Hillis, from Stewart Brand,
　　　　　　The Clock of the Long Now[1]

*My vision of the future no longer relies on a world
without troubles and cares. Rather it is a world where
the challenges are realizable. Such a vision is based on
a scenario in which the human imagination, drive, and
competence combine to meet the enormous hurdles of
. . . environmental restoration.*
　　　　—Peter Schwartz, *The Art of the Long View*[2]

Mark Dowie, in a book about the environmentalist movement at the
close of the twentieth century, tells a story whose essence is likely to
be familiar to most readers. The context is an international gathering
of environmentalists in 1993 in Esalen, California. This high-powered
group began its time together by going around the room, each person
introducing him- or herself, one by one. One of the last to speak was
Jeanette Armstrong, an Okanagan Indian from British Columbia. Here's
what Armstrong said:

Listening to those introductions confirmed what I have heard and feared about whites. Every introduction was about yourself, not about your community. You seem to have no community connections. If that's true, I'm sorry for you. In our culture, we identify ourselves in relation to our group. We don't know who we are except in relation to our family, our community, and the land that is our life. We don't know ourselves unless we know how nature works. Our language reflects the language of the birds and flowers and trees. I identify with my people and with the plants; and I am the river too. Our first law is the law of the natural world that gave us life. We cannot do anything that injures the natural world. We would be injuring ourselves. You can't imagine the pain your society creates by breaking up our connections to our land and our community. Grand Coulee Dam flooded the land of our ancestors, and we were "relocated." Our children were taken away to be educated at residential schools, and they returned without any sense of community. They didn't know how to relate to each other, or to plants and animals in a loving way. Your disconnections with your community ruin ours. I'm happy to be here with you, but mostly I feel grief for you. And I'm afraid for the world.[3]

I can only imagine the pain of being in the room at that moment and the awkward quiet that must have followed Armstrong's words and the difficulty of seeing oneself in the reflection of her mirror. But I can also imagine the thrill of self-discovery that she provided. Her words resonate with me: *We don't know who we are except in relation to our family, our community, and the land that is our life.* That is what this book has been all about.

I began this book with a story of a project where we put our foot down and said no to doing business the same old way. I focused the pages that followed in a more affirmative vein, looking at a number of principles a company can adopt that enable identification in relation to a group, that facilitate restoring who we are. The processes involved in managing *how* we work with one another inform *what* we do and *why.*

The actions involved in managing a sustainable business become integrated into the sustainable end products we provide.

Living Above the Store tries to evoke the centrifugal rippling effect of a pebble dropped in a body of water—as clichéd as that metaphor may be. We start with the place where we live and the people who share that place with us, taking stock of both in ways that enable us to recover our context and a better sense of self within that context. Part of the recovery of self involves restraint: restraining those external influences that over the years may have brought us considerable information but have inhibited our sense of curiosity and impoverished our capacity for wisdom.

The principle of restraint opens us up to a set of practices that foster collaborative learning and dialectical engagement. We don't all agree with one another. Nevertheless, our ongoing give-and-take resolves itself rather magically in a synthesis of values that also synthesizes our sense of who we are individually with who we are in a greater social context. At first that social context is the small circle of a company. We draw on our diverse differences and skills and life experiences to shape a stronger sense of collective spirit oriented toward a set of shared values and common purpose.

Instead of competing with other business firms, we compete with ourselves, struggling to shape a sustainable business that is in harmony with the natural world. As we work as a company toward that larger challenge, we shape covenants with key partners. The notion of *we* in restoring who we are is continually broadening to include all sectors of society, with the ideal of realizing a land-community ethic that is restorative for both humans and nature.

Managing this process has its challenges. Every additional ripple brings new voices and personalities and individual needs into the mix. Continual monitoring and tinkering with the sustainable business is called for, to ensure congruence of values and purpose among the constituents of this organically expanding community. More questions are asked, perhaps entirely new ones, perhaps old questions that suddenly have new relevance: Do we continue to have an abiding sense of place and of people? What does a land-community ethic mean to us these days?

Have we remained true to our commitment to engender meaning and purpose for all with whom we come into contact? Are we enabling our staff members and others to realize their highest potential?

How about we as a company? Are we still working toward realizing our highest potential? Can we push ourselves higher up the sustainability pyramid and still be in business? Have we sufficiently monitored the pace and nature of our growth as a company? Are we attending sufficiently to all aspects of our three performance organizers? Are we building true covenants in the community that run with the land? Are we leveraging our business to work deeply and collaboratively alongside the other sectors of society? Managing a sustainable business entails a restless questioning about how our values are evolving.

The questions, much like the repetitive but evolving story in the film *Groundhog Day*, always seem to return with renewed force and significance. This is also the case with numerous creative tensions that shape these questions and give them a compelling, dialectical force. Such tensions include the creative friction between a company's past history and the legacy it aspires to, between the essential nature of a company and what it is capable of, between the sense of meaning and purpose of the individual staff member and the sense of meaning and purpose for the company as a whole, having an optimal impact on the social order while minimizing our impact on nature, between abstract management principles and concrete management practices, between the needs of our land and the needs of our community. To manage a restorative business is to nurture these tensions in innovative, inspiring, productive, and fulfilling ways.

Managing a restorative business is about the uneasy synthesis of these tensions. It is about integrating the needs of land and community. It is also about integrating ourselves more firmly into place and people, assimilating each of us into a business culture in which we share a sense of purpose and mission. It is about incorporating the business culture into a larger community of placeholders, serving as stewards of both our land and our community. *Living Above the Store* is about integrating work into the other aspects of our lives.

A sustainable business puts down roots by locating itself in the context of people and place. It flourishes amidst diversity, with organisms jostling with one another and yet working in concert. A sustainable business comes into its own by realizing and synthesizing the diverse values of staff members. It matures as it succeeds in making its own sense of a land-community ethic shared by the larger social context, creating covenants that run with the land and shaping congruence among the sectors of society. Living as individuals, who we are as a business and who we are as a larger community are tied together.

Bo Burlingham has written about mission-driven companies such as ours that attempt to "build a better way of life in their own little corner of the globe." One problem Burlingham finds with such companies is that they devote little time to succession planning, little time to figuring out how to "nurture the qualities that had given it its mojo in the past."[4] Succession planning, however, seems to be a natural outgrowth of a bottom-up, centrifugal culture of shared leadership. It is something that always seems to be part of what we do, something to which I give ongoing thought in ways I am only partially conscious of. I am most aware of succession planning when I reflect upon the fact that for the first time in our almost seventy years as a company, a nonfamily member is likely to be heading the organization in the not-too-distant future. This prospect is a welcome one in many respects, enabling fresh nutrients into the mix in much the same way that a community revitalizes itself. Our ensemble approach to stewardship means that most of us already play leadership roles at different times and in disparate ways. In this way there exists not a succession plan as much as a succession process that is dynamic and ongoing. Everyone knows already the work that needs to be done and the intertwining roles we all play to make things work well. This book comes out of one of the roles I play as CEO, articulating and making more explicit what all of us already know.

So how does one pass along these restorative principles to the next generation of stewards of a sustainable business? Hopefully, by living those principles each day so they become part of the oxygen one breathes within our organization. Still, it's important to provide a more concrete articulation of this culture. After all, it would be a bit puzzling to instruct a newly hired staff member to simply "breathe the oxygen" of our company so as to take in the culture. Something more tangible is called for. What, then, would a set of operating instructions for managing a restorative business look like? Maybe something along the lines of the following set of charges:

Nourish the community. Make sure our staff is provided with the means to secure solid, healthy lives, with the capacity to eat nourishing foods; to live in places that are well built, safe, and secure; and to have ample time for the social company of friends and family. Beyond that provide the opportunity for those around us to realize their full potential, to be accorded dignity and respect, to live lives imbued with meaning, and to be nourished spiritually.

Listen to the heart.[5] So much of business today is taken up with analysis: futuristic scenario planning, strategic thinking about where the company should go, tactical initiatives for getting us there, metrics to evaluate our progress, policies to manage our mutual expectations, agendas to chart us through seemingly interminable meetings. But one day not too long ago, the only guide we had was "Do the right thing." It still is our primary guide. It is important not to allow analysis to stymie our sense of doing what's right.

Remember that nothing is extraneous. The materials forming this book are a flotsam and jetsam of stories told and pictures painted and philosophies expounded on and photographs taken and reminiscences shared. Like the old saying about the making of sausage, even the pig's tail goes into the mix. Be careful about cutting out and throwing away odd flywheels and gears that seem to have no function, because every piece of this business junkyard belongs. If we don't know what a piece is or what it does, it should be our charge to discover its purpose and figure out what use it can make of us, rather than discard it and lose the sense of its meaning.

Understand the story we are telling by our actions. Stories endure long after actual events occur. At least the best stories do, handed down from generation to generation with a loving attention to detail and precision. Poorer stories never get told at all, or when they do they lose power and context in a short period of time. Every business choice we make should be informed by the notion that we are creating a story that will endure.

Practice a set of _R_'s. Warren Bennis' framework—retreat, renew, return—is a good one, although we have added a fourth _R_ to the mix, _restore_. This four-R framework, while necessary, presumes a certain luxury of time on the part of stewards of a company to step away from business to focus on what is truly important. Not everyone, after all, has the luxury or desire to spend eighteen months on retreat in Africa.

An alternative four-R framework is something closer to Peter Senge's learning company, where ongoing reading, reflection, redirection, and restoration are all practiced. Too much emphasis on the first two (reading, reflection) creates an overly academic environment with a frustrating sense of analysis paralysis. Too much emphasis on the latter (particularly redirection) fosters a culture of trendy change management that leaves everyone feeling a bit hollow and aimless. Integrated into a participative management structure, these four _R_'s become a cornerstone of a sustainable business.

Allow for the improbability of connected minds.[6] Sometimes our own entrepreneurial exuberance gets the best of us. We have so many ventures in motion that we cease to cross-pollinate. In this flurry of entrepreneurial activity we become overly disciplined and consign tasks to specific departments that take sole ownership of them. Siloed behavior creeps in. A sharing of wisdom and experience is lost. But we can only truly realize who we are if we engage one another across functional roles. I am teased occasionally for likening our business to an ant colony, in which each type has its function but all manage to communicate and coordinate with one another. But I'll stick with that analogy. There is much to be learned from the ways in which ants share information or the ways in which honeybees optimize decision making or the ways in which flocks of birds precisely coordinate their movements.[7] We need to be like ants: each doing the heavy lifting that belies our small size, all knowing that our individual efforts coalesce into the needs of a much larger colony.

Stay within who we are. We are often asked if we can we take our core business group and rapidly expand. Sure we are scalable. We can do a much greater volume of work than we are doing today. But how about the quality of that work? Can we maintain quality if we scale up? What we build and where we build and how we build and with whom we build are questions of quality and sustenance provided, not volume and quantity. We have our own natural pace, our own natural rhythm, that governs what we do and who we are. We need to stay within that natural rhythm.

Celebrate. We have a tradition that when any accomplishment, large or small, personal or collective, has been reached, we clang this huge, brass ship captain's bell. And immediately business as usual stops so we can celebrate the moment. These are some of my favorite times at the company. So too are other informal or impromptu moments when laughter just seems to cut loose like some jazz improvisation. We're engaged in serious work and so often find ourselves in earnest discussions about the state of the environment or what the nature of real community entails. We sometimes forget to laugh, to savor the moment.

A personal note might accompany this set of charges, from the current steward of a restorative business to an incoming one. I imagine something along these lines.

Dear Steward:

This is something of a magical moment for us. It always is, when new voices are added to our mix. On behalf of my colleagues, I would like to tell you how excited we are that you have chosen us. We will do our best to rein in our excitement, so as not to overwhelm you at first. Whenever we have the opportunity to extend ourselves through the addition of others, we seem to want to download all of our thoughts and feelings and ideas at once. But we know from experience that this can be a bit overwhelming. You can lose yourself in the process. So sit a spell and let yourself recover from the long journey here. Take in some of your surroundings. It's better that way, to let yourself get the lay of the land at your own pace, so that you are able to realize for yourself the value you bring to all of us.

You are coming in to a company that has been in good operating order for some time. Check all the parts upon arrival. If you discover any problems, please don't hesitate to ask me or any of your colleagues. Some of us have been around a long time and may be able to answer a few of your questions regarding part of the company's more arcane mechanisms. Some of these mechanisms predate us, and where this is the case we rely on our vast supply of archived materials: stories that have been passed down from person to person, old photographs of people and projects we've been involved with, drawings and caricatures that capture a bit of the old spirit and humor of the place.

It will probably take you a while to get the hang of how all of this machinery works. It certainly did for us. In fact, I'd say we're still trying to figure out parts of it. No matter. You have lots of time, during which you'll not only begin experimenting with what this company can do, but you'll also have opportunities to test new things that we haven't thought, much less tried. I hope you find this company robust enough to meet these new challenges. The main thing to remember is: Take your time exploring. There is no rush. You don't have to prove yourself worthy of ownership. Your decision to cast your lot with us is reason enough. And we thank you for that deep expression of confidence. We realize the value you bring to our efforts and hope you will come to a similar realization over time. I hope we don't let you down.

You will find that the nature of this company works best when it is pulled by the overall needs of the larger environment. Deciding what those needs are is perhaps best left to you and your colleagues to figure out, in large part because those needs change. But in general I think you'll find that a commonsense approach to operations will serve you well. Add to the current configuration of parts and talent when it makes sense, not just because you can. Take on additional work when it fits in with the capacity of the company to make a difference. Focus on the quality of what you do, not the quantity. Respect the many differences among your colleagues. In the end those differences will be transcended by your shared values and a shared vision for the future. Focus on the deep covenantal relationships you are able to forge, not the flurry of contracts that will cross your desk, calling for signatures. Rely on manuals and policies only as a last resort, since your own sense of doing the right thing will, in large measure, serve you well.

Over the years I have found that engaging in a community of others who share a sense of meaning and purpose about what we do has been deeply restorative. By that I simply mean that this business has taught me, this business continues to teach me, the interconnectedness of all things. It has enabled me to integrate the strands of my own life in ways I would never have expected. I hope you find your engagement with us provides a similar opportunity to make connections among your colleagues, with the larger community of stakeholders and placeholders, and with the natural order of which we are all a part. In a very real sense, many of these connections find you. There's often a tendency among my colleagues and me to take many of the tensions at play within the company and impose a resolution by a sheer act of will or the feeling that we need to be decisive and not let these tensions continually hover over us. Resolutions, however, evolve of their own accord, pulling us along in their wake. Learning to let go and enable the strands of opinions and thoughts and passions to wash over you can be restorative, if you'll only let them.

There are no lifelong guarantees associated with this company and certainly no desire on the part of your colleagues for it to endure long after it has served its useful purpose. Just because this company has been around a long time does not make it great or worthy of lasting another good long time. The longevity of this company should be based instead on a standard of care: the care that you and your colleagues take in handling its many parts, the care that the business exercises in seeing that it remains relevant and purposeful, the care with which its activities dovetail with the needs of the larger environment.

I hope you start to become attached to this business we are sending your way. I have come to sense this attachment over time, feeling more than a little as though I'm living just above a family store. I can hear the voices of shoppers from the floor below, examining merchandise, asking questions about price and quality, exchanging simple conversation with the staff. No, I've not lost my sanity. It's part of the fabric within which this company is wrapped. Over time you'll probably begin to hear similar echoes. It comes with the territory. Is it doable, you may be asking yourself, to manage this sustainable business in the years and decades to come? In a word, yes.

ACKNOWLEDGMENTS

At the beginning of talks my colleagues and I give about our company practices specifically and about sustainable practices more generally, we start by presenting our host with a gift. It's a photographic collection of essays by a local photographer Jack Leigh, who captured life along the south Georgia coast. Shrimping, oystering, weather-beaten arboreal graveyards along our barrier islands, soft green marsh grasses and saw-toothed palmettos, and muscadine vines wrapped around centuries-old oaks: It's a captivating set of images called *The Land I'm Bound To*. And the title for us says it all. This is indeed the land we are all bound to. Presenting this collection of photographs to our host is our way of saying thank you for the gift of enabling us to engage with you, to learn from you.

I don't have a copy of Jack Leigh's book here to say thank you and to acknowledge the wisdom and guidance provided by so many folks who have brought me to this day. So perhaps this book—and the acknowledgments that follow—will suffice as a virtual return of the gifts provided me.

I am grateful for the guidance of Zelda Tenenbaum, our outside consultant on our HR practices. Many of the sustainable management practices discussed in this book are the result of processes Zelda guided us to institute and practice. I am also indebted to the nurturing provided by Ivan Bresgi—psychologist, teacher, mentor, friend. It was Ivan's constant coaching that led me to think more substantively about how all the pieces of a puzzle—one's life, engagement with family and friends, the elements of a company, the workings of a social system—can be integrated into a meaningful whole.

Phyllis Mueller, my patient, encyclopedic, and indomitable editor, worked alongside me through lousy prose, inscrutable business graphs, and general disorganized thinking on my part to shape an obtuse manuscript into what I hope is, in her words, "eminently readable." I am grateful for her gentle humor, knowledge of issues related to conservation, and her passion for organic and locally grown food, the last of which provided necessary sustenance during marathon editing sessions together. I am also deeply indebted to Patty McIntosh, head of the coastal division of The Georgia

Conservancy, for her encouragement to stick with this project, her cogent critiques of all drafts, and the knowledge and insights she brought to my better understanding of environmental issues. Much of my environmental research has been—and continues to be—guided by Patty, who, in a selfless effort to teach others about the priceless treasures along our Georgia coast, may not realize just how much she too is one of those treasures. I am also grateful for the help of Will Berson, also with The Georgia Conservancy, in understanding better the ecology of our region. Nirit Avnimelech-Melaver, Glenn Glass, Lydia Kukoff, Lisa Lilienthal, Nina Mizrachi, Katie Teel, and Marjorie Young also provided early encouragement and feedback on prior drafts, without which help this book would never have gotten off the ground. Frank McIntosh provided much-needed guidance and assistance in making the numerous graphs throughout this book more readable as well as visually compelling.

I also need to acknowledge the help provided by outside readers. *Living Above the Store* is not an academic book, but it nevertheless called for a type of peer review in a number of disciplines. I am grateful to John Vogel for vetting some of the more technical business issues discussed in this book; Steve Olson for providing critical information into the nature of values-driven organizations; Mark Gunther and Bill Dawers, who provided sharp and kind critiques of a rough draft of the manuscript; and Michael Singer for providing important insights into building a brain trust of professionals beyond the borders of a real estate company.

My colleagues at Melaver, Inc., many of whom are referenced in the pages that follow, essentially wrote this book through their ideas and practices. In many respects my efforts have been that of an organizational sociologist and scribe, observing and then capturing on paper what my colleagues say and do, day in and day out. So to Karen Stewart, Randy Peacock, Karen Hudsepth, Tommy Linstroth, Mary Day, Vivian Rahn, Brion Ehret, Rhett Mouchet, Scott Doksansky, Christine Russo, Camille Pope, Cathy Rodgers, Angela Lewis, Angela Walden, Trey Everett, Michael Frey, Lynn Beam, Anthony Wagner, Michael Bone, Amanda Reeves, et. al.: thank you. The same holds true for our close outside partners Sam Cook, Dan Monroe, Michael Skinner, Robb Stanley, and Earline Davis, all of whom have provided long-standing examples of what sustainable partnering entails. I owe a debt of gratitude to my classmates at the Kellogg School of Management for their camaraderie, collaborative spirit, and belief in me. A deep, special thanks is owed to Ben Sher, with whom my travels many years ago, both within books and without, have been a formative influence on my thinking about nature and community.

My acknowledgments would not be complete without recognizing the Melaver, Inc. outside board members—Ray Anderson, Jim Falick, Doug Kinney, and John Knott—for gently challenging me and my colleagues to realize our highest potential as a company. The same holds true for my family members—Norton, Betty, Millie, Tovah, and Ellen Melaver—who have helped set the vision for our business, who have had the patience to endure my very slow learning curve, and who have entrusted me and my colleagues to sustain this business for the next generation of stewards.

I would like to thank the entire team at Chelsea Green, a publishing company that stands for and practices the various principles elucidated in this book. I'm also grateful to Cynthia Zygmund and Literary Services, Inc., my agent, who found a perfect home for my manuscript. I would like to acknowledge the influence of others who have provided guidance, mentoring, and encouragement over the years: Hugh Hawkins, Robert Kiely, Brian McHale, Bob Berkebile, Jon March, Jeanne Anderson, Curry Wadsworth, Gregg Bayard, Jason Bregman, Richard Rowland, Sylvester Formey, Mike Everly, Bruce Gunter, Kelly Jordan, Yum Arnold, John Sibley, Dennis Creech, Paul Pressly, Helen Downing, Howard Morrison, and Chris Miller.

Most of the chapters in this book have their genesis in talks I have given over the past several years. I would like to thank the Tuck School of Business at Dartmouth College (introduction), Southface Institute (chapter one), the Board of Regents of the University of Georgia (chapter two), the Savannah area Chamber of Commerce (chapter three), the Harvard University Graduate School of Design (chapter four), and the Georgia Urban Forest Council (chapter five) for providing a forum for testing out early thoughts and concepts and challenging my thinking along the way.

NOTES

Introduction

1 Max De Pree, *Leadership Is an Art* (New York: Doubleday, 1987), p. 69.
2 Statistics on the built environment can be found on the USGBC website at www.usgbc.org .
3 For a more formal analysis of the Birmingham Fed project, see David Adams, Katherine Birnie, and John H. Vogel Jr., "The Birmingham Fed: A Green Building," (Hanover, N.H.: Tuck School of Business at Dartmouth, 2007).
4 Eric T. Freyfogle, *Why Conservation Is Failing and How We Can Regain Ground* (New Haven, Conn.: Yale University Press, 2006). Donald Worster, *The Wealth of Nature: Environmental History and The Ecological Imagination* (Oxford, England: Oxford University Press, 1993). Storm Cunningham, *The Restoration Economy: The Greatest New Growth Frontier; Immediate and Emerging Opportunities for Businesses, Communities, & Investors* (San Francisco: Berrett-Koehler Publishers, 2002).
5 John von Neumann and Oskar Morgenstern, *Theory of Games and Economic Behavior* (Princeton, N.J.: Princeton University Press, 1947).
6 Report of the Intergovernmental Panel on Climate Change, November 2007, cited in Peter Senge, Bryan Smith, Nina Kruschwitz, Joe Laur, Sara Schley, *The Necessary Revolution: How Individuals and Organizations Are Working Together to Create a Sustainable World* (New York: Doubleday, 2008), p. 168.
7 Joseph Romm, *Hell and High Water: The Global Warming Solution* (New York: HarperPerennial, 2007).
8 David Ehrenfeld, *The Arrogance of Humanism* (Oxford, England: Oxford University Press, 1978).
9 Peter Schwartz, *The Art of the Long View: Planning for the Future in an Uncertain World* (New York: Doubleday, 1991), p. 74.
10 Eric T. Freyfogle, *Bounded People, Boundless Lands: Envisioning a New Land Ethic* (Washington, D.C.: Island Press, 1998), p. 176.
11 William Greider, *The Soul of Capitalism: Opening Paths to a Moral Economy* (New York: Simon & Schuster, 2003), pp. 331–2.
12 Warren Bennis, *On Becoming a Leader* (New York: Basic Books, 2003).
13 Eugene Odum, *Ecological Vignettes: Ecological Approaches to Dealing with Human Predicaments* (Amsterdam: Overseas Publishers Association, 1988).
14 Stephen R. Covey, *The Seven Habits of Highly Effective People: Restoring the Character Ethic* (New York: Simon & Schuster, 1989).
15 See Daniel Kemmis, *Community and the Politics of Place* (Norman: University of Oklahoma Press, 1992).
16 Arie de Geus, *The Living Company: Habits for Survival in a Turbulent Business Environment* (Boston: Harvard Business School Press, 1997).
17 George Lakoff, *Don't Think of an Elephant: Know Your Values and Frame the Debate* (White River Junction, Vt.: Chelsea Green, 2004).

Chapter One

1 David W. Orr, *The Nature of Design: Ecology, Culture, and Human Intention* (New York: Oxford University Press, 2002), p. 32.
2 Tim Traver, *Sippewissett: Or, Life on a Salt Marsh* (White River Junction, Vt.: Chelsea Green Publishing Company, 2006), p. 137.
3 James Alan McPherson, "A Matter of Vocabulary," *Hue and Cry* (Boston: Little, Brown & Company, 1969), pp. 22–30.
4 Peter Schwartz, *The Art of the Long View: Planning for the Future in an Uncertain World* (New York: Doubleday, 1991), pp. 39–43. Murray Edelman, *The Politics of Misinformation* (Cambridge, England: Cambridge University Press, 2001), p. 4.

5 George Santayana, *The Life of Reason, Vol. 1: Reason in Common Sense* (New York: Prometheus Books, 1998). Originally published in 1905.

6 Orrin H. Pilkey and Mary Edna Fraser, *A Celebration of the World's Barrier Islands* (New York: Columbia University Press, 2003), p. 282.

7 Ibid., p. 38.

8 Lawrence S. Earley, *Looking for Longleaf: The Fall and Rise of an American Forest* (Chapel Hill: The University of North Carolina Press, 2004), p. 140.

9 Janisse Ray, *Pinhook: Finding Wholeness in a Fragmented Land* (White River Junction, Vt.: Chelsea Green Publishing, 2005), p. 22.

10 Ralph Nader, Foreword to James M. Fallows, *The Water Lords* (New York: Grossman, 1971), p. x.

11 Kenneth R. Krakow, *Georgia Place-Names* (Macon: Winship Press, 1975).

12 James M. Fallows, *The Water Lords* (New York: Grossman, 1971), p. 3.

13 David W. Orr, *The Nature of Design: Ecology, Culture, and Human Intention* (New York: Oxford University Press, 2002), p. 57.

14 William Cronon, *Changes in the Land: Indians, Colonists, and the Ecology of New England* (New York: Hill and Wang, 1983), ch. 3.

15 William Cronon, *Changes in the Land: Indians, Colonists, and the Ecology of New England* (New York: Hill and Wang, 1983), pp. 54–81.

16 Eric T. Freyfogle, *The Land We Share: Private Property and the Common Good* (Washington, D.C.: Island Press, 2003).

17 David Suzuki and Holly Dressel, *Good News for a Change: How Everyday People Are Helping the Planet* (Vancouver: Greystone Books, 2002), pp. 161–204 on the ineffectiveness of "modern" farming techniques in Bali.

18 Jared Diamond, *Collapse: How Societies Choose to Fail or Succeed* (New York: Viking, 2005), pp. 433–4.

19 The case for the longer staying power of locally owned businesses is made by Michael H. Shuman, *The Small-Mart Revolution: How Local Businesses Are Beating the Global Competition* (San Francisco: Berrett-Koehler Publishers, Inc., 2006); see especially pp. 35–62. See also Thomas H. Greco Jr., *Money: Understanding and Creating Alternatives to Legal Tender* (White River Junction, Vt.: Chelsea Green Publishing, 2001); see especially pp. 46–54.

20 It will be years before we are able to evaluate the involvement of Shangri-La with the Coral Cay Conservation's efforts to preserve the Sulu-Sulawesi Coral Triangle reefs in the Philippines.

21 Lester R. Brown, *Eco-Economy: Building an Economy for the Earth* (New York: W. W. Norton & Company, 2001). Donella Meadows et. al., *Limits to Growth: The 30-Year Update* (White River Junction, Vt.: Chelsea Green Publishing Company, 2004). David Suzuki and Amanda McConnell, *The Sacred Balance: Rediscovering Our Place in Nature* (Vancouver, B.C.: Greystone Books, 1997). Edward O. Wilson, *The Future of Life* (New York: Random House, 2002).

22 Jared Diamond, *Collapse: How Societies Choose to Fail or Succeed* (New York: Viking, 2005) lists failure to anticipate a problem ("creeping normalcy") and failure to respond to a problem once it arrives as two of the four critical failures of group decision making; p. 421.

23 Steven D. Levitt and Stephen J. Dunbar, *Freakonomics: A Rogue Economist Explores the Hidden Side of Everything* (New York: HarperCollins, 2005), pp. 13, 20–21, 89–90.

24 Janine Benyus, *Biomimicry: Innovation Inspired by Nature* (New York: HarperCollins, 1997). Rachel Carson, *Silent Spring* (Boston: Houghton Mifflin Company, 1962), p. 13. Eugene Odum, *Ecological Vignettes: Ecological Approaches to Dealing with Human Predicaments* (Amsterdam: Overseas Publishers Association, 1988). William Cronon, *Changes in the Land: Indians, Colonists, and the Ecology of New England* (New York: Hill and Wang, 1983). Pope John Paul II, 1990 Encyclical *Centesimus Annum,* quoted in Rod Dreher, *Crunchy Cons: How Birkenstocked Burkeans, Gun-Loving Organic Gardeners, Evangelical Free-Range Farmers, Hip Homeschooling Mamas, Right-Wing Nature Lovers, and Their Diverse Tribe of Countercultural Conservatives Plan to Save America (or at Least the Republican Party)* (New York: Crown Forum, 2006). Leopold Aldo, *A Sand County Almanac: With Essays on Conservation from Round River* (New York: Oxford University Press, 1949). Ian McHarg, *Design with Nature* (Garden City, N.J.: John Wiley & Sons, Inc. 1969), p. 26; Ted

Steinberg, *Down to Earth: Nature's Role in American History* (Oxford, England: Oxford University Press, 2002), p. 285. David Suzuki and Amanda McConnell, *The Sacred Balance: Rediscovering Our Place in Nature* (Vancouver, B.C.: Greystone Books, 1997), p. 194. Donald Worster, *The Wealth of Nature: Environmental History and the Ecological Imagination* (Oxford, England: Oxford University Press, 1993), pp. 14, 69, 218–19. Danah Zohar and Dr. Ian Marshall, *SQ: Connecting with Our Spiritual Intelligence* (New York: Bloomsbury Publishing, 2000), pp. 31–32. For a trenchant critique not only of anthropocentrism but our inability to step outside this viewpoint, see David Ehrenfeld, *The Arrogance of Humanism* (Oxford, England: Oxford University Press, 1978).

25 For specific examples, see Michael H. Shuman, *The Small-Mart Revolution: How Local Businesses Are Beating the Global Competition* (San Francisco: Berrett-Koehler Publishers, 2006), pp. 172–7.

26 Peter Senge, Bryan Smith, Nina Kruschwitz, Joe Laur, and Sara Schley, *The Necessary Revolution: How Individuals and Organizations Are Working Together to Create a Sustainable World* (New York: Doubleday, 2008), pp. 125–33.

27 The concepts *dharma* and *ayurveda* perhaps better capture the elements involved in an integrative orientation toward place, but I have chosen the term *integrative* since it will be of greater familiarity to most readers.

28 At the present time, more than 600 companies utilize CERES benchmarks,

29 Thomas Friedman, *The Lexus and the Olive Tree: Understanding Globalization* (New York: First Anchor Books, 2002), p. 302. UNP et. al., *World Resources 2005, The Wealth of the Poor: Managing Ecosystems to Fight Poverty* (Washington, D.C.: World Resources Institute, 2005). Jeffrey D. Sachs, *The End of Poverty: Economic Possibilities for Our Time* (New York: Penguin Group, 2005).

30 Gaston Bachelard, *The Poetics of Space: The Classic Look at How We Experience Intimate Places* (Boston: Beacon Press, 1958).

31 James C. Collins, *Good to Great: Why Some Companies Make the Leap . . . and Others Don't* (New York: HarperCollins Publishers, 2001), p. 64; 1997 McKinsey study cited in Bob Willard, *The Sustainability Advantage: Seven Business Case Studies of a Triple Bottom Line* (Gabriola Island, B.C.: New Society Publishers, 2002). Malcolm Gladwell, *The Tipping Point: How Little Things Can Make a Big Difference* (New York: Little, Brown & Company, 2000), p. 19. W. Chan Kim and Renee Mauborgne, *Blue Ocean Strategy: How to Create Uncontested Market Space and Make the Competition Irrelevant* (Boston: Harvard Business School Press, 2005), p. 171. Brian Natrass and Mary Altomare, *Dancing with the Tiger: Learning Sustainability Step by Natural Step* (Gabriola Island, B.C.: New Society Publishers, 2002), p. 243. Andrew Savitz and Karl Weber, *The Triple Bottom Line: How Today's Best-Run Companies Are Achieving Economic, Social, and Environmental Success—and How You Can Too* (San Francisco: Jossey-Bass, 2006), p. 271. John Kotter, *Leading Change*, cited in Nikos Mourkogiannis, *Purpose: The Starting Point of Great Companies* (New York: Palgrave Macmillan, 2006), p. 161. Peter Senge, *The Fifth Discipline: The Art & Practice of the Learning Organization* (New York: Doubleday, 1990).

32 Richard Florida, *The Rise of the Creative Class: And How It's Transforming Work, Leisure, Community, and Everyday Life* (New York: Basic Books, 2002), pp. 13, 34–5.

33 Jeffrey Hollender and Stephen Fenishcell, *What Matters Most: How a Small Group of Pioneers Is Teaching Social Responsibility to Big Business, and Why Big Business Is Listening* (New York: Basic Books, 2004), p. x.

34 Max De Pree, *Leadership Is an Art* (New York: Doubleday, 1987). Warren Bennis, *On Becoming a Leader* (New York: Basic Books, 2003), p. 142.

35 Ibid., p. 42.

36 Nikos Mourkogiannis, *Purpose: The Starting Point of Great Companies* (New York: Palgrave Macmillan, 2006), p. 6. David W. Orr, *Earth in Mind: On Education, Environment, and the Human Prospect* (Washington, D.C.: Island Press, 2004), p. 22.

37 For a more detailed discussion of centrifugal culture creation at Melaver, Inc., see Martin Melaver and Phyllis Mueller, *The Green Building Bottom Line* (New York: McGraw-Hill, 2008), chapters one and two.

38 Peter Brook, *The Empty Space: A Book about the Theatre: Deadly, Holy, Rough, Immediate* (London: MacGibbon & Kee, 1968).

39 Patrick Lencioni, *The Five Dysfunctions of a Team: A Leadership Fable* (San Francisco: Jossey-Bass, 2002).

40 For a fuller exploration of these processes, see Martin Melaver and Phyllis Mueller, *The Green Building Bottom Line* (New York: McGraw-Hill, 2008).

41 A cogent critique of teamwork in the modern corporation, as a type of fictional deep acting that unmoors the individual's sense of place and purpose, can be found in Richard Sennett, *The Corrosion of Character: The Personal Consequences of Work in the New Capitalism* (New York: W. W. Norton, 1998), pp. 107–17. I believe that while this critique has significant merit generally, the practice of teamwork grounded in a shared sense of values and purpose offers a different and more positive picture than the one Sennett proposes.

42 For an informative itemization of corporate initiatives of taking stock of people within a community, see Charles Landry, *The Creative City: A Toolkit for Urban Innovators* (London: Earthscan, 2000), p. 74.

43 Letitia E. Landon, *Romance and Reality* (London: Crosby, Nichols, Lee & Co., 1860), p. 245.

44 See Matthew Stewart, "The Management Myth," *Atlantic Monthly*, June 2006, on Frederick Winslow Taylor. Regarding the unification system, see Daniel J. Boorstin, *The Americans: The National Experience* (New York: Random House, 1965), pp. 26–34. Although Boorstin contends that the unification system signaled the specialization of machines, not workers, I would argue that the specialization of one entails the specialization of the other.

45 For a sober, pessimistic account of how a society conspires to preserve the status quo and the status of elites, see Murray Edelman, *The Politics of Misinformation* (Cambridge, England: Cambridge University Press, 2001), especially pp. 18–38.

46 Bob Willard, *The Sustainability Advantage: Seven Business Case Studies of a Triple Bottom Line* (Gabriola Island, B.C.: New Society Publishers, 2002).

47 Ibid.

48 Peter Schwartz, *The Art of the Long View: Planning for the Future in an Uncertain World* (New York: Doubleday, 1991), pp. 219–21, 237–9.

49 James Collins, *Good to Great: Why Some Companies Make the Leap . . . and Others Don't* (New York: HarperCollins Publishers, 2001). Nikos Mourkogiannis, *Purpose: The Starting Point of Great Companies* (New York: Palgrave Macmillan, 2006).

50 David W. Orr, *Earth in Mind: On Education, Environment, and the Human Prospect* (Washington, D.C.: Island Press, 2004), p. 71.

51 Bo Burlingham, *Small Giants: Companies That Choose to Be Great Instead of Big* (New York: Portfolio, 2005); John Grant, *The Green Marketing Manifesto* (Chichester, England: John Wiley & Sons, Ltd., 2007); Bill McKibben, *Deep Economy: The Wealth of Communities and the Durable Future* (New York: Time Books, Henry Holt & Co., 2007); Michael H. Shuman, *The Small-Mart Revolution: How Local Businesses Are Beating the Global Competition* (San Francisco: Berrett-Koehler Publishers, Inc., 2006).

52 Joseph L. Badaracco, *Questions of Character: Illuminating the Heart of Leadership through Literature* (Boston: Harvard Business School Press, 2006), p. 134.

53 Ted Nordhaus and Michael Shellenberger, *Break Through: From the Death of Environmentalism to the Politics of Possibility* (New York: Houghton Mifflin Company, 2007); Fred Krupp and Miriam Horn, *Earth: The Sequel; The Race To Reinvent Energy and Stop Global Warming* (New York: W. W. Norton & Co., 2008); Daniel C. Esty and Andrew S. Winston, *Green to Gold: How Smart Companies Use Environmental Strategy to Innovate, Create Value, and Build Competitive Advantage* (New Haven, Conn.: Yale University Press, 2006).

54 Paul Hawken, *Growing a Business* (New York: Fireside Books, 1987), p. 92.

55 E. F. Schumacher, *Small Is Beautiful: Economics as If People Mattered* (Point Roberts, WA: Hartley & Marks Publishers, 1973), pp. 10, 20, 193.

56 David Suzuki and Holly Dressel, *Good News for a Change: How Everyday People Are Helping the Planet* (Vancouver: Greystone Books, 2002). Hawken, *Growing a Business* (New York: Fireside Books, 1987), pp. 42, 52, 61. Bo Burlingham, *Small Giants: Companies That Choose to Be Great Instead of Big* (New York: Portfolio, 2005), p. 171.

57 Ryuzaburo Kaku, "The Path of Kyosei," in *Harvard Business Review*, *HBR on Corporate Responsibility* (Boston: Harvard Business School Publishing, 2003), p. 122.

58 Brian Natrass and Mary Altomare, *The Natural Step for Business: Wealth, Ecology, and the Evolutionary Corporation* (Gabriola Island, B.C.: New Society Publishers, 1999), and *Dancing with the Tiger: Learning Sustainability Step by Natural Step* (Gabriola Island, B.C.: New Society Publishers, 2002).

59 Nikos Mourkogiannis, *Purpose: The Starting Point of Great Companies* (New York: Palgrave Macmillan, 2006), citing John Kotter's key steps in change management, p. 161.

60 Peter Senge, Bryan Smith, Nina Kruschwitz, Joe Laur, and Sara Schley, *The Necessary Revolution: How Individuals and Organizations Are Working Together to Create a Sustainable World* (New York: Doubleday, 2008), p. 339.

61 The number 160 probably first came to be focused on in Stanley Milgram's so-called six degrees of separation experiment. See also Malcolm Gladwell, *The Tipping Point: How Little Things Can Make a Big Difference* (New York: Little, Brown & Company, 2000). Ed Zajac, Kellogg School of Management course on corporate governance.

62 Malcolm Gladwell, *The Tipping Point: How Little Things Can Make a Big Difference* (New York: Little, Brown & Company, 2000), p. 198.

63 An exceptional case is that of Gore Industries, which makes a point of limiting businesses and business units to 160 people. See also a discussion of Joe Cabral and Chatsworth Products in William Greider, *The Soul of Capitalism: Opening Paths to a Moral Economy* (New York: Simon & Schuster, 2003), p. 88.

64 Timothy Beatley and Kristy Manning, *The Ecology of Place: Planning for Environment, Economy, and Community* (Washington, D.C.: Island Press, 1997), p. 2.

65 Both companies have also come in for their fair share of criticism. See Naomi Klein, *No Logo: Taking Aim at the Brand Bullies* (New York: Picador, 1999), pp. 136–7, 239–43, 361. Robert B. Reich, *Supercapitalism: The Transformation of Business, Democracy, and Everyday Life* (New York: Alfred A. Knopf, 2007), pp. 194–5.

66 Brian Natrass and Mary Altomare, *The Natural Step for Business: Wealth, Ecology, and the Evolutionary Corporation* (Gabriola Island, B.C.: New Society Publishers, 1999) and *Dancing with the Tiger: Learning Sustainability Step by Natural Step* (Gabriola Island, B.C.: New Society Publishers, 2002). Bo Burlingham, *Small Giants: Companies That Choose to Be Great Instead of Big* (New York: Portfolio, 2005). David Suzuki and Holly Dressel, *Good News for a Change: How Everyday People Are Helping the Planet* (Vancouver: Greystone Books, 2002). Jeffrey Hollender and Stephen Fenishcell, *What Matters Most: How a Small Group of Pioneers Is Teaching Social Responsibility to Big Business, and Why Big Business Is Listening* (New York: Basic Books, 2004). Paul Hawken, *Growing a Business* (New York: Fireside Books, 1987).

Chapter Two

1 Wendell Berry, *The Unsettling of America* (San Franscisco: Sierra Club Books, 1986), p. 93.

2 James C. Collins, *Good to Great: Why Some Companies Make the Leap . . . and Others Don't* (New York: HarperCollins Publishers, 2001), particularly on the notion of Level 5 leadership, pp. 17–40. Warren Bennis, *On Becoming a Leader* (New York: Basic Books, 2003). Joseph L. Badaracco, *Questions of Character: Illuminating the Heart of Leadership through Literature* (Boston: Harvard Business School Press, 2006).

3 Ray Anderson and Bob Berkebile, clearly identify their transformation in terms of disruptive events. Stephen R. Covey, in "Three Roles of the Leader in the New Paradigm," in Frances Hesselbein et. al. *The Leader of the Future: New Visions, Strategies, and Practices for the Next Era* (San Francisco: Jossey-Bass Publishers, 1996), pp. 155–6, emphasizes pain as the key driver of personal change and the global economic demand for quality as the key driver of corporate change.

4 W. Chan Kim and Renee Mauborgne, *Blue Ocean Strategy: How to Create Uncontested Market Space and Make the Competition Irrelevant* (Boston: Harvard Business School Press, 2005).

5 The notion of "creative destruction" is Joseph Schumpeter's, discussed in Thomas Friedman, *The Lexus and the Olive Tree: Understanding Globalization* (New York: First Anchor Books, 2002), p. 11.

6 See also Stewart Brand, *The Clock of the Long Now: Time and Responsibility* (New York: Basic Books, 1999), p. 35.

7 Joseph Romm, *Cool Companies: How the Best Businesses Boost Profits and Productivity by Cutting Greenhouse Gas Emissions* (Washington, D.C.: Island Press, 1999), pp. 39–40. Jason F. McLennan, *The Philosophy of Sustainable Design: The Future of Architecture* (Kansas City, Mo.: Ecotone Publishing, 2004), pp. 209–224.

8 Peter Drucker, in a Foreword to Frances Hesselbein, ed., *The Leader of the Future: New Visions, Strategies, and Practices for the Next Era* (San Francisco: Jossey-Bass Publishers, 1996), p. xiii. Richard Leider, "The Ultimate Leadership Task," Hesselbein, *op. cit.*, pp. 193–198.

9 Robert F. Kennedy Jr., speech in Savannah, Georgia, Feb. 10, 2007. Warren Bennis, *On Becoming a Leader* (New York: Basic Books, 2003).

10 For a frank account of such "marquee envy," see David Gottfried, *Greed to Green: The Transformation of an Industry and a Life* (Berkeley, Cal: WorldBuild Publishing, 2007).

11 Jason F. McLennan, *The Philosophy of Sustainable Design: The Future of Architecture* (Kansas City, Mo.: Ecotone Publishing, 2004), p. 80.

12 Timothy Beatley and Kristy Manning, *The Ecology of Place: Planning for Environment, Economy, and Community* (Washington, D.C.: Island Press, 1977), p. 157.

13 Eric T. Freyfogle, *The Land We Share: Private Property and the Common Good* (Washington, D.C.: Island Press, 2003), p. 2.

14 Howard Frumkin et. al., *Urban Sprawl and Public Health: Designing, Planning, and Building for Healthy Communities* (Washington, D.C.: Island Press, 2004), p. xii.

15 Storm Cunningham, *The Restoration Economy: The Greatest New Growth Frontier; Immediate and Emerging Opportunities for Businesses, Communities & Investors* (San Francisco: Berrett-Koehler Publishers, 2002).

16 Sarah James and Torbjorn Lahti, *The Natural Step for Communities: How Cities and Towns Can Change to Sustainable Practices* (Gabriola Island, B.C.: New Society Publishers, 2004), p. 60.

17 David Suzuki and Amanda McConnell, *The Sacred Balance: Rediscovering Our Place in Nature* (Vancouver: Greystone Books, 1997), p. 102. On the loss of twenty-five square miles of the Louisiana delta every ten months, see Mike Tidwell, *Bayou Farewell: The Rich Life and Tragic Death of Louisiana's Cajun Coast* (New York: Random House, 2003).

18 Jason F. McLennan, *The Philosophy of Sustainable Design: The Future of Architecture* (Kansas City: Ecotone Publishing, 2004), p. 81.

19 Howard Frumkin et. al., *Urban Sprawl and Public Health: Designing, Planning, and Building For Healthy Communities* (Washington, D.C.: Island Press, 2004).

20 John Ward, *Perpetuating the Family Business: 50 Lessons Learned from Long Lasting, Successful Families in Business* (New York: Palgrave Macmillan, 2004).

21 Peter Senge in Frances Hesselbein et. al., eds., *The Leader of the Future: New Visions, Strategies, and Practices for the Next Era* (San Francisco: Jossey-Bass Publishers, 1996), p. 54.

22 For Waugh and Hewlett-Packard, see Marc Gunther, *Faith and Fortune: The Quiet Revolution to Reform American Business* (New York: Crown Publishing, 2004), pp. 180–197. For Flies and Costco, see Peter Senge, Bryan Smith, Nina Kruschwitz, Joe Laur, and Sara Schley, *The Necessary Revolution: How Individuals and Organizations Are Working Together to Create a Sustainable World* (New York: Doubleday, 2008), p. 269.

23 Peter Senge, Bryan Smith, Nina Kruschwitz, Joe Laur, and Sara Schley, *The Necessary Revolution: How Individuals and Organizations Are Working Together to Create a Sustainable World* (New York: Doubleday, 2008), pp. 285–92, 302, 323.

24 Andrew Savitz and Karl Weber, *The Triple Bottom Line: How Today's Best-Run Companies Are Achieving Economic, Social, and Environmental Success—and How You Can Too* (San Francisco: Jossey-Bass, 2006). Sarah James and Torbjorn Lahti, *The Natural Step for Communities: How Cities and Towns Can Change to Sustainable Practices* (Gabriola Island, B.C.: New Society Publishers, 2004).

25 John Abrams notes that letting go builds community within a company, facilitates empowerment, fosters belonging, enables people to evolve, and holds the greatest potential for the greatest financial returns. John Abrams, *The Company We Keep: Reinventing Small Business for People, Community, and Place* (White River Junction, Vt.: Chelsea Green, 2005), pp. 32, 44, 48.

26 Rachel Carson, *Silent Spring* (Boston: Houghton Mifflin Company, 1962), p. 13.
27 Max De Pree, *Leadership Is an Art* (New York: Doubleday, 1987), p. 32. Eric T. Freyfogle, *Bounded People, Boundless Land: Envisioning a New Land Ethic* (Washington, D.C.: Island Press, 1998), p. 31. David W. Orr, *Earth in Mind: On Education, Environment, and the Human Prospect* (Washington, D.C.: Island Press, 2004), ch. 14. David Suzuki and Amanda McConnell, *The Sacred Balance: Rediscovering Our Place in Nature* (Vancouver, B:C: Greystone Books, 1997), pp. 3–4. Edward O. Wilson, *Consilience: The Unity of Knowledge* (New York: Random House, 1998).
28 Upton Sinclair, *I, Candidate for Governor: And How I Got Licked* (Berkeley: University of California Press, 1934).
29 Frances Hesselbein et. al., eds., *The Leader of the Future: New Visions, Strategies, and Practices for the Next Era* (San Francisco: Jossey-Bass Publishers, 1996).
30 Edgar Schein, "Leadership and Organizational Culture," in Frances Hesselbein et. al., eds. *The Leader of the Future: New Visions, Strategies, and Practices for the Next Era* (San Francisco: Jossey-Bass Publishers, 1996).
31 Sarah James and Torbjorn Lahti, *The Natural Step for Communities: How Cities and Towns Can Change to Sustainable Practices* (Gabriola Island, B.C.: New Society Publishers, 2004). Andrew Savitz and Karl Weber, *The Triple Bottom Line: How Today's Best-Run Companies Are Achieving Economic, Social, and Environmental Success—and How You Can Too* (San Francisco: Jossey-Bass, 2006). Malcolm Gladwell, *The Tipping Point: How Little Things Can Make a Big Difference* (New York: Little, Brown & Company, 2000).
32 The term *groupthink* was coined by William H. Whyte in *Fortune* (1952). Irving Janis did extensive research on the concept, used to describe a type of group arrival at a decision by suppressing doubts and critical thinking
33 John Seely Brown, "Narrative as a Knowledge Medium in Organizations," in John Seely Brown, Stephen Denning, Katalina Groh, and Laurence Prusak, *Storytelling in Organizations: Why Storytelling Is Transforming 21st Century Organizations and Management* (Burlington, Vt.: Elsevier Butterworth-Heinemann, 2005), p. 76.
34 There are also a number of charters that adopt the precautionary principle as part of overall sustainable principles, including the Netherlands' National Environmental Policy Plan (NEPP), the United Nations' Earth Charter, the Rio Declaration (1992), the Helsinki Convention (1992), the Framework Convention on Climate Change (1992), and the Cartagena Protocol on Biosafety (2000). Andres R. Edwards, *The Sustainability Revolution: Portrait of a Paradigm Shift* (Gabriola Island, B.C.: New Society Publishers, 2005), pp. 37–46, 55–58.
35 Amy M. Patrick, "Apocalyptic or Precautionary? Revisioning Texts in Environmental Literature," in Amy Merrill Ingram, Ian Marshall, Daniel J. Philippon, and Adam W. Sweeting eds., *Coming into Contact: Explorations in Ecocritical Theory and Practice* (Athens: University of Georgia Press, 2007), pp. 141–53. Barry L. Johnson, "Adaptive Management: Scientifically Sound, Socially Challenged?," *Conservation Ecology,* 3 (2): 8, 1999.
36 Ted Steinberg, *Down to Earth: Nature's Role in American History* (Oxford, England: Oxford University Press, 2002), p. 285.
37 Nick Salafsky, Richard Margolius, and Kent H. Redford, *Adaptive Management: A Tool for Conservation Practitioners* (Biodiversity Support Program, 2001).
38 Janine M. Benyus, *Biomimicry: Innovation Inspired by Nature* (New York: HarperCollins, 1997), p. 263.
39 Ian L. McHarg, *Design with Nature* (Garden City, N.J.: John Wiley & Sons, 1969), p. 26. John Muir, *A Thousand-Mile Walk to the Gulf* (New York: Houghton Mifflin Company, 1916), p. 136. Aldo Leopold, *A Sand County Almanac: With Essays on Conservation from Round River* (New York: Oxford University Press, 1949), pp. xviii–xix.
40 Donald Worster, *The Wealth of Nature: Environmental History and the Ecological Imagination* (Oxford, England: Oxford University Press, 1993), p. 5.
41 Rachel Carson, *Silent Spring* (Boston: Houghton Mifflin Company, 1962), p. 127.
42 John Elkington and Pamela Hartigan, *The Power of Unreasonable People: How Social Entrepreneurs Create Markets That Change the World* (Boston: Harvard Business School Press, 2008), pp. 182–3, from e-mails between Mitchell Kapor and the authors.
43 Bo Burlingham, *Small Giants: Companies That Choose to Be Great Instead of Big* (New York: Portfolio, 2005), pp. 93–117. Jeffrey Hollender and Stephen Fenishcell, *What Matters*

Most: How a Small Group of Pioneers Is Teaching Social Responsibility to Big Business and Why Big Business Is Listening (New York: Basic Books, 2004), pp. 19, 233, 266, and concluding chapter.

44 Ibid. pp. xv, xvii, xix.

45 Max De Pree, *Leadership Is an Art* (New York: Doubleday, 1987), p. 42.

46 Bob Berkebile, interview in McGraw-Hill, "Green Building: SmartMarket Report 2006," pp. 32–33.

47 For a discussion of deep ecology, first promulgated by Norwegian philosopher and ecologist Arne Naess, see Andres R. Edwards, *The Sustainability Revolution: Portrait of a Paradigm Shift* (Gabriola Island, B.C.: New Society Publishers, 2005), pp. 113–122. See also Patrick Curry, *Ecological Ethics: An Introduction* (Cambridge, England: Polity Press, 2006), pp. 63–99.

48 Quoted in David W. Orr, *Earth in Mind: On Education, Environment, and the Human Prospect* (Washington, D.C.: Island Press, 2004), p. 140.

Chapter Three

1 Richard Goodman, *French Dirt: The Story of a Garden in the South of France* (Chapel Hill, N.C.: Algonquin Books of Chapel Hill, 2002), p. 165.

2 Richard Goodman, *French Dirt: The Story of a Garden in the South of France* (Chapel Hill, N.C.: Algonquin Books of Chapel Hill, 2002).

3 Rachel Bodle, "Everyone a Rainmaker," in *Insight* 8, no. 1 (Jan.–March 1994), p. 23. Arie De Geus, *The Living Company: Habits for Survival in a Turbulent Business Environment* (Boston: Harvard Business School Press, 1997), ch. 8.

4 On the three basic value propositions—customer intimacy, product leadership, and operational efficiency—see Michael Treacy and Fred Wiersema, "Customer Intimacy and Other Value Disciplines," *Harvard Business Review,* Jan.–Feb. 1993.

5 James C. Collins, *Good to Great: Why Some Companies Make the Leap . . . and Others Don't* (New York: HarperCollins Publishers, 2001), p. 98.

6 Thomas L. Friedman, *The World Is Flat: A Brief History of the Twenty-First Century* (New York: Farrar, Straus and Giroux, 2005), p. 451.

7 E. F. Schumacher, *Small Is Beautiful: Economics as If People Mattered* (Point Roberts, Wash.: Hartley & Marks Publishers, 1973), pp. 19–20.

8 The notion of E and O cultures was developed by Michael Beer and Nitin Nohria, "Cracking the Code of Change," *Harvard Business Review* , May–June 2000. The Solidarity-Sociability Matrix was developed by Rob Goffee and Gareth Jones, "What Holds the Modern Company Together?" *Harvard Business Review*, November–December 1996.

9 Max De Pree, *Leadership Is an Art* (New York: Doubleday, 1987), pp. 69–70. Dalai Lama and Howard C. Cutler, *The Art of Happiness: A Handbook for Living* (New York: Riverhead Books, 1998), pp. 51, 189. David Suzuki with Amanda McConnell, *The Sacred Balance: Rediscovering Our Place in Nature* (Vancouver, B.C.: Greystone Books, 1997), p. 207.

10 William Bridges, *Making Sense of Life's Transitions: Strategies for Coping with the Difficult, Painful, and Confusing Times in Your Life* (Cambridge, Mass.: Perseus Books, 1980), p. 52. Warren Bennis, *On Becoming a Leader* (New York: Basic Books, 2003), p. xxii. Max De Pree, *Leadership Is an Art* (New York: Doubleday, 1987), p. 69.

11 Joseph L. Badaracco, *Questions of Character: Illuminating the Heart of Leadership through Literature* (Boston: Harvard Business School Press, 2006), p. 130. Yvon Chouinard, *Let My People Go Surfing: The Education of a Reluctant Businessman* (New York: Penguin Press, 2005), p. 260.

12 Richard Florida, *The Rise of the Creative Class: And How It's Transforming Work, Leisure, Community, and Everyday Life* (New York: Basic Books, 2002), pp. 34–5. E. F. Schumacher, *Small Is Beautiful: Economics as If People Mattered* (Point Roberts, Wash.: Hartley & Marks Publishers, 1973), p. 193.

13 E. F. Schumacher, *Small Is Beautiful: Economics as If People Mattered* (Point Roberts, Wash.: Hartley & Marks Publishers, 1973), p. 10.

14 The discussion of Hall-Tonna's work is based on chapter five of Steve Olson, *The Ethics of Leadership* (unpublished dissertation: Emory University, 2007). Olson's excellent analysis is

drawn primarily from Brian P. Hall, *Values Shift: A Guide to Personal and Organizational Transformation* (Eugene, Ore: Wipf & Stock Publishers, 2006).

15 Lewis Thomas, *The Lives of a Cell: Notes of a Biology Watcher* (New York: Bantam, 1974), p. 133.

16 Warren Bennis, *On Becoming a Leader* (New York: Basic Books, 2003), p. 171.

17 Janine M. Benyus, *Biomimicry: Innovation Inspired by Nature* (New York: HarperCollins, 1997), p. 24.

18 Yvon Chouinard, *Let My People Go Surfing: The Education of a Reluctant Businessman* (New York: Penguin Press, 2005), p. 121. Paul Hawken, *Growing a Business* (New York: Fireside Books, 1987). Arie De Geus, *The Living Company: Habits for Survival in a Turbulent Business Environment* (Boston: Harvard Business School Press, 1997).

19 Daniel Pink, *Free-Agent Nation*, cited in Richard Florida, *The Rise of the Creative Class: And How It's Transforming Work, Leisure, Community, and Everyday Life* (New York: Basic Books, 2002).

20 Ivan Ilich, *Energy and Equity: Ideas in Progress* (London: Marion Boyars Publishers, 2001).

21 Robert Putnam, *Bowling Alone*, cited in Howard Frumkin et. al., *Urban Sprawl and Public Health: Designing, Planning, and Building for Healthy Communities* (Washington, D.C.: Island Press, 2004), p. 172.

22 Thomas L. Friedman, *The World Is Flat: A Brief History of the Twenty-First Century* (New York: Farrar, Straus and Giroux, 2005), p. 38.

23 Chris Anderson, *The Long Tail: Why the Future of Business Is Selling Less of More* (New York: Hyperion, 2006), p. 184.

24 The complete list of nine, in reverse order of importance, is as follows: (9) Numbers (subsidies, taxes, standards). (8) Material stocks and flows. (7) Regulating negative feedback loops. (6) Driving positive feedback loops. (5) Information flows. (4) The rules of the system (incentives, punishment, constraints). (3) The power of self-organization. (2) The goals of the system. (1) The mindset or paradigm out of which the goals, rules, feedback structure arise.

25 Donella Meadows, "Places to Intervene in a System," *Whole Earth Magazine*, Winter 1997.

26 Michael E. Porter, *Competitive Advantage: Creating and Sustaining Superior Performance* (New York: Simon & Schuster, 1985).

27 Esty and Winston argue that while Porter's analysis is still relevant, the ferocity of competition is such that business now needs to take into account environmental issues. See Daniel C. Esty and Andrew S. Winston, *Green to Gold: How Smart Companies Use Environmental Strategy to Innovate, Create Value, and Build Competitive Advantage* (New Haven, Conn.: Yale University Press, 2006), p. 98.

28 Peter Senge, Bryan Smith, Nina Kruschwitz, Joe Laur, and Sara Schley, *The Necessary Revolution: How Individuals and Organizations Are Working Together to Create a Sustainable World* (New York: Doubleday, 2008), p. 305.

29 Alfie Kohn, *No Contest: The Case against Competition* (Boston: Houghton Mifflin Company, 1986) argues that the notion of competing against oneself is a sloppy formulation, since what is being conveyed is a notion of internal striving and not competition in which one person's success depends on others' failures. What I am referring to as competing against oneself is most akin to Kohn's notion of intentional as opposed to structural competition. See pp. 3–5, 6, 89.

30 Andres R. Edwards, *The Sustainability Revolution: Portrait of a Paradigm Shift* (Gabriola Island, B.C.: New Society Publishers, 2005), p. 50. Daniel C. Esty and Andrew S. Winston, *Green to Gold: How Smart Companies Use Environmental Strategy to Innovate, Create Value, and Build Competitive Advantage* (New Haven, Conn.: Yale University Press, 2006). Andrew Savitz and Karl Weber, *The Triple Bottom Line: How Today's Best-Run Companies Are Achieving Economic, Social, and Environmental Success—and How You Can Too* (San Francisco: Jossey-Bass, 2006). Studies emphasizing collaboration over competition would include Alfie Kohn, *No Contest: The Case against Competition* (New York: Houghton Mifflin, 1992), and John Abrams, *The Company We Keep: Reinventing Small Business for People, Community, and Place* (White River Junction, Vt.: Chelsea Green Publishing, 2005), pp. 85–90.

31 Yvon Chouinard, *Let My People Go Surfing: The Education of a Reluctant Businessman* (New York: Penguin Press, 2005), p. 10.

32 W. Chan Kim and Renee Mauborgne, *Blue Ocean Strategy: How to Create Uncontested Market Space and Make the Competition Irrelevant* (Boston: Harvard Business School Press, 2005), pp. 185–90 on the sustainability and renewal of blue ocean strategy.

33 Alfie Kohn, *No Contest: The Case against Competition* (Boston: Houghton Mifflin Company, 1986), pp. 192–96.

34 Janisse Ray, *Ecology of a Cracker Childhood* (Minneapolis: Milkweed Editions, 1999), p. 211.

35 Michael Singer, e-mail to the author

36 William Butler Yeats, "Among School Children," original date of publication 1928, from *The Collected Poems of W.B. Yeats* (Hertfordshire, England: Wordsworth Editions Limited, 1994) p 183–5. "O body swayed to music, O brightening glance, how can we know the dancer from the dance?"

37 Cited in Peter Senge, *The Fifth Discipline: The Art & Practice of the Learning Organization* (New York: Doubleday, 1990), p. 217. It should be noted that Russell's analysis goes on to emphasize the key role that competition plays in this Zen-like condition he's describing. That would seem to be natural and inevitable, given the context within which he's describing things (basketball). Translated into a business context, however, I think the competition becomes more internalized as each member of the team pushes to maximize his or her potential in the interest of higher objectives set by the overall team/company.

Chapter Four

1 Dalai Lama and Howard C. Cutler, *The Art of Happiness: A Handbook for Living* (New York: Riverhead Books, 1998), p. 189.

2 Paul Coelho, *The Alchemist* (New York: HarperCollins, 1988), p. xiv.

3 For the legal definition of covenant, see William P. Statsky, *Legal Thesaurus/Legal Dictionary: A Resource for the Writer and Computer Researcher* (St. Paul, Minn.: West Publishing Company, 1985). For the real-estate definitions, see Daniel Oran and Mark Tosti, *Oran's Dictionary of the Law* (Cengage Delmar Learning, 2007).

4 Sustainable Fellwood has been registered with the U.S. Green Building Council's pilot program for LEED for Neighborhood Development (LEED-ND).

5 Donald Worster, *The Wealth of Nature: Environmental History and the Ecological Imagination* (Oxford, England: Oxford University Press, 1993), pp. 144, 153.

6 David W. Orr, *Earth in Mind: On Education, Environment, and the Human Prospect* (Washington, D.C.: Island Press, 2004), chapter 8 on virtue, pp. 60–63.

7 *New York Times Magazine*, Sunday, Feb. 25, 2007.

8 Sophisticated marketing tactics that complement such push tactics include what is called half finished frames, which invite the consumer to "participate by filling in the picture." See Richard Sennett, *The Culture of the New Capitalism* (New Haven, Conn.: Yale University Press, 2006), pp. 148–9.

9 A similar approach to individuating products so as to enhance branding is sometimes referred to as platform construction or gold-plating. See Richard Sennett, *The Culture of the New Capitalism* (New Haven, Conn.: Yale University Press, 2006), pp. 143–4.

10 Storm Cunningham, *The Restoration Economy: The Greatest New Growth Frontier; Immediate and Emerging Opportunities for Businesses, Communities & Investors* (San Francisco: Berrett-Koehler Publishers, 2002). "It's a lot easier to strategize—and to execute—when one's business is based on real needs." p. 51.

11 As this book was being prepared for publication, I came across a similar reworking of the Brundtland definition. See Michael H. Shuman, *The Small-Mart Revolution: How Local Businesses Are Beating the Global Competition* (San Francisco: Berrett-Koehler Publishers, Inc., 2006), p. 218.

12 Milton Friedman and Rose Friedman, *Free to Choose: A Personal Statement* (San Diego: Harcourt, 1970).

13 Brian Czech, in an irreverent and iconoclastic work entitled *Shoveling Fuel for a Runaway Train: Errant Economists, Shameful Spenders, and a Plan to Stop Them All* (Berkeley: University of California Press, 2000) focuses considerable attention on overconsumptive practices on the part of the purchaser. The top 1 percent of the nation's consumers, what

Czech labels the liquidating class, is largely to be reformed through shaming tactics. The steady-state class, the bottom 80 percent of the population, is considered to be the least of our worries, since their purchasing power lacks the wastefulness exhibited by others. And then there is the 19-percent amorphic class in the middle, for whom Czech holds out hope as the group most open to education and restraint.

14 This exercise first came to my attention as part of work we were doing with The Natural Step. I have since seen it referenced in John P. Kotter and Dan S. Cohen, *The Heart of Change: Real-Life Stories of How People Change Their Organizations* (Boston: Harvard Business School Press, 2002), p. 81.

15 Bill McKibben, *Deep Economy: The Wealth of Communities and the Durable Future* (New York: Times Books, Henry Holt & Company, 2007), p. 135.

16 B. Joseph Pine and James H. Gilmore, *The Experience Economy: Work Is Theater & Every Business Is a Stage* (Boston: Harvard University Press, 1999). Naomi Klein cites the tendency of companies such as Disney, Coke, Barnes & Noble, and Nike among many others to create stand-alone stores that mix shopping, amusement, and multimedia for "inspirational retail." Naomi Klein, *No Logo: Taking Aim at the Brand Bullies* (New York: Picador, 1999), p. 150.

17 John Kay and Aubrey Silberson, "Corporate Governance," in *National Institute Economic Review* (Aug. 1995), pp. 84–97. Michael Bradley, Cindy A. Schipani, Anant K. Sundaram, and James P. Walsh, "The Purposes and Accountability of the Corporation in Contemporary Society: **Corporate Governance at a Crossroads**," *Law and Contemporary Problems*, vol. 62, no. 3, Challenges to Corporate Governance (Summer 1999), pp. 9–86.

18 Robert Reich points out that the view and practice of stakeholder capitalism was discussed and to some degree practiced during the first half of the twentieth century, propounded by Walter Lippmann, Adolf A. Berle, and Gardiner C. Means. However, Reich contends, such a stakeholder view is not conducive to the way supercapitalism has evolved since the mid-1970s. See Robert B. Reich, *Supercapitalism: The Transformation of Business, Democracy, and Everyday Life* (New York: Alfred A. Knopf, 2007), pp. 26–27, 176–7.

19 A particularly cogent discussion of the evolution of American individualism as unique blend of spiritual and pragmatic elements can be found in Jeremy Rifkin, *The European Dream: How Europe's Vision of the Future Is Quietly Eclipsing the American Dream* (New York: Jeremy P. Tarcher/Penguin, 2004), pp. 24–26, 131–2.

20 William Cronon, *Changes in the Land: Indians, Colonists, and the Ecology of New England* (New York: Hill and Wang, 1983); Donald Worster, *The Wealth of Nature: Environmental History and The Ecological Imagination* (Oxford, England: Oxford University Press, 1993); Ted Steinberg, *Down to Earth: Nature's Role in American History* (Oxford, England: Oxford University Press, 2002); Eric Freyfogle, *The Land We Share: Private Property and the Common Good* (Washington, D.C.: Island Press, 2003); Jeremy Rifkin *The European Dream: How Europe's Vision of the Future Is Quietly Eclipsing the American Dream* (New York: Jeremy P. Tarcher/Penguin, 2004).

21 Mark Dowie, "In Law We Trust," *Orion*, July/August 2003.

22 Eric T. Freyfogle, *The Land We Share: Private Property and the Common Good* (Washington, D.C.: Island Press, 2003).

23 Samuel P. Hays, *Beauty, Health, and Permanence: Environmental Politics in the United States, 1955–1985* (Cambridge, England: Cambridge University Press, 1987). Robert F. Kennedy Jr., *Crimes against Nature: How George W. Bush and His Corporate Pals Are Plundering the Country and Hijacking Our Democracy* (New York: HarperCollins, 2004).

24 Eric T. Freyfogle, *The Land We Share: Private Property and the Common Good* (Washington, D.C.: Island Press, 2003), p. 246.

25 Jeffrey D. Sachs, *The End of Poverty: Economic Possibilities for Our Time* (New York: The Penguin Group, 2005) and *Common Wealth: Economics for a Crowded Planet* (New York: The Penguin Group, 2008).

26 Paul Hawken, *The Ecology of Commerce: A Declaration of Sustainability* (New York: HarperBusiness, 1993), pp. 75–90.

27 Matthew E. Kahn, *Green Cities: Urban Growth and the Environment* (Washington, D.C.: Island Press, 2006).

28 Samuel P. Hays, *Beauty, Health, and Permanence: Environmental Politics in the United States,*

1955–1985 (Cambridge, England: Cambridge University Press, 1987); William Greider, *The Soul of Capitalism: Opening Paths to a Moral Economy* (New York: Simon & Schuster, 2003).

29 Robert B. Reich, *Supercapitalism: The Transformation of Business, Democracy, and Everyday Life* (New York: Alfred A. Knopf, 2007); Sheldon S. Wolin, *Democracy Incorporated: Managed Democracy and the Specter of Inverted Totalitarianism* (Princeton, N.J.: Princeton University Press, 2008).

30 Jeffrey D. Sachs, *Common Wealth: Economics for a Crowded Planet* (New York: The Penguin Group, 2008) and Thomas L. Friedman, *Hot, Flat, and Crowded: Why We Need a Green Revolution—And How It Can Renew America* (New York: Farrar, Straus and Giroux, 2008).

31 Jeffrey D. Sachs, *Common Wealth: Economics for a Crowded Planet* (New York: The Penguin Group, 2008), p. 321. For a trenchant critique of Sachs's mien of humanitarianism, especially in the context of Bolivia, see Naomi Klein, *The Shock Doctrine: The Rise of Disaster Capitalism* (New York: Henry Holt & Co., 2007), pp. 142–68.

32 For a thorough investigation into various overarching sustainable principles adopted by numerous national, regional, and local charters see Andres R. Edwards, *The Sustainability Revolution: Portrait of a Paradigm Shift* (Gabriola Island, B.C.: New Society Publishers, 2005).

33 Timothy Beatley and Kristy Manning, *The Ecology of Place: Planning for Environment, Economy, and Community* (Washington, D.C.: Island Press, 1997), p. 2. Theodore Steinberg, *Slide Mountain: Or, The Folly of Owning Nature* (Berkeley: University of California Press, 1996). Amitai Etzioni, *The Spirit of Community* (New York: Touchstone, 1994). Eric T. Freyfogle, *Bounded People, Boundless Land: Envisioning a New Land Ethic* (Washington, D.C.: Island Press, 1998), pp. 37, 140. David Suzuki and Amanda McConnell, *The Sacred Balance: Rediscovering Our Place in Nature* (Vancouver, B.C.: Greystone Books, 1997), pp. 3–4, 175.

34 Timothy Beatley and Kristy Manning, *The Ecology of Place: Planning for Environment, Economy, and Community* (Washington, D.C.: Island Press, 1997), p. 195.

35 Eric T. Freyfogle, *The Land We Share: Private Property and the Common Good* (Washington, D.C.: Island Press, 2003), p. 138.

36 Edward O. Wilson, *Consilience: The Unity of Knowledge* (New York: Random House, 1998), pp. 303–4.

37 Ted Steinberg, *Down to Earth: Nature's Role in American History* (Oxford, England: Oxford University Press, 2002), p. 284.

38 David W. Orr, *Earth in Mind: On Education, Environment, and the Human Prospect* (Washington, D.C: Island Press, 2004), p. 210.

39 Daniel C. Esty and Andrew S. Winston, *Green to Gold: How Smart Companies Use Environmental Strategy to Innovate, Create Value, and Build Competitive Advantage* (New Haven, Conn.: Yale University Press, 2007), pp. 166–94.

40 John Elkington and Pamela Hartigan, *The Power of Unreasonable People: How Social Entrepreneurs Create Markets That Change the World* (Boston: Harvard Business School Press, 2008), pp. 184–6.

41 Janine M. Benyus, *Biomimicry: Innovation Inspired by Nature* (New York: HarperCollins, 1997).

42 David W. Orr, *Earth in Mind: On Education, Environment, and the Human Prospect* (Washington, D.C.: Island Press, 2004), p. 77. Donald Worster, *The Wealth of Nature: Environmental History and The Ecological Imagination* (Oxford, England: Oxford University Press, 1993), p. 75. Paul R. Ehrlich and Anne H. Ehrlich, *Betrayal of Science and Reason: How Anti-Environmental Rhetoric Threatens Our Future* (Washington, D.C.: Island Press, 1996), p. 31.

43 Martin Melaver and Phyllis Mueller, *The Green Building Bottom Line* (New York: McGraw-Hill, 2008).

44 John Abrams, *The Company We Keep: Reinventing Small Business for People, Community, and Place* (White River Junction, Vt.: Chelsea Green, 2005), devotes a chapter to these challenges. See chapter 4, "Balancing Multiple Bottom Lines," pp. 77–98.

45 Donald Worster, *The Wealth of Nature: Environmental History and the Ecological Imagination* (Oxford, England: Oxford University Press, 1993), p. 144.

46 Steve Olson on cycle-seven leadership, *The Ethics of Leadership* (unpublished dissertation: Emory University, 2007).

47 Discussed in Stewart Brand, *The Clock of the Long Now: The Ideas behind the World's Slowest Computer* (New York: Basic Books, 1999), p. 29. Brand references a 1978 paper by Boulding but does not cite the specific source.

48 Linda Clarkson, Vern Morrissette, and Gabriel Régallet, *Our Responsibility to the Seventh Generation*, (Winnipeg, MB: International Institute for Sustainable Development, 1992.)

49 Stewart Brand, *The Clock of the Long Now: The Ideas behind the World's Slowest Computer* (New York: Basic Books, 1999).

50 Lewis Thomas, *The Lives of a Cell: Notes of a Biology Watcher* (New York: Bantam, 1974), p. 15.

Chapter Five

1 Eugene Odum, *Ecological Vignettes: Ecological Approaches to Dealing with Human Predicaments* (Amsterdam: Overseas Publishers Association, 1988), p. 150.

2 David Sobel and Stewart Brand, among others, draw upon this same metaphor or concentric circles to illustrate the process of maturation; Sobel in terms of the development of a child into adulthood, and Brand in terms of the development of a civilization. See David Sobel, *Children's Special Places: Exploring the Role of Forts, Dens, and Bush Houses in Middle Childhood* (Detroit, Mich: Wayne State University Press, 2001), and Stewart Brand, *The Clock of the Long Now: The Ideas behind the World's Slowest Computer* (New York: Basic Books, 1999), pp. 34–39.

3 Jeremy Rifkin prefers the term *civil society organizations* (CSOs) since it encapsulates a broader notion of service than simple volunteerism. See Jeremy Rifkin, *The European Dream: How Europe's Vision of the Future Is Quietly Eclipsing the American Dream* (New York: Jeremy P. Tarcher/Penguin, 2004), pp. 234–46.

4 An equivalent concept to congruence is that of process philosophy or process politics. See Jeremy Rifkin, *The European Dream: How Europe's Vision of the Future Is Quietly Eclipsing the American Dream* (New York: Jeremy P. Tarcher/Penguin, 2004), pp. 220–1.

5 David C. Korten has something similar in mind in referring to the need for creative balance among civic, governmental, and economic sectors. See David C. Korten, *When Corporations Rule the World* (Bloomfield & San Francisco: Kumarian Press and Berrett-Koehler Publishers, 2001), pp. 102–4.

6 For an interesting discussion of both the significance of and our poor understanding of this quiet voice see Stephen Denning's discussion of George Steiner in John Seely Brown, Stephen Denning, Katalina Groh, and Laurence Prusak, *Storytelling in Organizations: Why Storytelling Is Transforming 21st Century Organizations and Management* (Burlington, Vt.: Elsevier Butterworth-Heinemann, 2005), pp. 114–5.

7 Some would argue that proactive planning has not been much of a positive influence either. See David Ehrenfeld, *The Arrogance of Humanism* (Oxford, England: Oxford University Press, 1978), pp. 53, 61. Ian McHarg, *Design with Nature* (Garden City, N.J.: John Wiley & Sons, 1969), p. 155. Ray Suarez, *The Old Neighborhood: What We Lost in the Great Suburban Migration, 1966–1999* (New York: Free Press, 1999), points out the contradiction between our lament for the sense of lost community and our apparent unwillingness to do much about it.

8 William McDonough and Michael Braungart, *Cradle to Cradle: Remaking the Way We Make Things* (New York: North Point Press, 2002), p. 44.

9 Tim Traver, *Sippewissett: Or, Life on a Salt Marsh* (White River Junction, Vt.: Chelsea Green Publishing, 2006), pp. 89–90.

10 Aldo Leopold, *A Sand County Almanac: With Essays on Conservation from Round River* (New York: Oxford University Press, 1949), p. 231.

11 Sometimes referred to as cores (key conservation areas), corridors (the areas linking core areas), and carnivores (high-growth human habitat areas).

12 Janisse Ray, *Pinhook: Finding Wholeness in a Fragmented Land* (White River Junction, Vt.: Chelsea Green Publishing, 2005).

13 John Muir, *A Thousand-Mile Walk to the Gulf* (New York: Houghton Mifflin Company, 1916), p. 212.

14 Paul Hawken, speeches before The Georgia Conservancy, Atlanta, September 2005, and at the U.S. Green Building Council's annual Greenbuild Conference, Atlanta, November 2005; Ray Anderson, in informal remarks preceding a brainstorming session of The Natural Step, Atlanta, February 2005.

15 I have been trying without success to locate the source of this anecdote

16 Jeremy Rifkin prefers the term *civil society organizations* (CSOs) to *nonprofit organizations*, because of the stronger emphasis on service rather than the connotation of volunteering. I would agree with Rifkin but have nevertheless stuck with the more conventional term *nonprofit organizations* since it is more familiar to most readers. See Jeremy Rifkin, *The European Dream: How Europe's Vision of the Future Is Quietly Eclipsing the American Dream* (New York: Jeremy P. Tarcher/Penguin, 2004), pp. 234–46.

17 See Charles Landry, *The Creative City: A Toolkit for Urban Innovators* (London: Earthscan, 2000), pp. 41–76.

18 Edward O. Wilson, *Consilience: The Unity of Knowledge* (New York: Random House, 1998). See also arguments by Dr. Sylvia Earle and Dr. George Woodwell, cited in Tim Traver, *Sippewissett: Or, Life on a Salt Marsh* (White River Junction, Vt.: Chelsea Green Publishing, 2006), p. 11.

19 Three relatively recent works by Mark Dowie, Eric Freyfogle, and Nordhaus/Shellenberger lay the blame squarely on the failure of the environmental community, albeit for different reasons. See Mark Dowie, *Losing Ground: American Environmentalism at the Close of the Twentieth Century* (Cambridge, Mass.: MIT Press, 1995); Eric T. Freyfogle, *Why Conservation Is Failing and How It Can Regain Ground* (New Haven, Conn: Yale University Press, 2006); Ted Nordhaus and Michael Shellenberger, *Break Through: From the Death of Environmentalism to the Politics of Possibility* (New York: Houghton Mifflin Company, 2007). For an alternative, big-picture perspective that lays the blame on a political system that has lost its way, see Robert B. Reich, *Supercapitalism: The Transformation of Business, Democracy, and Everyday Life* (New York: Alfred A. Knopf, 2007).

20 Edward O. Wilson, *Consilience: The Unity of Knowledge* (New York: Random House, 1998), p. 171.

21 Ibid, p. 186.

22 Ibid, p. 277.

23 For an extensive exploration of sector-based frictions see Samuel P. Hays, *Beauty, Health, and Permanence: Environmental Politics in the United States, 1955–1985* (Cambridge, England: Cambridge University Press, 1987).

24 Two studies have recently been published that make a compelling case for the fact that a large impediment to social and environmental justice policies actually stems from a too-close working relationship between two sectors, government and business. Both Sheldon Wolin and Robert Reich argue that this cozy relationship needs to be pried apart, a sentiment I wholly endorse. In the context of the argument I am making here about shaping congruence, I would contend that this unholy alliance between business and government is actually a sophisticated version of tribalism, in which business has learned to play the game well of co-opting government for its own ends. See Robert B. Reich, *Supercapitalism: The Transformation of Business, Democracy, and Everyday Life* (New York: Alfred A. Knopf, 2007) and Sheldon S. Wolin, *Democracy Incorporated: Managed Democracy and the Specter of Inverted Totalitarianism* (Princeton, N.J.: Princeton University Press, 2008).

25 Mike Tidwell, *Bayou Farewell: The Rich Life and Tragic Death of Louisiana's Cajun Coast* (New York: Random House, 2003).

26 For an interesting discussion of this conflation of natural versus humankind-induced events see Thomas L. Friedman, *Hot, Flat, and Crowded: Why We Need a Green Revolution—And How It Can Renew America* (New York: Farrar, Straus and Giroux, 2008), pp. 112-14.

27 Frances Hesselbein, ed., *The Leader of the Future: New Visions, Strategies, and Practices for the Next Era* (San Francisco: Jossey-Bass Publishers, 1996), p. 122.

28 Jeffrey D. Sachs, *The End of Poverty: Economic Possibilities for Our Time* (New York: The Penguin Group, 2005), p. 256. Robert B. Reich, *Supercapitalism: The Transformation of Business, Democracy, and Everyday Life* (New York: Alfred A. Knopf, 2007).

29 Mike Tidwell, *The Ravaging Tide: Strange Weather, Future Katrinas, and the Coming Death of America's Coastal Cities* (New York: Free Press, 2006), pp. 177–8.

30 David Suzuki and Holly Dressel, *Good News for a Change: How Everyday People Are Helping the Planet* (Vancouver: Greystone Books, 2002), p. 311ff.

31 David Suzuki and Holly Dressel, *Good News for a Change: How Everyday People Are Helping the Planet* (Vancouver: Greystone Books, 2002), p. 311ff.

32 Ibid., p. 233.

33 For various discussions of partnerships between businesses and other sectors see: Peter M. Senge, Bryan Smith, Nina Kruschwwitz, Joe Laur, and Sara Schley, *The Necessary Revolution: How Individuals and Organizations Are Working Together to Create a Sustainable World* (New York: Doubleday, 2008); Daniel C. Esty and Andrew S. Winston, *Green to Gold: How Smart Companies Use Environmental Strategy to Innovate, Create Value, and Build Competitive Advantage* (New Haven, Conn.: Yale University Press, 2006); Brian Dumaine, *The Plot to Save the Planet: How Serious Money, Visionary Entrepreneurs, and Corporate Titans Are Creating Real Solutions to Global Warming* (New York: Crown Publishing, 2008).

34 Edward O. Wilson, *The Future of Life* (New York: Random House, 2002), pp. 149–90.

35 Peter M. Senge, Bryan Smith, Nina Kruschwwitz, Joe Laur, and Sara Schley, *The Necessary Revolution: How Individuals and Organizations Are Working Together to Create a Sustainable World* (New York: Doubleday, 2008), p. 94.

36 Peter Senge, *The Fifth Discipline: The Art & Practice of the Learning Organization* (New York: Doubleday, 1990), p. 231.

37 E-mail correspondence with the author, July 10, 2008.

38 Murray Edelman, *The Politics of Misinformation* (Cambridge, England: Cambridge University Press, 2001), p. 111.

39 Ibid., p. 156.

40 Danah Zohar and Dr. Ian Marshall, *SQ: Connecting with Our Spiritual Intelligence* (New York: Bloomsbury Publishing, 2000), p. 5.

41 The phrase is from Eric T. Freyfogle, *Bounded People, Boundless Land: Envisioning a New Land Ethic* (Washington, D.C.: Island Press, 1998), p. 165.

42 Aldo Leopold, *A Sand County Almanac: With Essays on Conservation from Round River* (New York: Oxford University Press, 1949), p. 190.

43 Tommy Linstroth and Ryan Bell, *Local Action: The New Paradigm in Climate Change Policy* (Burlington: University of Vermont Press, 2007).

44 From Pope Pius XI, cited in Herman E. Daly and John B. Cobb, Jr., *For the Common Good* (Boston: Beacon, 1997), p. 17.

45 David Suzuki and Holly Dressel, *Good News for a Change: How Everyday People Are Helping the Planet* (Vancouver, B.C.: Greystone Books, 2002), p. 5.

46 Martin Melaver and Phyllis Mueller, *The Green Building Bottom Line* (New York: McGraw-Hill, 2008).

47 Jared Diamond, *Collapse How Societies Choose to Fail or Succeed* (New York: Viking, 2005), pp. 433–4.

48 Jeffrey Hollender and Stephen Fenishcell, *What Matters Most: How a Small Group of Pioneers Is Teaching Social Responsibility to Big Business, and Why Big Business Is Listening* (New York: Basic Books, 2004), p. 25

49 John Abrams, *The Company We Keep: Reinventing Small Business for People, Community, and Place* (White River Junction, Vt.: Chelsea Green, 2005), p. 158.

50 Malcolm Gladwell, *Blink: The Power of Thinking without Thinking* (New York: Little, Brown & Company, 2005), p. 52.

51 David Ehrenfeld, *The Arrogance of Humanism* (Oxford, England: Oxford University Press, 1978), pp. 16–17.

Chapter Six

1 Janisse Ray, *Ecology of a Cracker Childhood* (Minneapolis: Milkweed Editions, 1999), p. 29.

2 Jack Leigh, *The Land I'm Bound To* (New York: W. W. Norton & Co., 2000), p. 223.

3 John Muir, *A Thousand-Mile Walk to the Gulf* (New York: Houghton Mifflin Company, 1916), p. 164.

4 Daniel J. Boorstin, *The Americans: The National Experience*, cited in William Bridges, *Making Sense of Life's Transitions: Strategies for Coping with the Difficult, Painful, and Confusing Times in Your Life* (Cambridge, Mass: Perseus Books, 1980), p. 2.

5 Cited in an interview with Mike Tidwell, *Bayou Farewell: The Rich Life and Tragic Death of Louisiana's Cajun Coast* (New York: Random House, 2003), p. 211.

6 Alice Outwater, *Water: A Natural History* (New York: Basic Books, 1996).

7 Ted Steinberg, *Down to Earth: Nature's Role in American History* (Oxford, England: Oxford University Press, 2002), pp. 55–174. Alice Outwater, *Water: A Natural History* (New York: Basic Books, 1996), p. 87.

8 Though it begs certain hard questions beyond the scope of this work, I nevertheless find appealing Tom Horton's quiet blend of criticality and optimism when he notes, "The potential is there for a new era of responsibility in harvesting the bay, but the cold fact is that to date, we have never moved to manage any species on a sustainable basis before it crashed to historic depths." Tom Horton and David W. Harp, *Water's Way: Life along the Chesapeake* (Baltimore: The Johns Hopkins University Press, 1992), p. 88.

9 Ted Steinberg: "As historians and citizens, we need to embrace a more humble view of human agency. We must acknowledge the unpredictability involved in incorporating nature into human designs and, in so doing, bring natural forces to the fore of the historical process. . . . When it comes to the human control of nature, beware: Things rarely turn out the way they are supposed to." *Down to Earth: Nature's Role in American History* (Oxford, England: Oxford University Press, 2002), p. 285. On the notion of big bets, see David W. Orr, *Earth in Mind: On Education, Environment, and the Human Prospect* (Washington, D.C.: Island Press, 2004), p. 77.

10 Danah Zohar and Dr. Ian Marshall, *SQ: Connecting with Our Spiritual Intelligence* (New York: Bloomsbury Publishing, 2000), pp. 5, 41.

11 Cited in Steven D. Levitt and Stephen J. Dubner, *Freakonomics: A Rogue Economist Explores the Hidden Side of Everything* (New York: HarperCollins, 2005), pp. 89–90.

12 John Ward and Ivan Landsberg, Kellogg Family Business Seminar, Oct. 15–20, 2006.

13 Among many writings on the critical role of failure in learning entities, see Arie De Geus, *The Living Company: Habits for Survival in a Turbulent Business Environment* (Boston: Harvard Business School Press, 1997); Peter Senge, *The Fifth Discipline: The Art & Practice of the Learning Organization* (New York: Doubleday, 1990); Charles Landry, *The Creative City: A Toolkit for Urban Innovators* (London: Earthscan, 2000), pp. 152–3.

14 Wendell Berry, *The Unsettling of America* (San Francisco: Sierra Club Books, 1986), p. 53.

15 Warren Bennis, *On Becoming a Leader* (New York: Basic Books, 2003), p. 181.

16 UNP, *World Resources 2005, The Wealth of the Poor: Managing Ecosystems to Fight Poverty* (Washington, D.C.: World Resources Institute, 2005). Jeffrey D. Sachs, *The End of Poverty: Economic Possibilities for Our Time* (New York: Penguin Group, 2005). Paul Hawken, *Blessed Unrest: How the Largest Movement in the World Came into Being and Why No One Saw It Coming* (New York: Viking, 2007).

17 W. J. Bate, ed. *Samuel Johnson: Selected Essays from* The Rambler, Adventurer, *and* Idler (New Haven, Conn.: Yale University Press, 1968), p. 208.

18 I am indebted to my editor Phyllis Mueller for this interesting gloss on Serotinus, as well as for her research in defining the word as "late bloomer."

19 E. F. Schumacher, *Small Is Beautiful: Economics as If People Mattered* (Point Roberts, Wash.: Hartley & Marks Publishers, 1973), p. 252.

20 David Sobel, *Children's Special Places*, as described in Edward O. Wilson, *The Future of Life* (New York: Random House, 2002), p. 138.

21 Barbara Kingsolver, Steven L. Hopp, Camille Kingsolver, *Animal, Vegetable, Miracle: A Year of Food Life* (New York: HarperCollins, 2007), p. 212.

22 Donella H. Meadows, *The Global Citizen* (Washington, D.C.: Island Press, 1991), p. 16.

23 Coincidentally, I discovered after the fact that Donella Meadows found this analogy helpful. See Donella H. Meadows, *The Global Citizen* (Washington, D.C.: Island Press, 1991), pp. 262–3.

24 See Wikipedia entry for Alocholics Anonymous.

25 Wendell Berry, *The Unsettling of America* (San Francisco: Sierra Club Books, 1986), p. 18.

26 Mart A. Stewart, *"What Nature Suffers to Groe"*: Life, Labor, and Landscape on the Georgia *Coast, 1680–1920* (Athens: University of Georgia Press, 1996), p. 56.

27 Richard Florida, *The Rise of the Creative Class: And How It's Transforming Work, Leisure, Community, and Everyday Life* (New York: Basic Books, 2002), especially p. 15.

28 Robert F. Kennedy Jr. in a speech in Savannah, Georgia, on Feb. 10, 2007.

29 James Gustave Speth, *The Bridge at the Edge of the World: Capitalism, the Environment, and Crossing from Crisis to Sustainability* (New Haven, Conn.: Yale University Press, 2008), pp. 217–232.

30 The phrase comes from Eric T. Freyfogle, *Bounded People, Boundless Land: Envisioning a New Land Ethic* (Washington, D.C.: Island Press, 1998), p. xiv.

Conclusion

1 Stewart Brand, *The Clock of the Long Now: Time and Responsibility; The Ideas behind the World's Slowest Computer* (New York: Basic Books, 1999), p. 48. Original citation is Po Bronson, "The Long Now," *Wired* (May 1998), p. 118.

2 Peter Schwartz, *The Art of the Long View: Planning for the Future in an Uncertain World* (New York: Doubleday, 2001), p. 189.

3 Mark Dowie, *Losing Ground: American Environmentalism at the Close of the Twentieth Century* (Cambridge, Mass.: MIT Press, 1995), p. 234.

4 Bo Burlingham, *Small Giants: Companies That Choose to Be Great Instead of Big* (New York: Portfolio, 2005), pp. 117, 162.

5 I find compelling Edward Wilson's inversion of the usual primacy of rationality over emotion, a sentiment also echoed in David Ehrenfeld's *The Arrogance of Humanism* (Oxford, England: Oxford University Press, 1978) and in David Suzuki and Amanda McConnell, *The Sacred Balance: Rediscovering Our Place in Nature* (Vancouver: Greystone Books, 1997). Here is Wilson: "In order to pass through the bottleneck, a global land ethic is urgently needed. Not just any land ethic that might happen to enjoy agreeable sentiment, but one based on the best understanding of ourselves and the world around us that science and technology can provide. Surely the rest of life matters. Surely our stewardship is its only hope. We will be wise to listen carefully to the heart, then act with rational intention and all the tools we can gather and bring to bear." *The Future of Life* (New York: Random House, 2002), p. xxiii.

6 I wish this phrase were mine, but it comes from Lewis Thomas, *The Lives of a Cell: Notes of a Biology Watcher* (New York: Bantam, 1974), p. 133. Once I came across this phrase, nothing better seemed to capture the notion of serendipitous collaboration.

7 The intelligent, leaderless behavior of large groups in nature is discussed in Peter Miller, "Swarm Theory," *National Geographic*, July 2007, pp. 126–47.

BIBLIOGRAPHY

Abrams, John. *The Company We Keep: Reinventing Small Business for People, Community, and Place*. White River Junction, Vt.: Chelsea Green Publishing Co., 2005.

Anderson, Chris. *The Long Tail: Why the Future of Business Is Selling Less of More*. New York: Hyperion, 2006.

Anderson, Ray. *Mid-Course Correction: Toward a Sustainable Enterprise: The Interface Model*. White River Junction, Vt.: Chelsea Green Publishing Co., 1998.

Ariely, Dan. *Predictably Irrational: The Hidden Forces That Shape Our Decisions*. New York: HarperCollins, 2008.

Bachelard, Gaston. *The Poetics of Space: The Classic Look at How We Experience Intimate Places*. Boston: Beacon Press, 1958.

Badaracco, Joseph L. *Questions of Character: Illuminating the Heart of Leadership through Literature*. Boston: Harvard Business School Press, 2006.

Barrionuevo, Alexei. "For Good or Ill, Boom in Ethanol Reshapes Economy of Heartland." *New York Times*, June 25, 2006.

Bate, W. J. *Samuel Johnson: Selected Essays from the* Rambler, Adventurer, *and* Idler. New Haven, Conn.: Yale University Press, 1968.

Beatley, Timothy, and Kristy Manning. *The Ecology of Place: Planning for Environment, Economy, and Community*. Washington, DC: Island Press, 1997.

Beer, Michael and Nitin Nohria. "Cracking the Code of Change." *Harvard Business Review*, May 1, 2000.

Bennis, Warren. *On Becoming a Leader*. New York: Basic Books, 2003.

Benyus, Janine M. *Biomimicry: Innovation Inspired by Nature*. New York: HarperCollins, 1997.

Berry, Wendell. *The Unsettling of America*. San Francisco: Sierra Club Books, 1986.

Blanc, Paul D. *How Everyday Products Make People Sick: Toxins at Home and in the Workplace*. Berkeley: University of California Press, 2007.

Boorstin, Daniel J. *The Americans: The National Experience*. New York: Random House, 1965.

Bossidy, Larry, Ram Charan, and Charles Burck. *Execution: The Discipline of Getting Things Done*. New York: Random House, 2002.

Bourseiller, Phillippe. *365 Ways to Save the Earth*. New York: Harry N. Abrams, Inc., 2006.

Bradley, Michael, et al. "The Purposes and Accountability of the Corporation in Contemporary Society: Corporate Governance at a Crossroads." *Law and Contemporary Problems*, 1999: 9–86.

Brand, Stewart. *The Clock of the Long Now: Time and Responsibility; The Ideas Behind the World's Slowest Computer*. New York: Basic Books, 1999.

Bridges, William. *Making Sense of Life's Transitions: Strategies for Coping with the Difficult, Painful, and Confusing Times in Your Life*. Cambridge, Mass.: Perseus Books, 1980.

———. *Managing Transitions: Making the Most of Change*. Reading, Mass: Perseus Books, 1991.

Brown, John Seely, et al. *Storytelling in Organizations: Why Storytelling Is Transforming 21st Century Organizations and Management*. Burlington, Vt.: Elsevier Butterworth-Heinemann, 2005.

Brown, Lester R. *Eco-Economy: Building an Economy for the Earth*. New York: W. W. Norton & Company, 2001.

Burlingham, Bo. *Small Giants: Companies That Choose to Be Great Instead of Big*. New York: Portfolio, 2005.

Carson, Rachel. *Silent Spring*. Boston: Houghton Mifflin Company, 1962.

Carter, Jimmy. *Our Endangered Values: America's Moral Crisis*. New York: Simon & Schuster, 2005.

Chouinard, Yvon. *Let My People Go Surfing: The Education of a Reluctant Businessman*. New York: Penguin Press, 2005.

Coelho, Paulo, trans. by Alan R.Clarke. *The Alchemist*. New York: HarperCollins, 1988.

Collins, James C. *Good to Great: Why Some Companies Make the Leap . . . and Others Don't.* New York: HarperCollins Publishers, 2001.

Collins, James C., and Jerry I. Porras. *Built to Last: Successful Habits of Visionary Companies.* New York: HarperCollins, 1994.

Conrad, Joseph. *Heart of Darkness.* Hertfordshire, England: Wordsworth Editions Limited, 1998.

Covey, Stephen R. *The 7 Habits of Highly Effective People: Restoring the Character Ethic.* New York: Simon & Schuster, 1989.

Cowdrey, Albert E. *This Land, This South: An Environmental History.* Lexington: The University Press of Kentucky, 1996.

Craige, Betty Jean. *Eugene Odum: Ecosystem Ecologist & Environmentalist.* Athens: University of Georgia Press, 2001.

Cronon, William. *Changes in the Land: Indians, Colonists, and the Ecology of New England.* New York: Hill and Wang, 1983.

Cunningham, Storm. *The Restoration Economy: The Greatest New Growth Frontier; Immediate and Emerging Opportunities for Businesses, Communities & Investors.* San Francisco: Berrett-Koehler Publishers, 2002.

Curry, Patrick. *Ecological Ethics: An Introduction.* Cambridge, England: Polity, 2006.

Czech, Brian. *Shoveling Fuel for a Runaway Train; Errant Economists, Shameful Spenders, and a Plan to Stop Them All.* Berkeley: University of California Press, 2000.

Dalai Lama and Howard C.Cutler. *The Art of Happiness: A Handbook for Living.* New York: Riverhead Books, 1998.

Daly, Herman E., and John Cobb Jr.. *For the Common Good.* Boston: Beacon, 1997.

de Geus, Arie. *The Living Company: Habits for Survival in a Turbulent Business Environment.* Boston: Harvard Business School Press, 1997.

Denning, Stephen . *The Secret Language of Leadership: How Leaders Inspire Action through Narrative.* San Francisco: Jossey-Bass, 2007.

———. *Squirrel Inc.: A Fable of Leadership through Storytelling.* San Francisco: John Wiley & Sons, Inc., 2004.

De Pree, Max. *Leadership Is an Art.* New York: Doubleday, 1987.

Diamond, Jared. *Collapse: How Societies Choose To Fail or Succeed.* New York: Viking, 2005.

———. *Guns, Germs, and Steel: The Fates of Human Societies.* New York: W. W. Norton & Company, 1997.

Dowie, Mark. "In Law We Trust: Can Environmental Legislation Still Protect the Commons?" *Orion,* July/August, 2003.

———. *Losing Ground: American Environmentalism at the Close of the Twentieth Century.* Cambridge, Mass.: MIT Press, 1995.

Dreher, Rod. *Crunch Cons: How Birkenstocked Burkeans, Gun-Loving Organic Gardeners, Evangelical Free-Range Farmers, Hip Homeschooling Mamas, Right-Wing Nature Lovers, and Their Diverse Tribe of Countercultural Conservatives Plan to Save America (or At Least the Republican Party).* New York: Crown Forum, 2006.

Dumaine, Brian. *The Plot to Save the Planet: How Serious Money, Visionary Entrepreneurs, and Corporate Titans Are Creating Real Solutions to Global Warming.* New York: Crown Publishing, 2008.

Earley, Lawrence S. *Looking for Longleaf: The Fall and Rise of an American Forest.* Chapel Hill: The University of North Carolina Press, 2004.

Edelman, Murray. *The Politics of Misinformation.* Cambridge, England: Cambridge University Press, 2001.

Edwards, Andres R. *The Sustainability Revolution: Portrait of a Paradigm Shift.* Gabriola Island, B.C.: New Society Publishers, 2005.

Ehrenfeld, David. *The Arrogance of Humanism.* Oxford, England: Oxford University Press, 1978.

Ehrlich, Paul R., and Anne. H. Ehrlich. *Betrayal of Science and Reason: How Anti-Environmental Rhetoric Threatens Our Future.* Washington, D.C.: Island Press, 1996.

Eliade, Mircea, and Willard R. Trask. *The Myth of the Eternal Return: Or, Cosmos and History.* Princeton, N.J.: Princeton University Press, 1971.

Elkington, John, and Pamela Hartigan. *The Power of Unreasonable People: How Social Entrepreneurs Create Markets That Change the World.* Boston: Harvard Business School Press, 2008.

Esty, Daniel C., and Andrew S. Winston. *Green to Gold: How Smart Companies Use Environmental Strategy to Innovate, Create Value, and Build Competitive Advantage.* New Haven, Conn.: Yale University Press, 2006.

Fallows, James M. *The Water Lords.* New York: Grossman, 1971.

Florida, Richard. *The Rise of the Creative Class: And How It's Transforming Work, Leisure, Community, and Everyday Life.* New York: Basic Books, 2002.

Freyfogle, Eric T. *Bounded People, Boundless Lands: Envisioning a New Land Ethic.* Washington, D.C.: Island Press, 1998.

———. *The Land We Share: Private Property and the Common Good.* Washington, D.C.: Island Press, 2003.

———. *Why Conservation Is Failing and How It Can Regain Ground.* New Haven, Conn.: Yale University Press, 2006.

Friedman, Milton, and Rose Friedman. *Free to Choose: A Personal Statement.* San Diego: Harcourt, 1970.

Friedman, Thomas L. *Hot, Flat, and Crowded: Why We Need a Green Revolution—And How It Can Renew America.* New York: Farrar, Straus and Giroux, 2008.

——— *The Lexus and the Olive Tree: Understanding Globalization.* New York: First Anchor Books, 2002.

———. *The World Is Flat: A Brief History of the Twenty-First Century.* New York: Farrar, Straus and Giroux, 2005.

Frumkin, Howard, Lawrence Frank, and Richard Jackson. *Urban Sprawl and Public Health: Designing, Planning, and Building for Healthy Communities.* Washington, D.C.: Island Press, 2004.

Gilbert, Elizabeth. *Eat, Pray, Love.* New York: Penguin, 2006.

Gladwell, Malcolm. *Blink: The Power of Thinking without Thinking.* New York: Little, Brown and Company, 2005.

———. *The Tipping Point: How Little Things Can Make a Big Difference.* New York: Back Bay Books/Little, Brown and Company, 2000.

Goffee, Rob, and Gareth Jones. "What Holds the Modern Company Together?" *Harvard Business Review,* Nov. 1, 1996.

Goleman, Daniel. *Emotional Intelligence.* New York: Bantam Books, 1995.

Goodell, Jeff. *Big Coal: The Dirty Secret behind America's Energy Future.* Boston: Houghton Mifflin Company, 2006.

Goodman, Richard. *French Dirt: The Story of a Garden in the South of France.* Chapel Hill, N.C.: Algonquin Books of Chapel Hill, 2002.

Gore, Al. *An Inconvenient Truth: The Planetary Emergency of Global Warming and What We Can Do about It.* Emmaus, Pa.: Rodale, 2006.

Gottfried, David. *Greed to Green: The Transformation of an Industry and a Life.* Berkeley, Cal.: WorldBuild Publishing, 2007.

Grant, John. *The Green Marketing Manifesto.* Chichester, England: John Wiley & Sons, Ltd., 2007.

Greco, Jr. Thomas H. *Money: Understanding and Creating Alternatives to Legal Tender.* White River Junction, Vt.: Chelsea Green Publishing, 2001.

Greider, William. *The Soul of Capitalism: Opening Paths to a Moral Economy.* New York: Simon & Schuster, 2003.

Grodin, Seth. *All Marketers Are Liars: The Power of Telling Authentic Stories in a Low-Trust World.* New York: Portfolio, 2005.

Gunther, Marc. *Faith and Fortune: The Quiet Revolution to Reform American Business.* New York: Crown Publishing, 2004.

Harrow, Lisa. *What Can I Do? An Alphabet for Living.* White River Junction, Vt.: Chelsea Green Publishing, 2006.

Harvard Business Review on Corporate Responsibility. Boston: Harvard Business School Publishing, 2003.

Hawken, Paul. *Blessed Unrest: How the Largest Movement in the World Came into Being and Why No One Saw It Coming.* New York: Viking, 2007.

———. *The Ecology of Commerce: A Declaration of Sustainability.* New York: HarperBusiness, 1993.

————. *Growing a Business*. New York: Fireside Books, 1987.

Hawken, Paul, Amory Lovins, and L. Hunter Lovins. *Natural Capitalism: Creating the Next Industrial Revolution*. Boston: Little, Brown and Company, 1999.

Hays, Samuel P. *Beauty, Health, and Permanence: Environmental Politics in the United States, 1955–1985*. Cambridge, England: Cambridge University Press, 1987.

Hesselbein, Frances, Marshall Goldsmith, and Richard Beckhard, eds. *The Leader of the Future: New Visions, Strategies, and Practices for the Next Era*. San Francisco: Jossey-Bass Publishers, 1996.

Hirshberg, Gary. *Stirring It Up: How to Make Money and Save the World*. New York: Hyperion, 2008.

Hollender, Jeffrey, and Stephen Fenishcell. *What Matters Most: How a Small Group of Pioneers Is Teaching Social Responsibility to Big Business, and Why Big Business Is Listening*. New York: Basic Books, 2004.

Horton, Tom, and David W. Harp. *Water's Way: Life along the Chesapeake*. Baltimore: The Johns Hopkins University Press, 1992.

Ilich, Ivan. *Energy and Equity (Ideas in Progress)*. London: Marion Boyars Publishers, 2001.

Ingram, Annie Merrill et al. *Coming into Contact: Explorations in Ecocritical Theory and Practice*. Athens: University of Georgia Press, 2007.

Jacobs, Jane. *The Death and Life of Great American Cities*. New York: Random House, 1961.

James, Sarah, and Torbjorn Lahti. *The Natural Step for Communities: How Cities and Towns Can Change to Sustainable Practices*. Gabriola Island, B.C.: New Society Publishers, 2004.

Johansson, Frans. *The Medici Effect: What Elephants and Epidemics Can Teach Us About Innovation*. Boston: Harvard Business School Press, 2006.

Kahn, Matthew E. *Green Cities: Urban Growth and the Environment*. Washington, D.C.: Brookings Institution Press, 2006.

Kay, John, and Aubrey Silberson. "Corporate Governance." *National Institute Economic Review*, August 1, 1995.

Kelley, Tom, and Jonathan Littman. *The Ten Faces of Innovation: IDEO's Strategies for Beating the Devil's Advocate & Driving Creativity throughout Your Organization*. New York: Doubleday, 2005.

Kemmis, Daniel. *Community and the Politics of Place*. Norman: University of Oklahoma Press, 1992.

Kennedy, Robert F. Jr. *Crimes against Nature: How George W. Bush and His Corporate Pals Are Plundering the Country and Hijacking Our Democracy*. New York: HarperCollins, 2004.

Kermode, Frank. *The Classic: Literary Images of Permanence and Change*. Cambridge, Mass: Harvard University Press, 1983.

Kidder, Tracy. *Mountains beyond Mountains: The Quest of Dr. Paul Farmer, a Man Who Would Cure the World*. New York: Random House, 2004.

Kim, W. Chan, and Renee Mauborgne. *Blue Ocean Strategy: How to Create Uncontested Market Space and Make the Competition Irrelevant*. Boston: Harvard Business School Press, 2005.

Kingsolver, Barbara, Steven L. Hopp, and Camille Kingsolver. *Animal, Vegetable, Miracle: A Year of Food Life*. New York: HarperCollins, 2007.

Klein, Naomi. *No Logo: Taking Aim at the Brand Bullies*. New York: Picador, 1999.

————. *The Shock Doctrine: The Rise of Disaster Capitalism*. New York: Henry Holt and Company, 2007.

Kohn, Alfie. *No Contest: The Case against Competition*. Boston: Houghton Mifflin Company, 1986.

Korten, David C. *When Corporations Rule the World*. Bloomfield, Conn., & San Francisco: Kumarian Press & Berrett-Koehler Publishers, 1995.

Kotter, John P. and Dan S. Cohen. *The Heart of Change: Real-Life Stories of How People Change Their Organizations*. Boston: Harvard Business School Press, 2002.

Krakow, Kenneth R. *Georgia Place-Names*. Macon, Ga.: Winship Press, 1975.

Krupp, Fred, and Miriam Horn. *Earth: The Sequel; The Race to Reinvent Energy and Stop Global Warming*. New York: W. W. Norton & Company, 2008.

Kunstler, James Howard. *The Geography of Nowhere: The Rise and Decline of America's Man-Made Landscape*. New York: Touchstone, 1993.

Lakoff, George. *Don't Think of an Elephant: Know Your Values and Frame the Debate.* White River Junction, Vt.: Chelsea Green, 2004.

Landry, Charles. *The Creative City: A Toolkit for Urban Innovators.* London: Earthscan, 2000.

Leigh, Jack. *The Land I'm Bound To.* New York: W. W. Norton & Co., 2000.

Lencioni, Patrick. *The Five Dysfunctions of a Team: A Leadership Fable.* San Francisco: Jossey-Bass, 2002.

Leopold, Aldo. *A Sand County Almanac; With Essays on Conservation from Round River.* New York: Oxford University Press, 1949.

Levitt, Steven D., and Stephen J. Dubner. *Freakonomics: A Rogue Economist Explores the Hidden Side of Everything.* New York: HarperCollins, 2005.

Linstroth, Tommy and Ryan Bell. *Local Action: The New Paradigm in Climate Change Policy.* Burlington: University of Vermont Press, 2007.

Louv, Richard. *Last Child in the Woods: Saving Our Children from Nature-Deficit Disorder.* Chapel Hill, N.C.: Algonquin Books of Chapel Hill, 2006.

Lovins, Amory B., et al. *Winning the Oil Endgame: Innovation for Profits, Jobs, and Security.* Snowmass, CO: Rocky Mountain Institute, 2005.

Lowenstein, Roger. *When Genius Failed: The Rise and Fall of Long-Term Capital Management.* New York: Random House, 2000.

Maathai, Wangari Muta. *Unbowed: A Memoir.* New York: Alfred A. Knopf, 2006.

Maslow, Abraham H. *Motivation and Personality,* third ed. New York: Longman, 1954.

McDonough, William, and Michael Braungart. *Cradle to Cradle: Remaking the Way We Make Things.* New York: North Point Press, 2002.

McHarg, Ian L. *Design with Nature.* Garden City, N.Y.: John Wiley & Sons, Inc., 1969.

McKibben, Bill. *Deep Economy: The Wealth of Communities and the Durable Future.* New York: Times Books, Henry Holt and Company, 2007.

Mclennan, Jason F. *The Philosophy of Sustainable Design: The Future of Architecture.* Kansas City, Mo.: Ecotone Publishing, 2004.

McPhee, John. *Encounters with the Archdruid.* New York: Farrar, Straus and Giroux, 1971.

McPherson, James Alan. *Hue and Cry: Short Stories.* Boston: Little Brown & Company, 1969.

Meadows, Donella. "Places to Intervene in a System." *Whole Earth Magazine,* Winter, 1997.

Meadows, Donella H. *The Global Citizen.* Washington, D.C.: Island Press, 1991.

Meadows, Donella, Jorgan Randers, and Dennis Meadows. *Limits to Growth: The 30-Year Update.* White River Junction, Vt.: Chelsea Green Publishing, 2004.

Melaver, Martin and Phyllis Mueller. *The Green Building Bottom Line.* New York: McGraw Hill, 2008.

Melville, Herman. *Moby-Dick; or The Whale.* New York: Harper and Brothers, 1851.

Miller, Peter. "Swarm Theory." *National Geographic,* July, 2007: 126-47.

Mourkogiannis, Nikos. *Purpose: The Starting Point of Great Companies.* New York: Palgrave Macmillan, 2006.

Muir, John. *A Thousand-Mile Walk to the Gulf.* New York: Houghton Mifflin Company, 1916.

Nattrass, Brian, and Mary Altomare. *Dancing with the Tiger: Learning Sustainability Step by Natural Step.* Gabriola Island, B.C.: New Society Publishers, 2002.

———. *The Natural Step for Business: Wealth, Ecology, and the Evolutionary Corporation.* Gabriola Island, B.C.: New Society Publishers, 1999.

Neuwirth, Robert. *Shadow Cities: A Billion Squatters, A New Urban World.* New York: Routledge, Taylor & Francis Group, 2006.

New York Times editorial staff. "Responsible Use of Eminent Domain." *New York Times,* June 26, 2006.

Nordhaus, Ted, and Michael Shellenberger. *Break Through: From the Death of Environmentalism to the Politics of Possibility.* New York: Houghton Mifflin Company, 2007.

Odum, Eugene. *Ecological Vignettes: Ecological Approaches to Dealing with Human Predicaments.* Amsterdam: Overseas Publishers Association, 1988.

Olson, Steve. *The Ethics of Leadership.* Atlanta: Unpublished Ph.D dissertation, Emory University, 2007.

Orr, David W. *Earth in Mind: On Education, Environment, and the Human Prospect.* Washington, D.C.: Island Press, 2004.

———. *The Nature of Design: Ecology, Culture, and Human Intention.* New York: Oxford University Press, 2002.

Ottman, Jacqueline A. *Green Marketing: Opportunity for Innovation,* second ed. New York: BookSurge LLC, 1993.

Outwater, Alice. *Water: A Natural History.* New York: Basic Books, 1996.

Pilkey, Orrin H., and Mary Edna Fraser. *A Celebration of the World's Barrier Islands.* New York: Columbia University Press, 2003.

Pine, B. Joseph, and James H. Gilmore. *The Experience Economy: Work Is Theater & Every Business Is a Stage.* Cambridge, Mass.: Harvard University Press, 1999.

Pitts, Adrian. *Planning and Design Strategies For Sustainability and Profit: Pragmatic Sustainable Design on Building and Urban Scales.* Burlington, Vt.: Architectural Press, 2004.

Pollan, Michael. *The Omnivore's Dilemma: A Natural History of Four Meals.* New York: Penguin Books, 2006.

Porter, Michael E. *Competitive Advantage: Creating and Sustaining Superior Performance.* New York: Simon & Schuster, 1985.

Quinn, Daniel. *Ishmael: An Adventure of the Mind and Spirit.* New York: Bantam/Turner, 1992.

———. *The Story of B: An Adventure of the Mind and Spirit.* New York: Bantam, 1996.

Ray, Janisse. *Ecology of a Cracker Childhood.* Minneapolis, Minn.: Milkweed Editions, 1999.

———. *Pinhook: Finding Wholeness in a Fragmented Land.* White River Junction, Vt.: Chelsea Green Publishing, 2005.

Reich, Robert B. *Supercapitalism: The Transformation of Business, Democracy, and Everyday Life.* New York: Alfred A. Knopf, 2007.

Reisner, Marc. *Cadillac Desert: The American West and Its Disappearing Water.* London: Viking Penguin, 1986.

Rifkin, Jeremy. *The European Dream: How Europe's Vision of the Future Is Quietly Eclipsing the American Dream.* New York: Jeremy P. Tarcher/Penguin, 2004.

Rivoli, Pietra. *The Travels of a T-Shirt in the Global Economy.* Hoboken: John Wiley & Sons, Inc., 2005.

Rogers, Heather. *Gone Tomorrow: The Hidden Life of Garbage.* New York: The New Press, 2005.

Romm, Joseph. *Cool Companies: How the Best Businesses Boost Profits and Productivity by Cutting Greenhouse Gas Emissions.* Washington, D.C.: Island Press, 1999.

———. *Hell and High Water: The Global Warming Solution.* New York: HarperPerennial, 2007.

Sachs, Jeffrey D. *Common Wealth: Economics for a Crowded Planet.* New York: The Penguin Press, 2008.

———. *The End of Poverty: Economic Possibilities for Our Time.* New York: Penguin Group, 2005.

Savannah Unit of the Georgia Writer's Project of the Work Projects Administration. *Drums and Shadows: Survival Studies among the Georgia Coastal Negroes.* Athens: University of Georgia Press, 1940.

Savitz, Andrew, and Karl Weber. *The Triple Bottom Line: How Today's Best-Run Companies Are Achieving Economic, Social, and Environmental Success—and How You Can Too.* San Francisco: Jossey-Bass, 2006.

Schumacher, E. F. *Small Is Beautiful: Economics as If People Mattered,* twenty-fifth anniversary edition, with preface by James Robertson and Introduction by Paul Hawken, ed. Point Roberts, Wash.: Hartley & Marks Publishers, 1999.

Schwartz, Peter. *The Art of the Long View: Planning for the Future in an Uncertain World.* New York: Doubleday, 1991.

Senge, Peter M. *The Fifth Discipline: The Art & Practice of the Learning Organization.* New York: Doubleday, 1990.

Senge, Peter M., et al. *The Necessary Revolution: How Individuals and Organizations Are Working Together to Create a Sustainable World.* New York: Doubleday, 2008.

Sennett, Richard. *The Corrosion of Character: The Personal Consequences of Work in the New Capitalism.* New York: W. W. Norton, 1998.

———. *The Culture of the New Capitalism.* New Haven, Conn. Yale University Press, 2006.

Shepard, Paul. *Nature and Madness.* Athens: University of Georgia Press, 1982.

Shuman, Michael H. *The Small-Mart Revolution: How Local Businesses Are Beating the Global Competition.* San Francisco: Berrett-Koehler Publishers, Inc., 2006.

Sobel, David. *Children's Special Places: Exploring the Role of Forts, Dens, and Bush Houses in Middle Childhood*. Detroit, Mich: Wayne State University Press, 2001.

Speth, James Gustave. *The Bridge at the Edge of the World: Capitalism, the Environment, and Crossing from Crisis to Sustainability*. New Haven, Conn.: Yale University Press, 2008.

Statsky, William P. *Legal Thesaurus/Legal Dictionary: A Resource for the Writer and Computer Researcher*. St. Paul, Minn.: West Publishing Company, 1985.

Steinberg, Ted. *Down to Earth: Nature's Role in American History*. Oxford, England: Oxford University Press, 2002.

Stewart, Mart A. *"What Nature Suffers to Groe": Life, Labor, and Landscape on the Georgia Coast, 1680–1920*. Athens: University of Georgia Press, 1996.

Stewart, Matthew. "The Management Myth." *The Atlantic Monthly*, January 6, 2006.

Suarez, Ray. *The Old Neighborhood: What We Lost in the Great Suburban Migration, 1966–1999*. New York: The Free Press, 1999.

Suzuki, David, and Holly Dressel. *Good News for A Change: How Everyday People Are Helping the Planet*. Vancouver, B.C.: Greystone Books, 2002.

Suzuki, David, and Amanda McConnell. *The Sacred Balance: Rediscovering Our Place in Nature*. Vancouver, B.C.: Greystone Books, 1997.

Tal, Alon. *Speaking of Earth: Environmental Speeches That Moved the World*. New Brunswick, N.J.: Rutgers University Press, 2006.

Thomas, Lewis. *The Lives of a Cell: Notes of a Biology Watcher*. New York: Bantam, 1974.

Thoreau, Henry David. *Walden; or, Life in the Woods*. Boston: Ticknor & Fields, 1854.

Tidwell, Mike. *Bayou Farewell: The Rich Life and Tragic Death of Louisiana's Cajun Coast*. New York: Random House, 2003.

———. *The Ravaging Tide: Strange Weather, Future Katrinas, and the Coming Death of America's Coastal Cities*. New York: Free Press, 2006.

Traver, Tim. *Sippewissett: Or, Life on a Salt Marsh*. White River Junction, Vt.: Chelsea Green Publishing, 2006.

Treacy, Michael, and Fred Wiersema. "Customer Intimacy and Other Value Disciplines." *Harvard Business Review*, January 1, 1993.

UNP et al. *World Resources 2005, The Wealth of the Poor: Managing Ecosystems to Fight Poverty*. Washington, D.C.: World Resources Institute, 2005.

Wachtel, Paul L. *The Poverty of Affluence: A Psychological Portrait of the American Way of Life*. Gabriola Island, B.C.: New Society Publishers, 1989.

Walker, Alice. *In Love and Trouble; Stories of Black Women*. New York: Harcourt, Brace & Jovanovich, 1973.

Ward, John. *Perpetuating the Family Business: 50 Lessons Learned form Long Lasting, Successful Families in Business*. New York: Palgrave Macmillan, 2004.

Weisman, Alan. *Gaviotas: A Village to Reinvent the World*. White River Junction, Vt.: Chelsea Green Publishing, 1998.

———. *The World Without Us*. New York: St. Martin's Press, 2007.

Willard, Bob. *The Sustainability Advantage: Seven Business Case Studies of a Triple Bottom Line*. Gabriola Island, B.C.: New Society Publishers, 2002.

Wilson, Edward O. *The Future of Life*. New York: Random House, 2002.

———. *Consilience: The Unity of Knowledge*. New York: Random House, 1998.

Wolin, Sheldon S. *Democracy Incorporated: Managed Democracy and the Specter of Inverted Totalitarianism*. Princeton, N.J.: Princeton University Press, 2008.

Worster, Donald. *The Wealth of Nature: Environmental History and the Ecological Imagination*. Oxford, England: Oxford University Press, 1993.

Yudelson, Jerry. *Green Building A to Z: Understanding the Language of Green Building*. Gabriola Island, B.C.: New Society Publishers, 2007.

Zohar, Danah, and Ian Marshall. *SQ: Connecting with Our Spiritual Intelligence*. New York: Bloomsbury Publishing, 2000.

INDEX

Note: page numbers followed by f refer to Figures

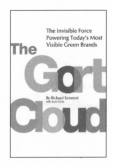
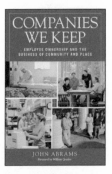